THE POLITICS OF PUBLIC MANAGEMENT:
THE HRDC AUDIT OF GRANTS AND CONTRIBUTIONS

The Politics of Public Management is a 'textbook case' in public administration. In this study David Good describes and analyses in depth the events and circumstances of the scandal surrounding the grants and contributions audit at Human Resources Development Canada (HRDC), which dominated media, parliamentary, and public attention for many months. Good argues that the HRDC crisis of 2000 was the result of a complex series of factors, which transformed a fixable administrative matter into a scandal that generated media headlines alleging that the government had lost close to $1 billion in misallocated funds. The author contextualizes this crisis by looking at the dichotomies and contradictions inherent in public administration, and by proposing that certain trade-offs must be made in the administration of any public organization.

Good skilfully weaves together into a coherent and comprehensible whole both theoretical and practical considerations in his analysis, drawing on recent literature in the field and capturing for the reader the nuances and complexities of public administration. The first and only extensive critical examination to date of the events surrounding the scandal at HRDC, this text offers an original and groundbreaking contribution to current scholarship on public administration and management in Canada.

DAVID A. GOOD is an adjunct professor of Public Administration at the University of Victoria.

The Institute of Public Administration of Canada Series in Public Management and Governance

Editor: Donald Savoie

This series is sponsored by the Institute of Public Administration of Canada as part of its commitment to encourage research on issues in Canadian public administration, public sector management, and public policy. It also seeks to foster wider knowledge and understanding among practitioners, academics, and the general public.

Networks of Knowledge: Collaborative Innovation in International Learning, Janice Stein, Richard Stren, Joy Fitzgibbon, and Melissa Maclean

The National Research Council in the Innovative Policy Era: Changing Hierarchies, Networks, and Markets, G. Bruce Doern and Richard Levesque

Beyond Service: State Workers, Public Policy, and the Prospects for Democratic Administration, Greg McElligott

A Law unto Itself: How the Ontario Municipal Board Has Developed and Applied Land Use Planning Policy, John G. Chipman

Health Care, Entitlement, and Citizenship, Candace Redden

Between Colliding Worlds: The Ambiguous Existence of Government Agencies for Aboriginal and Women's Policy, Jonathan Malloy

The Politics of Public Management: The HRDC Audit of Grants and Contributions, David A. Good

The Politics of
Public Management

The HRDC Audit of
Grants and Contributions

DAVID A. GOOD

IPAC
The Institute of
Public Administration of Canada

IAPC
L'Institut d'administration
publique du Canada

UNIVERSITY OF TORONTO PRESS
Toronto Buffalo London

© University of Toronto Press Incorporated 2003
Toronto Buffalo London
Printed in Canada

ISBN 0-8020-8805-8 (cloth)
ISBN 0-8020-8587-3 (paper)

Printed on acid-free paper

National Library of Canada Cataloguing in Publication

Good, David A.
  The politics of public management : the HRDC audit of grants and
  contributions / David A. Good.

  (The Institute of Public Administration of Canada series in public
  management and governance)
  Includes bibliographical references and index.
  ISBN 0-8020-8805-8 (bound).   ISBN 0-8020-8587-3 (pbk.)

  1. Canada. Human Resources Development Canada – Appropriations and
  expenditures.   2. Canada. Human Resources Development Canada –
  Auditing.   I. Institute of Public Administraiton of Canada   II. Title.
  III. Series: Institute of Public Administraiton of Canada series in public
  management and governance

  JL75.G66 2003   354.9′2439′0971   C2003-901474-6

University of Toronto Press acknowledges the financial assistance to its publishing program of the Canada Council for the Arts and the Ontario Arts
Council.

University of Toronto Press acknowledges the financial support for its publishing activities of the Government of Canada through the Book Publishing
Industry Development Program (BPIDP).

To the memory of my mother and father,
Rhea and Edward Good

Contents

Foreword

We often lament the dearth of literature produced by practitioners of public administration because it is only they who can provide first-hand knowledge of how things actually work in government. No one is in a better position to explain how decisions are actually made in government, to report on the give and take between politicians and career officials and between policy positions, or to capture lessons learned to improve government operations. There is only a handful of solid studies produced by former politicians and public servants that have made an important contribution to the literature. We can now add David Good's book to the list.

The Politics of Public Management: The HRDC Audit of Grants and Contributions provides answers to a number of questions about the so-called HRDC scandal. But it does much more than that. It takes us backstage where we see that public administration is anything but simple, although it can be made to appear so. The book brings to life how and why government decides, and the environment in which this takes place. In particular, it sheds light on how a crisis can take shape and spin out of control, as well as how it can be managed. If one wants a case study to demonstrate that the new public management holds more appeal on paper than in practice, one needs to look no further than this book. The House of Commons is above all a partisan milieu where administrative matters can, in a matter of a ten-second clip on the evening news, be transformed into a highly charged political crisis. That the administrative matter may turn out to be much less serious than at first envisaged is not important. What is important is scoring political points and if career officials or the truth are caught in the crossfire, then so be it.

David Good has clearly demonstrated that it is possible for practitioners to tell their story and to do so with an admirable degree of detachment and scholarship. Indeed, this book stands as a model for others. It does not reveal state secrets, it is highly respectful of public servants and politicians, and it avoids the temptation to rewrite history. It tells it like it was and it does this with dexterity and respect.

Donald J. Savoie, Editor
Canadian Public Administration Series

Preface

Despite the term public administration, the public rarely sees the actual work of most public administrators. Public administrators usually go about their work in the relative obscurity of large governmental organizations and the anonymity of the public service. While citizens occasionally come into contact with public servants in their dealings with governments on matters of services and benefits, most citizens spend more time with shopkeepers than they do with public service providers. Matters of public administration rarely rise to a level of national attention of the public, the media, and Parliament. The release of the internal administrative audit of the grants and contributions programs of Human Resources Development Canada (HRDC) was an exception. It has provided the basis for this book on public administration.

This book has been written for practitioners and students of public administration. As a former practitioner, I participated in and was exposed to any number of significant issues of public administration and public policy over my thirty years in the public service of Canada. Because there was seemingly no end to the pace and scope of these issues and the requirement for attention by senior public servants, there was little or no time for reflection and re-examination of the events after they had passed. It was always on to the next set of new issues. The great strength of practitioners is their ability to make things work. Their weakness is having too few opportunities to reflect on their practice in order to make things work better.

As a student of public administration, I have found that there have been too few opportunities to bring together academics and practitioners to examine what it is that public administrators actually do in their day-to-day work. With a few exceptions it is rare for an academic to spend much time inside government. While happily there has been an increasing amount of public sector research carried out by academics with the active engagement of practitioners, much of this work focuses on the big reforms of new public management or government restructuring. Students and academics have had relatively limited opportunity to take a fine-grained first-hand look at the actual happenings of public administration and to adapt and refine their conceptual and analytical tools in the process. The great strength of students and academics is their ability to critically apply their conceptual thinking to complex world events and to extract important learnings. Their weakness is having too few opportunities to get inside specific organizations and particular events to better understand why things are the way they are and how improvements can be successfully implemented.

When I completed my PhD in Public Policy at the University of California (Berkeley), my mentor and dissertation adviser, the renowned Aaron Wildavsky, lamented that too few former public servants with analytical understanding ever write about their important experiences once they have completed their tour of duty in government. Since I opted to begin my career in the public service in the practice of public policy, with the intention of later moving to academia in the study and teaching of the field, I felt compelled more than ever to heed Aaron's advice. I concluded that I did not simply want to write about my experiences but rather to reflect upon and put into context a significant public issue that could provide important insights into public administration. Of all the experiences I have had in the federal government, the administrative audit of the HRDC grants and contributions programs provides the most significant area for study because it contains so many of the fundamental issues of contemporary public administration.

I have written this book because I believe a careful and timely examination of the circumstances surrounding the HRDC audit of its grants and contributions has much to teach practitioners and students about how public administration is practised and how the practice could be improved. The case itself provides a useful springboard for considering important questions about public management reform.

This book draws upon what I have experienced and learned during my thirty years in the Canadian federal public service, fifteen of which were in six assistant deputy minister positions. Over my career I have worked in six departments, for twelve governments, both Liberal and Conservative, and for nineteen ministers. I have worked in areas of policy, program, operations, and administration, spending half of my career in central agencies and the other half in line departments. What I have learned has come from both successes and failures. I learned that government is first and foremost about an endless series of contradictions and dichotomies; it is in constant search for productive trade-offs and defensible compromises across many competing and praiseworthy objectives.

As a budding policy analyst, my experience in the early 1970s in the newly created Ministry of State for Urban Affairs – an agency of considerable research and analytical capacity but devoid of programs – taught me that knowledge is not necessarily power. More than just sound policy analysis was required for effective government action. My experiences with the Treasury Board Secretariat in the mid-1970s and again in the early 1990s taught me about the importance of public money. While many talk about the 'power of the purse,' the centrality of the budget process is not always what it is cracked up to be. There are instruments other than public money to pursue public purposes. At the Privy Council Office, working at the centre of government in the early 1980s in the Priorities and Planning Secretariat, I came to understand how influencing the policy-making process shaped the policies that emerged. Influence from the centre, however, was not the only determinant in shaping what government actually did. At the Ministry of State for Social Development I learned the strategic value of having the overview on the government's social policies, but I soon came to realize that both the devil and the opportunities lie in the program details. With the Department of Fisheries and Oceans I came to see how each new policy initiative temporarily resolved old problems but also created new ones. After several years, I came to realize through some first-hand experience that if the problems created were smaller than the problems resolved then progress was being made.

As fate would have it, immediately before and during the grants and contributions audit crisis, I was an assistant deputy minister at HRDC in Ottawa. From 1995 until 1997 I had responsibilities for finance and administration within the department, and from 1997 to 2000 I had, among other things, national responsibility for the grants and contributions programs of the department. These five years were a time of intensive activity. More recently, I have had the opportunity to reflect from a distance. As an adjunct professor of public administration at the University of Victoria I have been able to look back over the events surrounding the grants and contributions audit.

Some will question my objectivity in writing a book about public administration in an area where I have been a direct and visible participant. Some might well say that I am just rewriting history to 'tell my side of the story' in an effort to absolve myself from any responsibility or blame. As the former assistant deputy minister for the Human Resources Investment Branch in charge of the grants and contributions, I shouldered an important responsibility. My purpose in writing, however, is not to attribute blame or to absolve myself of responsibility. As an academic, I have felt compelled to write about the HRDC grants and contributions crisis because I believe it has much to teach us about public administration and public management reform.

Some former colleagues may view this book as too close in distance and in time. For a few in government, the events and their fallout may still be too fresh, but for most others these events have long passed, receding into distant memory and overtaken by the relentless flow of new challenges. Time is critical to learning in public administration, because most learning takes place through trial and error. There are important benefits to be gained by speeding up this otherwise slow trial-and-error learning process and by exposing the learnings to the test of public scrutiny.

There are many ways to focus on the grants and contributions crisis in order to find out what it has to teach us. If we want to understand why specific events and circumstances in public administration occur the way they do, focusing on the personalities and predispositions of the central players will be most effective. If we want to better understand the broad pattern of changes in public administration and the forces that shape these patterns, then focusing on the roles and relations among the players is the more productive course. This book focuses on the latter and not on the former. Learning for the future from the past requires that we look closely at what we can change and not what we might wish to replay.

There are many perspectives that one can take in examining past events and attempting to unearth future learnings. In a case as complex as this, and in an area as subtle as public administration, any single perspective is likely to prove inadequate, possibly serving only to reinforce the initial predispositions of the author. In this book, I therefore take several perspectives in an effort to have a broad and comprehensive understanding of the grants and contributions audit and of public administration. I look underneath public administration at its inherent dichotomies and contradictions. I look back and examine the context of public sector reform in the government of Canada over the 1990s and how it influenced subsequent events. I examine the grants and contributions audit from the outside looking in, describing how the media viewed and shaped the events. I analyse the grants and contributions audit from the inside looking out, explaining how the department grappled with a crisis in public administration. I provide an in-depth examination of how the highly visible direct employment programs called the Transitional Jobs Fund (TJF) and the Canada Jobs Fund (CJF) were administered. I look beyond this specific case and assess its wider implications for public management reform and improved accountability within government. I look ahead and to the future and indicate the urgent changes that must be made by each participant if improvements in public administration are to be to the benefit of all. And, finally, I look inside myself and provide a postscript about what I have personally learned from the experience and what I would have done differently.

In undertaking this work, from its early conceptual stage through to publication, I have incurred many debts. I am especially indebted to Donald Savoie, who was a very early and strong supporter of the idea, a candid and dependable critic of the manuscript, and a resourceful and trusted adviser throughout the process. Peter Aucoin read an early and partial draft, offered numerous suggestions for improvement, posed probing questions, and was generous in his encouragement. Sharon Sutherland, who read an early draft was candid in her critique, suggested areas for further investigation, and was most kind in sharing with me a draft of her article entitled 'Biggest Scandal in Canadian History: HRDC Audit Starts Probity War.'

I want to thank the many academics and former public servants who read versions of the entire manuscript and generously offered comments, criticisms, and suggestions for improvement. I am especially grateful to Emmanuel Brunet-Jailly, Barry Carin, Rod Dobell, Arthur Kroeger, John Langford, Evert Lindquist, Susan Phillips, Gordon Smith, and David Zussman. I also want to thank the two anonymous reviewers selected by the University of Toronto Press for their important comments and helpful suggestions. I thank Meredith Edwards, Jim McDavid, Gilles Paquet, and Michael Prince for their ideas and advice.

I had the extraordinary benefit of many comments and critiques on the manuscript from current public servants ranging from front-line employees, middle managers, and senior executives, through to those at the top of major government departments and at the centre of government. Some of them were central participants in the grants and contributions controversy, others participated around the edges, and still others observed the events from greater distance. Many of the them provided detailed, thorough, and extensive comments. I thank them all for their most careful reading of the manuscript, their criticisms, comments, and suggestions as well as for their advice and counsel. Had I taken all the advice I received, this book would not exist.

Many thanks to Virgil Duff at the University of Toronto Press for his advice and support. I owe a special thanks to my copy editor, Beth McAuley, whose numerous editorial suggestions helped to greatly improve the book.

As a former public servant I have a considerable obligation to my many friends and former colleagues and practitioners in the Government of Canada who supported me during a critical time in the HRDC grants and contributions audit crisis. I thank them for their support. I hope they recognize in this book some of the world in which they work and that they will consider and debate the suggestions for improvement.

To my current students in public administration, I express my thanks for giving me the opportunity to teach as well as to learn. Trial and error is a good teacher. Needless to say, I am responsible for the errors of fact and interpretation that remain in this book. Finally, I wish to acknowledge and thank my wonderful wife, Gilda, for her steadfast support and for never once asking when was I going to finish.

Victoria, British Columbia
January 2003

THE POLITICS OF PUBLIC MANAGEMENT:
THE HRDC AUDIT OF GRANTS AND CONTRIBUTIONS

Introduction

One noted academic has described the events surrounding the audit of the administration of grants and contributions programs of Human Resources Development Canada (HRDC) as a 'textbook case in public administration.'[1] If it is indeed a textbook case, it is hardly surprising since the audit and the government's response dominated media, parliamentary, and public attention over a lengthy period, leaping into the public's consciousness in the early days of the new millennium, and remaining in the public eye into the federal election campaign at the end of that same year. The issue, although largely pertaining to one government department, touched the central features of the administrative and political apparatus of government, dominated the entire department and its minister, became the focus of attention of the opposition and the media, took centre stage in question period in the House of Commons from February until June 2000, and was a significant preoccupation for Prime Minister Jean Chrétien. The audit triggered more than 800 questions directed to the Minister of HRDC, Jane Stewart, in question period; 17,000 pages of information about specific grants and contributions posted on the HRDC Web site; 100,000 pages released to the media and opposition under access-to-information legislation; several internal and external reviews, taskforces, and reports; and a separate examination by the Auditor General. Never before had an audit of any type, yet alone an internal administrative audit by a department of its own programs, triggered such visible and sustained political and public reaction.

This case involves HRDC, its grants and contributions programs, and the administrative audit of these programs by the department's Internal Audit Bureau. HRDC is a large and complex department of the federal government with expenditures in 1998–99 of $57.7 billion, representing

Table 1: 1998–99 HRDC Total Planned Spending*

Program	1998–99 Total Planned Spending (millions of dollars)
Corporate Services Program	108.9
Human Resources Investment and Insurance Program	2,110.1
Labour Program	107.0
Income Security Program	23,022.0
Employment Insurance	13,804.8
Canada Pension Plan	18,389.2
Other**	235.7
Total Planned Spending	57,777.7

*1998–99 expenditures are referenced because the Internal HRDC Grants and Contributions Audit was based upon that year.
**Includes small amounts for initiatives announced in the 1998 Budget, items not in the Main Estimates or the 1998 Budget, and Employee Benefit Plan recoverable from the Employment Insurance and Canada Pension Accounts.
Source: Adapted from Figure 1: 'Spending Authorities – Human Resources Development, Ministry Summary, Part 11 of the Estimates,' in HRDC 1998–99 Estimates, A Report on Plans and Priorities.

more than half of the total expenditures of the federal government.[2] As the table 1 indicates, its mandate touches nearly every aspect of human and social development, ranging from income support and pensions for the elderly, to employment insurance for the unemployed and assistance for students in post-secondary education, to a large and diverse range of grants and contributions relating to employment, training, and social development.

The department administers a significant portion of the government's grants and contributions programs.[3] In 1998–99, HRDC expended nearly $3.3 billion on grants and contributions, which included federal transfer payments to provincial governments based on federal-provincial agreements and federal legislation in such areas as labour market agreements and assistance for persons with disabilities; more discretionary contributions for direct employment measures such as the Transitional Jobs Fund; and direct grants to community organizations for promoting literacy initiatives. The following eight program areas use grants and contributions:

1 *Labour Market Training Programs* ($2,207 million). These programs include Employment Benefits and Support Measures such as targeted

wage subsidies, self-employment initiatives, job creation partnerships, skills development, employment assistance services, labour market partnerships, and research and innovation; the opportunities fund for persons with disabilities; fisheries adjustment and restructuring; and The Atlantic Groundfish Strategy (TAGS).

2 *Transitional Jobs Fund* ($125 million).[4] A program to encourage the creation of sustainable jobs in areas of high unemployment.

3 *Youth Programs* ($287 million). These programs give young Canadians work experience, skills, and information in making the transition from school to work.

4 *Aboriginal Training Programs* ($282 million). These programs take the form of fifty-four agreements with Aboriginal organizations to deliver training to Aboriginals under the Aboriginal Human Resources Development Strategy.

5 *Human Resource Partnerships* ($58 million). These partnerships are agreements with sector councils that represent business, labour, and educators to develop human resource strategies in such sectors as the steel industry, tourism, automotive repair, information technology, and so on.

6 *Social Development Programs* ($254 million). The programs include assistance for persons with disabilities and other initiatives for research and development, and demonstration projects to test out best practices in child-care delivery, and partnerships and innovations with the voluntary sector.

7 *Learning and Literacy* ($48 million). This program includes grants to organizations that promote literacy by increasing public awareness and developing innovative practices, demonstration projects to adopt new learning technologies, and partnership arrangements with provinces and national learning organizations to promote lifelong learning.

8 *Labour Programs* ($2 million). This small program includes contributions to labour and other organizations in order to promote safe and productive work environments.

Each of these eight program areas was included in the administrative audit undertaken by the Internal Audit Bureau of HRDC. However, only programs representing approximately $1 billion in expenditures (less than one-third of the total expenditures on grants and contributions) were included in the audit. All programs in the areas of the Transitional Jobs Fund, Youth Programs, Aboriginal Training Programs, Human

Resource Partnerships, Learning and Literacy, and Labour were included. In the Social Development area, the program for persons with disabilities was not included. In Labour Market Training, large expenditure programs for such initiatives as labour market agreements with provincial and territorial government, fisheries restructuring, and TAGS were not included.[5]

The audit, perhaps better called the 'file review,' looked at a purportedly random sample of 459 project files of various grants and contributions programs from these eight program areas. While the audit documentation noted that the programs 'represent(ed) approximately $1 billion in annual federal spending,'[6] the audit was not a financial audit of the projects. Instead, it was a 'paper review' of the extent and nature of the documentation contained in the 459 project files. The results of the audit are detailed in chapter 2, but, in essence, the audit found that the documentation contained in the project files was deficient, missing such items as application forms, cash flow forecasts, and descriptions of expected results.

Any 'textbook case' provides the opportunity to assess the chain of events from a wider perspective than the day-to-day actions and reactions of government, the media, and the public. It can put the issues into a broader context that provides an opportunity for learning about the specifics of the case. If the case is sufficiently rich and if the events and context can be linked, it can result in greater understanding about the practice of public administration in a democratic government. It can help us to better understand where public administration ends and politics starts, why matters that touch public money are so contentious, how errors are made and reported, how public impressions are created, and how accountability is rendered. At the very least, this case should shed some light on a number of the practical dilemmas that public administrators face in their day-to-day jobs and provide a deeper understanding of how public administration is actually practised.

This case touches a number of fundamental questions that are central to the practice of public administration in changing times. How are discretionary grants and contributions programs, which are sufficiently flexible to improve service yet vulnerable to abuse, best administered? Why are employment and job creation programs so difficult to administer? What are the appropriate roles for Members of Parliament in the delivery of government programs? What are the promises as well as the pitfalls of greater emphasis being placed on performance and results and lesser emphasis on administrative processes and program inputs?

What are the limitations of partnerships in service delivery? As operations and decision-making are pushed down and out to service providers, what is the capacity of an audit to provide reliable and accurate information up and in to central decision-makers? Is too much being expected from an audit? How does the intense scrutiny of the media shape the practice of public administration? How are mistakes best detected and corrected? How are responsibility assumed, accountability rendered, and blame apportioned?

I describe both the context for the administration of grants and contributions within HRDC and the events as they unfolded after the public release of the internal audit. The context begins in the early 1990s, with the public service reforms of Public Service 2000 before HRDC was created in 1993. It includes the fundamental restructuring of programs and the reductions in expenditures undertaken as part of the government-wide effort of the Program Review in 1994 and 1995. The context includes the series of undertakings to put in place new initiatives in public management within the department throughout much of the 1990s, up to and including the completion of the grants and contributions audit. The context, therefore, describes the operating framework for the department.

The events begin with the decision to conduct the internal departmental audit and include the release of the audit in mid-January 2000, and end with the Auditor General's report on HRDC's administration of its grants and contributions programs in October 2000. These events are described in terms of how they unfolded and were actually reported by the media. Particular emphasis is placed on the first eight weeks following the release of the internal audit. With the release of the audit, the media reported a 'billion dollar boondoggle.' Several months later, after reviewing some 17,000 individual project files, the department reported that the amount of outstanding debts owing to the government was only $85,000, a figure the Auditor General did not dispute in his report. Clearly the 'loss of a billion dollars' is the stuff of politics, whereas $85,000 in government overpayments is the stuff of public administration. Little wonder that the media, the opposition, and the public would focus on the first number and not the second.

There are clear limits to any case study. Based on 'lessons learned the hard way' from teaching students at the London School of Economics, Christopher Hood reminds us that 'the case-study approach to studying management is only effective if it can be related to a larger conceptual scheme.'[7] Therefore, both the context and the events are examined against the backdrop of the fundamental changes taking place in public administration over the past decade – changes that saw the government move from traditional public administration practices to a new public management approach. While there is a considerable body of literature about the new public management reforms that many governments have announced and are now putting in place, there is relatively little that addresses their effectiveness. Those that do, not surprisingly, conclude that the best answer to whether a reform is successful is, 'It depends.'[8] The purpose of this book is not to assess the new public management reforms or to attribute events of the HRDC audit to these or other reforms. Rather, it is to describe how one department of government went about doing its day-to-day work of administering and auditing its grants and contributions programs within the context of these far-reaching, government-wide changes.

This case raises the fundamental question, What is the true reality surrounding the crisis of the HRDC grants and contributions audit? There are two views on this matter. One view is that there were real and major problems in the management and control of grants and contributions programs and these problems were reflected in the results of the internal audit. The seeds of these inevitable problems were found in the preceding decade of turbulent change and budget and personnel cuts within the department and within the government. The other view is that there were no significant problems in the management and control of grants and contributions. The seeds of the resulting public 'problem' were the unfortunate combination of a poor quality audit purporting unsubstantiated conclusions, the mishandling of the public release of the internal audit by the department, and overly zealous media – all within a highly politically charged environment.

The first view starts from the premise that if governments take dramatic actions there are likely to be significant consequences, even if some of them are unintended. The cutting of 20 per cent of the department's employees and the re-engineering of the service delivery system under the general dictum that service to the public be maintained had real consequences, as did an additional transfer of 10 per cent of the departmental employees to several provincial governments as part of the new labour market agreements. The elimination of administrative barriers, the cutting of red tape, and the focus on program results as opposed to administrative processes also had significant consequences. The emphasis on partnerships, especially the role of Members of Parliament in advising on the choice of projects under the Transitional Jobs

Fund, had important ramifications. In short, a significant reduction in staff, dramatic program changes and restructuring, a determined effort to improve service to the public, the elimination of administrative processes, and the expanded role of Members of Parliament all contributed to a significant weakening of the management and control of the grants and contributions expenditures.

The second view starts from the premise that a high-profile public release of a low-quality internal audit into a charged political environment at a time of intense media competition is likely to lead to major problems for the department. This view holds that there was not a breakdown in the control of grants and contributions expenditures. Instead, there was a series of miscalculations by the department in the face of a highly competitive and aggressive media. Simply put, the department and the minister underestimated the media's reaction to the public release of an internal audit and overestimated their capacity to quickly provide detailed information in response to an onslaught of questions by a probing media and a relentless opposition.

Oh, that public administration could be this simple and conclusions about events this clear. Unlike the game of *Clue*, in which we find that the murder was committed by Colonel Mustard in the dining room with the revolver, matters of public administration are never so straightforward. Like most things, what you look at and where you view it from determine what you see. Administration, politics, and the media are no exceptions. That is why in this book I look at the HRDC audit from many different places.

I begin in chapter 1 by looking underneath public administration. Far from a story of the routine punctuated by periods of reform, it has increasingly become a seemingly endless stream of reform and change, occasioned by momentary interludes of routine and stability. New public management reforms are the products of old public administration problems. Nothing is ever permanently solved once and for all. Instead, at best, issues of public management are temporarily resolved under one form only to emerge later under another. Each new reform not only begets new problems but also often carries with it the seeds of its own decay. Reforms in public management involve a series of dichotomies and contradictions. Sometimes when we empower the front line, we lose control at the centre, only to subsequently tighten central control and rebureaucratize the front line. We have learned the hard way that proposals for administrative reorganization are not only costly but also contradictory.[9] For public administrators, these dichotomies and contractions are fundamental dilemmas in the search for both balance and choice. Sometimes these dichotomies and contradictions can be dealt with through balance and adjustment. At other times they cannot be reconciled and require tough choices, hard trade-offs, and important sacrifices.

Chapter 2 looks back over the 1990s and describes the public sector reforms that took place within the Canadian federal government. During this time, the federal government moved from traditional public administration to what has been described as a 'Canadian model' of public management. This was the framework within which HRDC operated. In this chapter, we see how HRDC grappled with the dichotomies and contradictions inherent in the government's approach to reforms, developed and implemented programs, and delivered services and benefits. For the department, it was not just a matter of balancing competing pressures and reconciling differing positions, it very often required hard, difficult trade-offs. In short, something had to be given up in order to get something else. These balances and trade-offs are described in terms of the dilemmas and contradictions inherent in cutting departmental administration while trying to maintain quality service to the public; empowering front-line staff while securing results from programs; breaking administrative barriers and constraints in order to achieve results; devolving programs to provincial governments and third-party delivery agents while attempting to ensure performance; developing flexible partnerships with private and voluntary sector organizations while maintaining accountability; and attempting to use an internal audit to secure timely, reliable, and accurate information for managing increasingly flexible grants and contributions programs.

Chapter 3 is the outside looking in and describes how the media not only reported but also shaped the events following the public release of the internal audit. I describe the techniques the media used to report the story, and compare and contrast the media's interpretation of the events with other interpretations. When the outside media look in on the government, they do not hold up a clean mirror to the department that reflects back the reality of public administration. Instead, it is a world of the 'distorted mirror' in which journalists and news organizations are not passive and neutral reflectors of reality but active agents that change, magnify, and intensify the reflection. This chapter describes what makes 'news' in public administration and shows how the daily deadlines of the media require superficiality and selectivity. By focusing on the underlying characteristics of newsworthiness, we can see how the release of the internal audit was reported by using well-established media techniques – simplification, dramatization, personalization, pre-formed storylines, and casting unexpected events as if they were part of the initial story.

The fundamental issues around which the events of the HRDC audit evolved over the course of eight months are foreshadowed by the media in the first twenty-four hours after the release of the internal audit. First impressions of the media became lasting impressions of the public. Over the course of these eight months, the media's spotlight would move from one new issue to another. If the internal world of public management is one of gradually securing trade-offs and balances in the face of contradictions and paradoxes, the external world of the media is one of quickly formulating impressions and conclusions based on deep-seated attitudes and predispositions about the nature of government and bureaucracy. While internal trade-offs and balances take time to achieve, the external impressions and conclusions are formed almost instanteously. As public management is increasingly performed in a fish bowl, the media amplify and magnify its dichotomies and contradictions and accelerates its reforms.

Chapter 4 is the inside looking out. It describes the events in terms of what the department and the government faced with the release of the internal audit – a crisis in public administration. To analyse these events, I apply a framework of crisis management in government for dealing with a lack of confidence in elected and non-elected public officials and a lack of control by the department. The framework charts the course of the crisis and the calculations and the miscalculations by the department. It describes the interplay of the forces of confidence and the forces of restoration, and how the forces of restoration operated slowly and disjointedly and eventually moved the department beyond the crisis and returned it to a state of 'business as usual.' But this was not the same business as before the crisis, nor was the business done in the same way. It is often during periods of great stress, and sometimes in periods of crisis, that administrative reforms are undertaken in an effort to restore confidence and secure control. As the analysis indicates, it is during these times when there is the greatest risk of systemic overreaction as the administrative reforms, like the infamous pendulum, swing too far in one direction. Hence, there is a subsequent need for a deliberate and planned readjustment and rebalancing. In this sense, administrative reform can be seen to sometimes carry the seeds of its own decay.

Chapter 5 takes a closer look at the most contentious and visible programs that formed a small part of the grants and contributions audit – the one hundred million dollar, not one billion dollar, Transitional Jobs Fund (TJF) and the Canada Jobs Fund (CJF). I explore in detail these programs that the media incorrectly labelled as 'the billion dollar job fund' by examining the limits to partnership arrangements between government and public and private sector organizations. I discuss how the inevitable tensions and potential contradictions between flexibility and the achievement of results, on the one hand, and accountability and control, on the other, are played out under the glare of the media. Most important, I examine the formal role of Members of Parliament in advising the government on the approval and implementation of TJF and CJF projects as part of the partnership arrangements, and the implications that this had for public servants, ministers, and government and opposition MPs in making accountability more complicated and more confused. This case indicates that there are important limits to partnerships and significant limits on the role that Members of Parliament can and should play in such programs. If governments and their partners do not skillfully determine the boundaries for such partnerships, they will be clumsily drawn by opposition parties, the media, and internal and external auditors.

Chapter 6 looks around and outside the specifics of the HRDC audit. It focuses on the larger issues of public management that go beyond this individual case, and it analyses the implications of the HRDC audit for the 'Canadian model' of public management as it has been conceived and is being implemented by the federal government in the context of Canadian politics. I describe the importance of a professional public service as the distinguishing feature of the 'Canadian model' and examine some of the model's limitations, especially why strengthening and improving accountability is so important yet so seemingly difficult to achieve. Accountability itself, however, contains dichotomies and contradictions, and is viewed differently by different people for different purposes. There is accountability for control of abuse, accountability for assurance of performance, and accountability for learning by organizations. The need to balance these different perspectives on accountability is and will continue to be a major challenge for public servants and politicians as they implement the 'Canadian model' of public management within the reality of Canadian politics.

In chapter 7, I look ahead and to the future, and conclude that there must be a better way, but where do we begin? Do we need to rescue politics from administration or administration from politics? The clue to understanding is to know that there can be no dichotomy or separation between politics and administration. I conclude that all major players in public administration – public servants, auditors, ministers, Members of Parliament, and the media – must be prepared to adjust a bit if anyone is to adjust at all. It is not a matter of imposing a single overriding reform on everyone – this does not exist nor can it be done. Instead, it is a matter of getting each player to realize that individual adjustments can lead to better collective outcomes for all in the form of improved public management.

It is essential that we speak up and speak out for a better way to administer our public programs. Public servants need to speak administrative truth to political power. Public servants, especially the leaders, need to explain administrative dichotomies and contradictions to politicians. Within the public service, everyone needs the opportunity to speak to everyone else about values and ethics in government. Auditors need to curtail their audit rhetoric and speak with a greater sense of humility about the limitations of their audits. They need to speak to politicians about the realities and constraints that are an everyday part of the public administrator's environment. Ministers need to listen to public administration advice and they need to speak for and politically defend public management reforms. Members of Parliament need to keep ministers accountable and public servants answerable, and they need to speak more to policy and less to administration. Finally, the media need to speak accurately and fairly in their reporting.

CHAPTER ONE

Looking Underneath
Dichotomies and Contradictions in Public Administration

Peter Hennessy, the thoughtful observer of British government, has written that 'the history of Whitehall is a story of long periods of routine punctuated by occasional orgies of reform when the system broke down, or, as in the greatest reform of all in the mid-nineteenth century, when scandal and outraged public opinion moved those in authority ... to inquire and then to act.'[1] Donald Savoie has noted that 'one is tempted to turn Peter Hennessy's observation around and argue that since the early 1980's, we have seen everywhere ... orgies of reform punctuated by brief periods of the routine.'[2] Indeed, change in public administration today is ongoing and relentless, with each new wave of administrative reform following previous reforms in rapid succession. As the waves rush to the beach they flow back only to be met by a continuous series of new waves and changes, which in turn are shaped by the outward flow of water. It seems that public administration is not a tranquil sea of off shore water but a coastal zone where water moves in many directions at the same time.

There is little doubt that public administration and public management in Canada, as it is elsewhere, is undergoing fundamental and significant change. The pace of these changes or reforms has quickened significantly and the scope is considerable, touching nearly every aspect of public management – policy and values, programs and expenditures, consultation and collaboration, organization and delivery, human resources, administration, and information technology, accountability and transparency, and audit and evaluation.

Each Administrative Reform Carries the Seeds of Its Own Decay

While the continued pressures for change in public administration is recognized, less understood and appreciated is the growing realization that the new administrative reforms are the products of old administrative problems. In this sense, each new reform can be seen as a reaction to the shortcomings of the previous reform efforts. Reform begets reform. Christopher Hood has described how each administrative reform carries not only intrinsic limits but also the seeds of its own decay.[3] Progress is therefore measured in relation to the magnitude of the old problems resolved (nothing is ever totally solved) compared with the new ones created. By this standard, if the problems created are smaller than the problem resolved, progress is being made.

That there are intrinsic limits and constraints in public administration and that there are often inherent dilemmas and contradictions are not new. Peter Aucoin in his comparative analysis of new public management begins his work by explaining the coexistence of 'a constant state of tension' between 'responsible government as party government' and 'good government and career public service.'[4] In the early 1970s, Charles Perrow[5] pointed out that bureaucratic processes are beset with dilemmas and to organize one way inevitably means to pay a serious price in another. Christopher Hood and Michael Jackson argue that administrative 'doctrines often come in contradictory pairs.'[6] In a recent assessment of public management reforms across a number of countries, Guy Peters explored the inherent contradictions in the reform process, observing that 'contradictions and paradox are an increasingly important part of thinking about management more generally.' He concludes, rather optimistically, that 'the sets of contradictions are in reality a statement of the need for balance, rather than a statement of the need to choose.'[7]

In another of his essays, Peter Aucoin has written persuasively about 'paradoxes and pendulums' in public administrative reform.[8] Gareth Morgan, in studying organizations analyses the challenge of 'managing paradox' as a 'struggle of opposites' where 'the very act of seeking to empower staff is likely to mobilize awareness of existing modes of control, which, in turn, undermines the drive toward empowerment.'[9] Kenneth Ruscio describes 'the paradox created by reformers who want to simultaneously give public managers greater flexibility and make them more accountable.'[10] Kenneth Kernaghan, Brian Marson, and Sandford Borins, in their book on the new public organization, describe the field of public administration as 'permeated by tensions, contradictions, paradoxes, and inconsistencies'[11] and point to the need for balance. Christopher Pollitt and Geert Bouckaert, in their recent comparative analysis of public management reforms in ten countries explicitly address the question of 'trade-offs, balances, limits, dilemmas, and paradoxes.' They observe that 'certain trade-offs and dilemmas are exceedingly common in administrative change, so that the achievement of one or two particular ends might well be "paid for" by a lowered performance in other respects.'[12] Although they agree with Peters and others that some contradictions and paradoxes can be dealt with by finding the appropriate balance, they allow that 'sometimes what sounds to be an incompatibility *is* an incompatibility, which cannot be reconciled.'[13] In short, there must be a trade-off. Something must be given up in order to achieve something else.

Pollitt and Bouckaert have compiled a list of 'contradictions' within management reforms that are seemingly incompatible. They focus on the substance of the management reforms rather than on the processes through which they are implemented. This is a significant restriction, although they are the first to acknowledge that implementation is important. As the authors put it, 'a fundamentally sound reform can be "messed up" through poor implementation and the worst effects of an unsound reform can be obscured, delayed or otherwise diluted by shrewd management.'[14] The ten contradictions, which include four at the level of system-wide reform in public administration and six at the level of specific operations, are summarized here:

1 Improve quality vs. cut costs.
2 Increase political control of bureaucracy vs. free up and empower managers to service clients and citizens.
3 Promote flexibility and innovation vs. increase citizen trust and therefore governmental legitimacy.
4 Give priority to making savings vs. give priority to improving the performance of the public sector.
5 'Responsibilize' government vs. reduce the tasks that government is involved with.
6 Motivate staff and promote cultural change vs. downsize and weaken.
7 Reduce the burden of internal scrutiny and associated paperwork vs. sharpen managerial accountability.
8 Create more single-purpose agencies vs. improve horizontal coordination.
9 Decentralize management authority vs. improve program coordination.
10 Increase effectiveness vs. sharpen managerial accountability.

While the authors undertake a brief conceptual analysis of each contradiction, they do not examine how these contradictions would actually be dealt with on the ground as actual politicians and public servants go about developing and implementing policies and programs in the face of real world circumstances. On the basis of their conceptual analysis, the authors conclude that some of these apparent contradictions are indeed real ones. For example, some like *motivate staff vs. downsize staff* are viewed as inescapable contradictions. Others like *internal scrutiny vs. sharpen managerial accountability* are seen as a question of balance, and still others like *increased control of bureaucracy vs. free up and empower managers to service clients and citizens* are determined to be compatible but only in a perfect world. In the 'real world,' they require trade-offs that become so sharp as to be contradictions. For example, in this last case, the authors indicate that three demanding and unrealistic conditions would be required in order that there not be a contradiction. First, politicians would have to refrain from interfering in management. Second, priorities and targets handed down by political leaders would have to be clear and congruent with the demands of citizens. Third, different service delivery organizations would all work within the same shared objectives, targets, and procedures. As we will see in the HRDC case, these conditions are rarely, if ever, attained in the real world. As a result, public servants are left with the difficult task: choosing one objective at the cost of foregoing the achievement of another. Choice in public administration is often a matter of balance, but it can also be a question of hard trade-offs.

Christopher Pollitt, who has studied how public administration is actually implemented in the UK government, has described the 'breaking up of the monolithic ministries' through the Next Steps reforms of the 1980s and 1990s as a 'solution to one set of problems,' which then required a preoccupation with greater integration and 'joining-up' of government to 'solve the downside' problems that were created. As he puts it:

> There is something of a trade-off here, or a kinder way to put it would be to say that there is a balancing act going on. You can not have full joined-upness (of government) and maximum decentralization and devolution simultaneously, you have to pitch your tent somewhere.[15]

The question of 'where to pitch your tent' to achieve an appropriate balance in public administration is not just the concern of academics and a preoccupation of public servants. In the aftermath of the release of the HRDC audit, the difficult task of achieving balance was recognized both by politicians and the Auditor General. The House of Commons Standing Committee on Human Resources and the Status of Persons with Disabilities, after a lengthy series of hearings involving a steady stream of diverse witnesses, concluded in its final majority report in June 2000 that 'maintaining a balance of efficiency, flexibility and sound financial management is a significant challenge to public service managers.'[16] The Auditor General, in his audit of HRDC grants and contributions in October 2000, acknowledged the difficulties in securing balance, concluding that 'there is no simple answer to what the ideal balance should be.'[17]

These paradoxical tensions and contradictions permeate the practice of public administration. One of the most vivid examples involves the Transitional Jobs Fund (TJF), a program that was the subject of the HRDC internal administrative audit and, with the audit's public release, became characterized by the opposition and media as representing the entire grants and contributions programs of the department. The design of TJF and its successor, the Canada Jobs Fund (CJF), contained underlying dichotomies and contradictions that required a skillful balancing act, but when that balance was no longer possible, the hard trade-offs that had to be made were exposed. At the heart of this program was an irreconcilable internal tension that was interpreted externally as a contradiction between better service and strengthened control.

At first, the irreconcilable tension in the TJF program was internally manageable. Public servants looked for balance and found innovative ways to reconcile service flexibility and increased discretion *with* accountability for outputs and the achievement of results. One of these innovations was creating an important role for Members of Parliament, which would involve them in the selection of projects for their constituencies so that the program would be more sensitive to the unique needs of their communities. Another innovation was identifying program results in the form of sustainable jobs that were created and verifying these results through independent program evaluations. The administration of the program also involved a minimum of fixed rules and input controls so that the program could be tailored to the different labour market conditions in different communities and thereby increase the likelihood of creating jobs.

In order to maximize the likelihood of achieving results in the form of sustainable jobs in regions with high unemployment, the geographic regions for program eligibility were flexible and open to interpretation by HRDC regional officials. For example, the eligibility guidelines permitted several definitions of high-unemployment regions. These defini-tions included eligibility in twenty out of fifty-four large employment insurance (EI) regions in the country that had unemployment rates above 12 per cent. Eligibility also included areas or 'pockets' with high unemployment over 12 per cent and that were located within the larger EI regions where unemployment was less than 12 per cent. There was also an eligibility criterion for communities with unique needs – for example, high unemployment in Aboriginal or persons with disabilities communities. There were also 'spin-off benefits' in which projects were available for low-unemployment regions (less than 12 per cent) if they produced jobs in the immediately surrounding regions of high unem-ployment (greater than 12 per cent). Overall, accountability for TJF was focused on what was achieved by way of program outputs rather than on the control of program inputs.

But time and the highly public events associated with the release of the internal audit and the relentless opposition and media criticism changed the context, mobilized new forces, and upset the precarious balance. In the new context, the pendulum dramatically shifted as accountability was defined exclusively in terms of program inputs and financial controls and not in terms of the results achieved. Program flex-ibility as a way to respond to different local conditions came to be seen as special treatment, a lack of transparency, and inequity in accessing the programs.

If academics, politicians, and auditors can recognize the difficulties in these dilemmas, what does this mean for public servants who must actu-ally practice public management in the real world? Are inherent contra-dictions and harsh trade-offs always the inevitable end-point of public management reform? When is there real room for balance? Why is this balance so hard to achieve? How is balance achieved in practice? Why does there appear to be balance at one point in time only to be dramatically rebalanced at a later time? Why is balance hardest to achieve when it is needed the most, during periods of rapid change within government?

When it comes to questions of achieving and maintaining balance, most public servants do not think about dichotomies and contradic-tions. They think about 'the swinging pendulum' and, indeed, they often speak from their own experience of 'the pendulum swinging too far.' Although they do not express their concerns the same way they implicitly agree with Peters who notes that 'the danger in administrative reform appears to arise in selecting one part of the dichotomy to the exclusion of the other.'[18] It's as if the heavy pendulum of administrative change, once it has become unstuck after 'long periods of routine,' gathers momentum during 'the occasional orgies of reform' and then swings back with such force that it undermines the very reform that is under way.

Why is each administrative reform a reaction to the failures of the previous reforms? Why are we surprised to see that the forces of administrative reform have swung the pendulum too far only to discover upon closer examination that we are now surprised for having been initially surprised? When reform is sometimes achieved, why is it so difficult to maintain? Why does it seem to take so long to 'get things going' only to see them go 'too far'? Why do some reforms start up and then quickly peter out as merely 'the flavour of the month,' while others are institutionalized and remain in place well beyond the period for which they are useful?

These are difficult questions. Some of which are addressed when I examine HRDC and its internal audit of the administration of its grants and contributions programs. The focus, therefore, is not aimed at the higher level of how the department went about implementing new reforms in public management. Rather, it is aimed at the lower level of how the department went about doing its normal work of administering grants and contributions and of undertaking its regular internal audits, all within the context of significant and dramatic changes in public administration.

First Impressions: The Public Release of the Internal Audit

On 19 January 2000, HRDC released a thirty-three-page internal audit of the administration of its grants and contribution programs undertaken by its own Internal Audit Bureau. The audit, or perhaps better referred to as a 'file review,' looked at a purportedly random sample of 459 project files from eight major grants and contributions programs,[19] delivered through regional offices and national headquarters. While the audit documentation indicated that the programs 'represent(ed) approximately $1 billion in annual federal spending,'[20] the audit was not a financial audit of the projects. Instead, it was a 'paper review' of the extent and nature of the documentation contained in 459 project files. Furthermore, the audit purported to 'assess the management and delivery of the grants and contributions.' Accompanying the audit was a press release indicating the audit had revealed 'a number of areas requiring improvement ... including project monitoring, contracting procedures and general financial practices.'

The press release emphasized that HRDC had 'already taken action to improve the administrative standards,' had put in place 'a comprehensive Action Plan,' and would be 'working hand in hand with the Auditor General as he conduct[ed] his government-wide review of grants and contributions.' Indeed, fifteen of the thirty-three pages detailed the department's action plan to remedy the situation, which the press release highlighted and which included the establishment within the department of a new national grants and contributions performance tracking directorate; clear direction to employees on proper management; supplemental training sessions for staff; holding managers accountable to ensure that proper procedures are followed; and the development of new management information systems. In addition to the release of the audit on 19 January, there was a 'technical briefing' of the media by senior officials of HRDC at 10:00 a.m. in the upstairs lounge of the National Press Building; a media scrum by Minister Jane Stewart at 1:30 p.m. in the foyer of the House of Commons; and follow-up interviews with the Minister by the national media that evening.

At the technical briefing, officials[21] described the results of the internal audit and the department's action plan that was underway. In response to the comment that holding a technical briefing on an internal audit was unusual and that its release at a time when the House of Commons was not in session was a deliberate strategy to pre-empt a subsequent leak of the audit, officials emphasized the importance of being 'open and transparent'[22] about the administrative problems and marshalling employees within the department to solve the problems. It was also confirmed that no officials were dismissed as a result of the audit findings.

At the media scrum, the Minister explained that the audit indicated that 'there is sloppy administration and that we need to do a better job of ensuring that our files are complete, decisions that are made are clear and the justification for those decisions is part and parcel of the files.'[23] In response to the question of whether 'heads would roll,' the Minister answered, '[T]his is not a witch hunt. This is about making sure we improve our administrative practices, that we track, that we train, that we do spots audits, that I measure my officials' performance reports about how well they make progress in this regard.' The Minister did not answer the question on the cost to Canadians of the shortcomings at HRDC, saying instead that 'I want to make sure, from a go-for-ward point of view, that the paper work is there.'

During a live interview on CBC Radio's *As It Happens*, a comment to the Minister was made pointing out that 'this may be the worst report card of a government department ... and you commissioned it.' In response, the Minister emphasized that she had instructed the deputy minister to take it seriously, that she wanted to see results in the short term, and that there would be no new grants and contributions monies flowing until there had been verification by departmental senior financial officers. She went on to defend the programs, emphasizing that they 'really make a difference in the lives of individuals and communities ... and if the integrity of these programs is undermined because of administrative sloppiness ... there is no way I could sweep this under the carpet.' In response to the observation that funding had been provided to hotel owners in the Prime Minister's riding, the Minister said, '[T]here's absolutely no indication from this report that there is any political influence or undue activity.'[24]

That night the national electronic media gave the item top billing. At 7:00 p.m. in its lead news story, *CBC Newsworld* referred to a 'stunning admission from the federal government.' *CBC National* referred in its top story to 'stunning revelations about government mismanagement on a monumental scale.' A reporter indicated that 'opposition critics [were] demanding that [the Minister] resign.' The assistant auditor general of the Office of the Auditor General for Canada observed: 'It's pretty pervasive and it's pretty serious. Once that kind of paperwork isn't there, anything can happen. There could be abuse, or there could be no abuse. You have no way of knowing.' Local Ottawa television summed up by saying, '[G]overnment officials are admitting they basically lost track of roughly a billion dollars.' Global Television referred to 'shocking revelations today' but included a clip from a Canadian Labour Congress spokesperson who cautioned that 'no matter how outrageous the administration of programs [is], we don't want to throw out the baby with the bathwater.'

That same day, the Opposition, which for some time had been strongly criticizing the government for its handling of the Transitional Jobs Fund (TJF), immediately jumped on the audit. Reform Member of Parliament and HRDC critic Diane Ablonczy declared that 'this program [TJF] is so deeply flawed; it is so corrupt. It's being used as a political slush-fund, with no accountability at all. I think it should be scrapped.'[25]

The next morning the print media across the country were seized by the issue. The 20 January 2000 headlines to their stories read:

- 'Bureaucrats mismanaged $3 billion, Ottawa says: Audit reveals mess in grant-giving process.' *The Globe and Mail*
- 'Audit finds Ottawa sloppy with job grants: 80% of projects that received money were never reviewed.' *National Post*
- 'Department loses track of $1 billion: sloppy records preclude monitoring of federal grants.' *Ottawa Citizen*
- 'Grant program out of control: Human Resources flunks audit.' *The London Free Press*
- 'Un monumental fouillis administratif.' *La Presse* (Montreal)
- 'Ottawa admits huge flaws in job grant programs.' *The Chronicle-Herald* (Halifax)
- 'Audit reveals bungling: Many Human Resource programs mismanaged.' *The Edmonton Sun*
- 'Sloppy records keep public from knowing if $1 billion in federal grants wrongly spent.' *The Vancouver Sun*

A reporter in *The Globe and Mail,* citing a regional HRDC official, noted that 'HRDC bureaucrats blamed cuts to their budgets in the mid-1990s for the administrative mess.' He also observed that 'Ms Stewart's job was made easier by the fact that she was not responsible for HRDC when the audited projects were approved' and by the fact that her deputy minister at the time the approvals were made 'now heads the entire civil service, as the Clerk of the Privy Council.' A *National Post* reporter noted that the Minister 'conceded ... massive flaws in the way the government hands out job creation grants,' adding that 'the report comes after months of denials.' The reporter reminded readers that last year the *National Post* 'published a series of articles revealing how companies in the Prime Minister's riding received millions worth of grants, even though their owners could no longer afford to pay their debts, had criminal records or troubles with the law and poor business records.' He questioned the motivation behind the decision to release the audit, suggesting that it was closely linked to the access to information (ATI) request by the opposition Reform Party. He concluded that 'the disclosure of the scathing audit and decision to adopt an action plan to correct the problems' comes in advance of the Auditor General's 'full-scale' review. This latter point was also noted in stories in the Holllinger press,

La Presse, and *Le Devoir.* The Information Commissioner noted that he was not surprised by the audit findings, concluding that it reflected inadequate management of government files. He indicated in a CBC Radio interview that 'the file management system within the government has collapsed and continues to collapse, and at this stage I don't see any enthusiasm within the government to tackle these problems.'

If the immediate media reports were highly critical of the Minister and her department, so too were the e-mails and letters the Minister received from citizens who heard about the audit on the evening news or from reading their morning newspapers. Their central concern revolved around the perception that somehow the government had lost '$1 billion' and so the Minister should resign and bureaucrats should be fired.

Within less than twenty-four hours, the fundamental issues around which the grants and contributions audit would revolve over the course of the next year were taking hold. These first impressions, whether accurate or not, would become lasting impressions despite the constant efforts of the Minister, her departmental officials, the Prime Minister, and others to explain otherwise. These impressions would shape where and how the media shone its spotlight as the events unfolded and as the face and complexion of the issues continuously shifted and changed.

The media reporting would start with the impression that '$1 billion' in public money had been lost. It would then focus on variations to this overall theme. It would treat all grants and contributions programs as job-creation programs, when only one-tenth of the total money was spent on these programs. It would focus on those 'bungling bureaucrats' who were 'to be paid bonuses for cleaning up the mess,' and would put the spotlight on 'who knew what, when and where' and on 'whose head should roll.' It would begin to make charges of a strategic, pre-emptive release of the internal audit by government in advance of an access to information request. It would focus on the previous minister of HRDC, the previous deputy minister, and the grants and contributions programs in other departments, especially the Canadian International Development Agency (CIDA) and the Department of Indian Affairs and Northern Development (DIAND). It would focus on the Prime Minister and job projects in his riding, and it would allege political influence and interference in the awarding of grants and contributions. It would sharply question the neutrality of the public service. It would turn to charges of criminal behaviour by recipients of government grants and contributions and police investigations. It would question the integrity and effectiveness of all grants and contributions programs, and as the department implemented corrective actions, it would raise concerns about the rebureaucratization of government, the dramatic increase in checking and rechecking of project applications, and the inability of some sponsors to receive their funding. It would lead to the unanimous call by the Parliamentary Committee of Human Resources Development to terminate the Canada Jobs Fund and disband the entire department.

These impressions go to the heart of the central themes of public administration and how it is changing in response to the new challenges facing government. If the internal world of public management is one of balance and trade-offs in the face of contradictions and paradoxes, then the external world is one of first impressions and conclusions in the face of deep-seated attitudes and predispositions about the nature of government and bureaucracy. If public servants attempt to resolve contradictions (some might say hide them), the media attempt to expose them. If the internal balance and trade-offs take considerable time to achieve, the external impressions and conclusions are formed instantaneously. The resolution of the contradictions and paradoxes and their attendant complicated explanations that preoccupy public servants are not news and are not of interest to the outside world or the media, but exposure of the contradictions themselves and the impressions they leave are. On the outside there is little or no time to explain or reconcile the contradictions and paradoxes. Public impressions are and must be formed quickly, and once formed they are hard to change.

Nearly a year after the release of the internal audit report, Arthur Kroeger, a highly respected former deputy minister of many federal departments, reflected on the events in a public speech. He noted that 'there are some important aspects of the affair that have received far less attention than they deserve, with the result that a seriously distorted picture is now firmly established in the public's mind.'[26] But, we get ahead of ourselves. Before we can describe the events that unfolded following the release of the audit on 19 January 2000 through to the Auditor General's Report on 17 October that same year, it is necessary to review the political and administrative context for HRDC, its grants and contributions programs, and its internal audit. The political and administrative context for the department finds its origins in the government's public sector reform initiatives that were a central feature of the 1990s.

CHAPTER TWO

Looking Back

The Context for Public Sector Reform

This chapter sets out the context for public sector reform that HRDC faced during the 1990s. The time period covers the creation of the department in 1993, the mid-1990s when the department delivered and administered its newly consolidated grants and contributions programs, up to and including the administrative audit of these programs in the late 1990s. It starts with the prevailing management philosophy of the day, describes the pressures on the department and government in the wake of fundamental government restructuring, and analyses how officials grappled with these changes as they implemented certain features of public management reform. In addition, the activities leading up to the audit and the final preparations for the public release of the internal audit are described. The central theme is not so much how officials found a sense of ongoing balance through this time of enormous change, but rather how they made tough trade-offs in turbulent times while catching their breath and rebalancing themselves during infrequent and brief intervals of calm.

I use the term public sector reform to convey the broad scope and far-reaching nature of the changes within government and the public service that were initiated during the 1990s. There were the major management reforms that began with Public Service 2000 in the early 1990s and carried forward by other management reform initiatives throughout the decade. There were also the sweeping changes in the machinery of government through the government's major reorganization in 1993, resulting in the creation of HRDC from the parts of five other departments. There was also the government's Program Review for 'Getting Government Right' in 1995, which included the most significant restructuring of government programs and deficit reduction efforts ever undertaken by a federal government. Throughout this period, the state of the federation was a matter of pressing national attention. In the early 1990s, both the Meech Lake and Charlottetown Accords failed to achieve constitutional reform, and in 1995 the federalist forces won a narrow victory in the 1995 Quebec referendum for sovereignty-association. In addition, the federal government transferred several program responsibilities to the provincial and territorial governments, the most important of which were the labour market development programs from HRDC.

Not only were each of these reforms significant in there own right but, perhaps not surprisingly, given the lengthy period of change involving two separate governments of different political stripes, they were not well aligned. As described by Ian Clark, a former secretary of the Treasury Board, their ordering was 'backward':

> Administrative reform preceded government restructuring, which preceded program review. In an ideal world, a government would decide 'what programs' it wanted to deliver, then 'which institutions' should be responsible for delivery, and then 'what management regime' was best suited to delivering the programs.[1]

It is particularly significant, however, that the ordering of these reforms had major implications for the way in which public servants in all departments, including HRDC, went about their day-to-day work of administering and delivering programs, weeding out programs that were no longer effective, cutting budgets and personnel, streamlining their operations, getting reliable feedback on program results and operations, and motivating overworked staff. It was not a matter of following a single blue print to implement a single project; rather, it was a matter of making a series of adjustments and changes to many projects and plans as larger events and circumstances unfolded.

Public Service 2000, which was launched in the early 1990s, set the management philosophy for the newly created HRDC in 1993. This public service reform was predicated on the view that removing or reducing management constraints would improve performance in government. At the time, this was a widely held view within government and one that was shared by the Auditor General.[2] As John Edwards, the former manager of Public Service 2000, has written:

> The primary factor that led to the launch of PS 2000 was the growing frustration, particularly throughout management ranks, at what were perceived

as excessive red tape and controls. As the public service absorbed a succession of budget cuts and sought to 'do more with less,' there was a widely held conviction that committed managers were being undermined by a culture based over(ly) much on rules – that following the rules was viewed as more important than getting results.[3]

In the words of a recent report issued by the Office of the Auditor General reflecting on public service management reform, Public Service 2000 'saw the need to move the public service orientation away from process and risk aversion to focus on more innovation, service quality, and results – to an organization with authority more decentralized and greater emphasis on using and nurturing the skills and potential of its workforce.'[4]

While public service reform was launched by Public Service 2000 and set a pattern for change, the philosophy of Public Service 2000 did not dominate the entire decade. The shaky start and un-coordinated approach in the early 1990s showed signs of greater coherency in the second part of the decade. Peter Aucoin, in a recent comparative analysis, concedes that 'the sequencing of initiatives, including the Program Review, the policy capacity and modernizing service delivery initiatives, La Relève and the articulation of the results-based management framework, reflected a more strategic and coordinated approach to public service reform than had been the case in the first part of the decade.'[5] Over the course of the decade, HRDC embraced each of these initiatives and in a number of areas – such as policy capacity, modernizing service delivery, and instituting a results-based management regime – was a leader within the public service.

There can be little argument with the observation that the creation of the Department of Human Resources Development 'represented by far the most significant development arising out of the June 1993 reorganization and consolidation of cabinet portfolios.'[6] The new department was large – $69 billion in expenditures in 1993–94 – representing half of the government's expenditure budget.[7] Far more significant than size, however, was the vast array and complexity of the program responsibilities assigned to the newly created department. Its programs touched nearly every aspect of human and social development. Just listing its areas of responsibility is daunting: investment in children in their early years and the reduction of child poverty; post-secondary education through student loans; assistance for youth in making the critical transition from school to work and securing their first job; skills upgrading and training for those in the labour force; protection and insurance for the temporarily unemployed; employment programs for groups at risk, such as youth, Aboriginals, persons with disabilities, and seasonal and chronically unemployed workers; adjustment programs for older workers and for those in regional resource industries experiencing dramatic downturns, such as the fishery; literacy programs for workers and children; regulations to ensure a safe and productive workplace for workers; reconciliation of labour-management disputes in industries falling under federal jurisdiction; income security programs for all elderly, including the elderly poor; and a system of universal retirement pensions for older Canadians.

The complexity of the department stems from the scope of the activities found in the five originating departments. HRDC was an amalgam of the Employment and Insurance Branches of the Canada Employment and Immigration Commission (CEIC), the entire Department of Labour, significant components of the Secretary of State, major programs of the Department of Health and Welfare, including direct transfer payments to individual Canadians, and selected programs of the Department of Multiculturalism and Citizenship. Each of the founding departments and most of the programs transferred to the new HRDC contained grants and contributions programs that were important instruments for achieving particular objectives across the broad area of human development.

The eight major grants and contributions programs, which were delivered by HRDC and subsequently became the subject of the internal administrative audit, found their origins in these five founding departments. Most of the grants and contributions were labour market training programs, initially delivered by CEIC and designed to meet the needs of particular Canadians such as persons with disabilities, Aboriginals, youth, new entrants to the workforce, women, and low-skilled workers. Only 10 per cent were direct job creation programs in the form of the Transitional Jobs Fund (TJF), designed to encourage sustainable jobs in regions of high unemployment. Others were social development programs originating from the Department of Health and Welfare; learning and literacy programs from the Secretary of State and the Department of Multiculturalism and Citizenship; and a few others from the Department of Labour. Over several years, these programs evolved and changed to meet the emerging needs of citizens, and their design and delivery were shaped by the changing management philosophy of the day and the evolving priorities of the government.

The comprehensive efforts of the Liberal government in 1995 to 'Get Government Right' through significant restructuring and to 'put its fiscal house in order' through dramatic reductions in expenditures had a particularly significant impact on HRDC. This was a department unlike many others, not just in size but more important in its diversity and complexity. It was a major policy department, created by the Conservative government to consolidate government organizations. The Liberal government reinforced and continued the department with the implicit objective of providing a counterweight to the well-established and sophisticated policy capacity of the Department of Finance. HRDC was also a major program delivery department, which permitted the government of the day to directly reach and touch Canadians through statutory programs involving direct transfers payment to individuals and through discretionary, non-statutory grants and contributions programs providing benefits to organizations and individuals. For a new department, that was the major player in both the formulation of social and human development policy and in the delivery of programs and services directly to Canadians, the 1990s was a period of unprecedented policy, program, expenditure, and administrative change. As the 'social face' of the federal government, the newly established HRDC was at the centre of these changes, not just in the sense that it was leading these changes, but also by responding, adjusting, and adapting to a broader set of fundamental fiscal, economic, social, and political forces.

The ink was still wet on the plans of the Transition and Renewal Secretariat, responsible for moulding the five departments into one, when the newly appointed HRDC minister launched a major social security review in 1994.[8] Although the review did not focus on the department's grants and contributions programs, it did examine a broad range of options for completely restructuring all its statutory programs – social assistance, employment insurance, employment benefits, pensions, and student loans. After one year, this overly ambitious comprehensive reform, which had preoccupied the minister and much of the department, collided with the fiscal reality of deficit reduction and the imperative of budget cuts in the government-wide Program Review. The result: the comprehensive effort of a total social security review was dead. All that remained on the table was the prospect of a fiscally driven reform of employment insurance.

Up to that point, the department was exempt from the government's Program Review on the understanding between the Ministers of HRDC and Finance that the high-profile and comprehensive review of social security programs would yield 'the required savings to the fisc.' As a consequence, there was no review within the department of the programs and operations outside social security. When it became clear in early 1995 that no savings would be realized from the social security review in time for announcement in the upcoming February 1995 budget, the Minister of Finance imposed on the department a substantial expenditure reduction of $1.1 billion annually, consisting of reductions in programs and reductions in personnel. More specifically, the budget cut included a $900-million reduction in employment programs and a 20 per cent cut of its 25,000 staff over three years, yielding $200 million in annual savings.[9]

HRDC embarked upon this immediate and urgent challenge against the backdrop of the spirit of Public Service 2000, which called for the removal and reduction of constraints and red tape that had long frustrated public service mangers in achieving results. More broadly, this exercise was undertaken in the context of reforms in public management, the benefits of which were being extolled by practitioners and leaders in Ottawa, and by many leading academics. The apparent success of such reform initiatives in other countries, particularly the Westminster systems of Australia, New Zealand, and the United Kingdom, reinforced the view that constraints could be removed and services improved during a period of restructuring and expenditure reduction. It is important, however, to note that the reforms in these countries to remove constraints were not triggered by public servants, as was the case in Canada, but by politicians who, in the words of Aucoin, perceived public service bureaucracies to be 'obstacles to governmental reform' and thereby 'a major part of "the problem" of governance.'[10] In Canada, the problem was not a public service that was unresponsive to the needs of the government, but rather a long-standing tradition of internal public service rules and constraints that stood in the way of achieving results.

The concept for these reforms found their origins in the new public management literature,[11] although neither the Conservative Mulroney government nor the Liberal Chrétien government ever formally endorsed new public management. Public servants almost never used the term 'new public management,' but instead spoke of public service reform or public sector reform. Sandford Borins has described the idea of new public management as

nothing less than a normative re-conceptualization of public administration consisting of several inter-related components: providing high-quality services that citizens value; increasing the autonomy of public managers, particularly from central agency controls; measuring and rewarding organizations and individuals on the basis of whether they meet demanding performance targets; making available the human and technological resources that managers need to perform well; and, appreciative of the virtues of competition, maintaining an open-minded attitude about which public purposes should be performed by the private sector, rather than the public sector.[12]

He goes on to add that 'some important results will flow from this agenda: innovative bureaucracies that provide better service, produced at lower cost by public servants whose morale has improved.'[13] Some of these claims may or may not be realized; it is never possible to know for sure, because no public administrative reform is ever introduced on a clean sheet. Instead, reforms are always undertaken, in part more often than in whole, against the backdrop of the mess and clutter of everyday life. In public administration nothing is ever neat and tidy.

Cutting Administration While Maintaining Quality Service

In March 1995, HRDC officials knew that it was not a matter of making things neat and tidy around the department but of doing some major spring-cleaning. To secure 'Program Review' savings of $900 million annually the department and its minister took bold steps by eliminating and reducing programs on a permanent basis. Programs under the Canada Jobs Strategy and Strategic Initiatives were eliminated. The Program for Older Workers Assistance was eliminated and transfers to the provinces under the Vocational Rehabilitation for Disabled Persons were frozen. In short, if these activities were priorities then others should do them. Given the magnitude of these program eliminations and reductions, the minister and the department had no appetite for further program cuts.

When it comes to budget reductions, it is often assumed that eliminating programs, rather than reducing operations, is the most important and significant decision. Ironically, it is the decisions concerning service delivery and operations that can sometimes turn out to have the farthest-reaching implications. Faced with the immediate need to reduce staff by 5,000 and achieve $200 million in savings, the department launched a series of mutually reinforcing initiatives that flowed directly from the reforms in public management. The initiatives focused on restructuring and improving service delivery, increasing productivity, improving and measuring program performance, streamlining administration and reducing overhead, eliminating 'red tape,' and empowering employees. Underpinning this was the recognition of the need to invest in the department's human resources through leadership and skills training and in information technology to support its service delivery.

This work began in earnest against the backdrop of one very important requirement – while expenditure savings were to be achieved and the number of personnel reduced, service to the public was to be maintained. Despite attempts to reconcile it, this contradiction remained. Achieving expenditure targets was the dominant concern of the Minister of Finance and maintaining or even enhancing service to citizens was the dominant concern of departmental ministers. While ministers were prepared to see some programs eliminated or reduced and others transferred to the provinces or privatized, they were not prepared to see the service levels reduced for the national programs that would remain. This included many of the important programs delivered by HRDC that directly touched people, such as employment insurance and training programs for the unemployed, old age security payments for the elderly, income supplements for the elderly poor, and loans for post-secondary students. As it would turn out, this assumption – to maintain service levels to the public – would not only significantly shape what was done but would also have unforeseen consequences on the future operation of the department.

With a focus on maintaining service to the public, officials turned their attention to achieving savings through reducing administration and support functions and restructuring the department's service delivery network. They focused on what is normally called 'overhead' or, as referred to by some in HRDC, 'the frozen middle.' Administration and support services are often an easy target in budget reduction exercises, largely because there are no supportive constituencies external to government and those few on the inside are too busy protecting their own programs and resources. What did it actually mean to cut administration and support services? It required significant reductions and, in some cases, the elimination of complete functions in such areas as finance, accounting, audit and review, post audit, records keeping, administration, clerical services, access to information and privacy, operational planning, communications, evaluation, and program support. Because the reductions targeted these areas and not program delivery, the actual magnitude of the reductions made to these administrative and support functions was much greater than the required 20 per cent. These reductions were made to the headquarters in Hull, to the ten regional head-quarters located in each province, and to the many service delivery units across the country.

What is required when a department cuts its 'overhead'? There is little doubt that it means the elimination of 'deadwood,' the weeding out of inefficient operations, and the termination of unnecessary or duplicating functions. It also requires that the department make investments and adjustments through information technology and process improvements to deal with these changes and thereby maintain or perhaps increase organizational efficiency. In short, a rebalancing takes place. But reductions of this magnitude, the results of which need to be delivered quickly, also mean that some necessary and indeed essential functions and personnel are removed. Experienced clerical staff, with memories for administrative detail and responsibilities for ensuring project files are complete and orderly, are no longer there. There are fewer 'checkers' to 'check up' on and make sure that administrative procedures are followed. Fewer internal auditors are there to find errors that administrators can correct in a timely manner without the distorting glare of media. There are fewer and less experienced communications officers to maintain open and professional links with the media and to quickly and accurately answer their probing questions. The fewer, remaining financial officers must answer ever increasingly more technical and complex questions with which they have had little experience. Operational review teams that at one time conducted regular office reviews to ensure financial and program compliance are no longer there. In the Ontario region, for example, the Operational Review and Management Support (ORAMS) unit that conducted non-financial audits and reviewed operational and decision-making processes on behalf of the regional assistant deputy minister was eliminated. Fewer program officers were required to monitor many more project files. Fewer systems experts were available to put in place the computer information systems for automating service delivery.

If there is one area of government where experienced personnel matter most it is in administrative and support functions.[14] It is in these functions where the employees tend to be older and have more experience in one single area than is the case in policy, program, or service delivery. Their valued-added expertise comes not just from what they know but from knowledge tested by experience. It is the experienced and seasoned financial officer who knows how to find the right balance in providing candid advice to the program officer about how to avoid offending the procedures in the manual while still meeting the needs of the program and its clients. While corporate memory is important in most government functions, when it comes to administration, it is critical. When it is lost, balance is more difficult to maintain and there is greater risk of organizational error. Lest anyone be sceptical about the importance of preserving corporate memory in the public service, it is now a key component of the federal government's recently launched strategy for 'a public service learning organization.'[15]

The departure of the 5,000 employees from the department was made easier through the use of two government-wide workforce adjustment measures – early retirement incentives (ERI) and early departure incentives (EDI).[16] The ERI, available to employees between fifty and sixty years of age, provided a significant incentive since it eliminated the pension penalty for those employees under fifty-five years of age with less than thirty years of service. The EDI offered cash payment in return for resignation from the public service. These two programs were provided to employees on a volunteer basis and the department had little control over which employees left. This resulted in the department losing a disproportionately larger share of its experienced employees who had a long history in the support and delivery of grants and contributions programs. In addition, in the face of a record-high number of claimants for unemployment insurance benefits in 1996–97, those employees who were cross-trained in both insurance and employment programs were required to work exclusively on insurance. This further reduced the number of employees who could support employment grants and contributions programs. In short, with the downsizing of employees, the department lost much of its 'corporate memory' in administration and support functions.

In the mid-1990s, the department completely re-engineered its service delivery network by replacing 450 Canada Employment Centres with 100 'parent' offices of Human Resource Centres Canada (HRCCs) and 200 satellite offices.[17] Maintaining service levels required a number of things – one-stop, single-window service; extensive use of electronic service through the use of kiosks; strengthening and expanding telephone call centres; partnerships with service providers; and contracting with private sector delivery partners in the more remote areas of the country where offices were being closed. One-stop service required cross-training among staff so that those employees responsible for the delivery of employment and training programs could also help those with an increasing workload of employment insurance claims. Kiosks and call centres required capital investments, and more private sector partnerships meant more complicated accountability in service delivery arrangements. Underlying all of this was the need for better information and, hence, more documentation.

The department strengthened its field operations by appointing 100 directors at the 'executive one' level to manage the Human Resource Centres. They were delegated increased responsibility for program approval and budgets and were encouraged to be innovative and responsive to citizens' needs. Against the backdrop of a tradition of rigid program and administrative criteria, managers were encouraged to be flexible within the parameters of the legislation, regulations, and the reduced number of program and administrative policies and procedures. It was recognized that partnerships with business and social development organizations in the diverse communities across the country were critical in the delivery of quality service to citizens. A new level and scale of local partnership arrangements began, including the $100 million Transitional Jobs Fund.

The manner in which the department embraced partnerships had far-reaching implications on the way it managed its grants and contributions programs. This is best illustrated in the partnership arrangements developed for the approval and delivery of projects under the Transitional Jobs Fund. Project development and decision-making authority was devolved to the regional and local level. HRCC directors and their staff were closely involved with private and voluntary sector sponsors in the formulation of projects, and the HRDC regional directors-general were largely responsible for recommending projects for the approval of the Minister. Private sector sponsors were expected to contribute to the projects, with the government focused on levering private money through public funds to create jobs in areas of high unemployment. The partnership arrangements were clearly community and locally focused with regional and local public officials afforded considerable flexibility within broad guidelines in the assessment and determination of projects. To ensure projects could be tailored to the unique local circumstances, Members of Parliament played a formal role in advising the Minister on the approval of individual projects within their ridings. Provinces were important partners in the process and their concurrence was required for projects to proceed.

As partnerships with business and voluntary sector organizations became increasingly used as a means to deliver federal grants and contributions programs to individuals and communities, new issues of accountability were raised. As the following exchange reveals, when the Clerk of the Privy Council appeared at the Standing Committee investigating the grants and contributions audit, not every Member of Parliament shared the same enthusiasm for partnerships as did the public service:

Member of Parliament: 'Whenever we get into partnerships, we get into trouble and particularly because we lose control. I never know who is in charge. For example, if a businessman puts in three quarters of the investment and we put in one quarter and then he decides to move, how could we possibly stop him when three quarters of the money is his?'

Secretary to the Cabinet and Clerk of the Privy Council: '... there are many complexities to the accountability process. The partnership that the honourable member refers to adds to that complexity. That is not a call to go back to simple federal delivery of programs because I think we are potentially much more powerful and effective when we work in partnership.'[18]

The department, as part of a government-wide initiative to improve the quality of service delivery to Canadians, accelerated its efforts to develop and publish service standards for its core programs in the areas of employment insurance, old age security payments, guaranteed income supplements for the elderly poor, and employment benefits and measures.[19] The department launched 'A Quality Services Journey,' which emphasized 'innovative changes in service delivery, advanced technology and an empowered and more autonomous local management with greater authority and maximum flexibility.'[20] In 1997, the department made a commitment that it would publish service standards for all points of service by 1998. The high priority that employees attached to this initiative was confirmed in the approving words of the Auditor General in his April 2000 report, in which he noted that the department 'has made considerable progress in addressing service quality.'[21] This was part of the quality-service movement that was not only sweeping HRDC, the federal government, and other governments in Canada, but also nearly every other modern government throughout the Western world. In the federal government the quality-service movement was aggressively championed by the Treasury Board Secretariat and had strong and highly visible support from the President of the Treasury Board and other ministers. With improved service standards in place, ministers were more prone to enhance or at least protect the level of service to the public and had no appetite for its reduction.

The inherent contradiction between cutting staff and maintaining service delivery was generally recognized but not easily reconciled. There were different views on the dilemma as reflected by officials in different parts of the organization – the centre vs. the regions, policy vs. operations, and programs vs. service delivery. The closer the officials looked, the more apparent it became that it was not a question of finding balance but of making trade-offs. There were only so many savings that could be achieved from restructuring the service delivery network. And even at that, some smaller and remote offices had to be closed and their services contracted out, and others changed to provide service via electronic kiosks. There were, of course, some efficiency savings to be realized. Some balance was invariably found by cutting out unnecessary and duplicating support functions, redesigning the entire service network, and eliminating counter-productive program and administrative procedures and processes. But, given the magnitude of the required reductions, these actions only took the department so far. In the end, risks had to be calculated and difficult trade-offs made, sometimes explicitly but more often implicitly. That meant sacrificing something immediately with the hope of restoring balance in the future. What officials gave up was administrative and support capacity both in the field and at national headquarters that underpinned the management of grants and contributions programs.

At a more sophisticated level, some advocate the need to build redundancy and productive overlap into organizations so that they have the capacity to respond to unexpected shocks and events.[22] Some argue convincingly that organizations should build in 'an optimal level of redundancy.' In practice, however, it is always difficult to argue for redundancy in public sector organizations and especially at a time of dramatic downsizing. It is also very difficult to successfully argue for redundancy in administrative functions that are all too often viewed as 'overhead' at best and 'counter-productive' at worst. There is rarely a constituency outside or inside government that is prepared to argue for strengthening the administrative capacity of government at any time. During a period of downsizing, administration becomes the target to be cut, not the area to be protected.

Empowering Staff While Achieving Results

Leadership skills and training for employees was an essential component of HRDC's overall strategy for dealing with change. By the mid-1990s, it was clear that the Public Service 2000 initiative had failed to make any government-wide breakthrough in the area of human resources management. This failure only encouraged large departments like HRDC to initiate their own reforms within the constraints of existing legislation and centrally imposed rules. Against the backdrop of a history of limited success of government-wide performance-based pay reforms in Canada and elsewhere,[23] HRDC turned its energy to developing the leadership skills of its employees. It started at the top with its executives and managers and then turned to its front-line employees.

The department developed a leadership profile that drew its inspiration from the new approaches to human resources that were part of the new public management reforms.[24] The new leadership profile was strongly promoted by the most senior executives and enjoyed the wide support and commitment of managers and staff, many of whom had been advocating the need for greater flexibility, innovation, and empowerment in the management of their operations. Not only did the leadership profile set the tone for executive and employee behaviour, but it also formed the basis for executive compensation. Managers would 'walk the talk' and be compensated for it as well.

The one-page profile contained five central statements of prescribed behaviour that resonated with employees: 'taking ownership of change, supporting people, breaking constraints, making it happen, and investing in partnerships.' These prescriptions reinforced employees' existing behaviour, encouraged others to adjust, and created the expectation that executives and managers would now be operating under this new framework. The profile elaborated the expectations with such bold expressions as:

- driving change with courage and confidence so ideas, events and processes are challenged and people feel supported,
- enable and show support for people to question the status quo and take risks,
- promoting and trying new ideas and accepting the responsibility when things go wrong,
- unleashing people to think boldly and implement new ways of doing business, letting go of control oriented processes so teams take initiatives and accept accountability for results,
- building relationships with internal and external partners based on mutually acceptable conditions to improve client service, and
- setting personal agendas aside to deal with issues in an objective manner and act on inputs from clients, partners and colleagues.[25]

The importance of the leadership profile to employees was reinforced through annual performance reviews, regular meetings, staff retreats and conferences at all levels in the department, and through day-to-day work. The profile was also integrated into the training of executives, managers, and front-line employees.

As the department encouraged its employees to challenge processes, procedural constraints and controls, it also asked that they give more attention to achieving results. In the mid- to late 1990s, measuring and reporting on program results increasingly became a key feature of government-wide efforts to improve performance reporting. As Evert Lindquist observes, '1997 was the year for "results" in the nation's capi-tal,'[26] with all federal departments agencies required to submit perfor-mance reports to Parliament. In 1996, in advance of this government-wide initiative, HRDC revamped its program results and performance system, putting in place a new 'Results-Based Accountability Frame-work.' In the place of an antiquated system of dozens of overlapping and little-used indicators of program performance, it established twelve key performance measures for its four major program areas, along with a series of secondary measures to monitor operations. Fewer, but better indicators offered the prospect that program performance would actu-ally be measured and that the results would be reported to, and actually used by, senior managers to monitor performance and make improve-ments and adjustments. For employment and training programs, the department established two measures. The first was a measure of the number of clients returning to work as a consequence of the training or counselling initiative undertaken. The second, which was a derivative of the first, was the savings to the employment insurance account as a con-sequence of the client receiving income benefits for a shorter period of time.

The department was an innovator in the development and use of per-formance measures, going beyond other departments and agencies in government. HRDC quickly made its measures operational, which were reported quarterly on a regional and program basis to its Management Board, chaired by the deputy minister. In setting its new 'Results-Based Accountability Framework,' the department was exceptionally explicit about how its employees should now operate:

Human Resource Centres of Canada (HRCCs) will operate in an environ-ment that is characterized by: decentralized service delivery, relaxed bureaucratic controls, and increased flexibility for managing resources and programs to optimize service to the public. Armed with the latest in information technology, HRCC managers will be freed to focus on the client and to determine how best to meet client needs efficiently and effectively. Results will be the principal measure of success in this environment, rather than the means of achieving them. However, increased local level authority and flexibility need to be balanced by a clear set of management accountabilities. Managers require a clear vision of what they will be held accountable for, what results are expected of them, and how these results will be measured and used.[27]

Even if managers and employees only believed half of what they read, there was little doubt that emphasis would now be placed on achieving agreed-upon results with less emphasis placed on administrative processes and procedures. As the performance measures were implemented, there could be little doubt in the minds of employees as to their importance, since they were used, along with other results, such as the efficiency and accuracy in processing employment insurance claims, by the Management Board in assessing the annual performance and compensation for HRCC directors. The balance to be struck seemed clear to employees and managers – they would be rewarded for the program results they achieved and not for the administrative procedures they met.

Breaking Barriers to Achieve Results

Encouraging managers to focus on and to be accountable for program results was balanced with the need to provide them with more flexibility so they could actually achieve these results. Managers had long operated under a 'rule-bound' system of input constraints, despite evidence in theory and practice that many of these input constraints were unnecessary for proper control and, in many instances, impeded managers in the achievement of program results. These constraints, which were well known to seasoned managers, were found across the entire spectrum of administrative functions – finance, human resources, accounting, facilities and assets, procurement, monitoring, assessment, and program and service delivery. The idea of removing these constraints found its origins in the Public Service 2000. Although by the mid-1990s the credibility of Public Service 2000 had been significantly eroded in the eyes of public servants because of expenditure cuts, wage freezes, strikes, and governments reorganizations, there continued to a strongly held view that constraints which impeded the effective management of departments needed to be removed or reduced.

Throughout the early and mid-1990s, there were a number of important initiatives undertaken by the central agencies to remove unnecessary government-wide constraints and rules and to provide individual departments and agencies with increased flexibility and authority in the management and delivery of programs and services. For example, in the area of resource management, the Treasury Board put in place more flexible procedures that included single operating budgets; the elimination of person-year controls on departments; carrying forward to the following fiscal year up to 5 per cent of a department's budget for operating expenditures; increased retention for departments of funds raised from cost recovery; consolidation of vote structures in the expenditure estimates; streamlining procurement; greater flexibility in the management of real property; the elimination and streamlining of central administrative directives in areas like travel; and the optional use of a number of the government's common services like translation and Crown assets. While progress in reforming and streamlining the human resources function was significantly less successful, some changes were made in the areas of staffing, employees' benefits, and training and development. It was against the backdrop of these government-wide administrative reforms that HRDC launched its own internal efforts to cut its red tape and eliminate unnecessary constraints in management.

To streamline its administration and operations and facilitate local flexibility in program delivery, HRDC launched a high-profile initiative entitled 'Breaking the Barriers.' The initiative, which was promoted by HRDC's most senior executives and which resonated strongly with HRDC employees, focused on the immediate elimination of administrative barriers. The initiative was closely linked to and balanced with the focus on the achievement of program results, and was presented to staff not as an initiative to break rules but rather to eliminate unnecessary procedures and processes that stood in the way of achieving those results. As the assistant deputy minister, Finance and Administration, explained: 'We are not just breaking barriers for the sake of breaking barriers. We are eliminating barriers in order to help managers get results. If we expect managers to be accountable, to improve service and to get results from the programs they manage, then they should expect that corporate services will eliminate the unnecessary barriers that stand in the way.'[28]

'Breaking the Barriers' was particularly well received by administrative and service delivery staff, both at headquarters and in the ten regions of the department. After decades of piling more constraints on top of more rules, it was now time for managers to identify and eliminate barriers that were unnecessary and stood in the way of serving the client and achieving results. This popular initiative produced seven reports in rapid succession that were widely distributed and read by employees. Within a short time, forty-three separate barriers were eliminated, such as simplifying youth employment program approvals; eliminating 250 financial codes; streamlining financial allotments; increasing local-office purchase authorities; simplifying government employee travel policy; and increasing direct deposits of clients' training allowances. The initiative was so successful that it was duplicated and distributed government-wide by the Treasury Board Secretariat on its Web site and in hard copy under the 'Breaking the Barriers' banner. Deputy ministers in all departments were briefed on the initiative at a weekly Deputies Breakfast chaired by the Clerk of the Privy Council. In the introduction to the Treasury Board Secretariat report, *Breaking the Barriers: Innovation in the Public Interest*, the Clerk of the Privy Council challenged public servants to 'relentlessly pursue the elimination of self-inflicted impediments to improved service delivery – such as bureaucratic red tape, turf protection and the fear of change.'[29]

Devolving Training Programs to the Provinces and Territories

The major policy initiative of the Liberal government to devolve labour market training programs to the provincial and territorial governments fundamentally changed the grants and contributions programs in HRDC.[30] This massive realignment of the responsibility for the design and delivery of training programs within the federation found its genesis in the establishment of new tools in support of labour market training under Part 11 of the new Employment Insurance (EI) Act of 1996. These so-called Part 11 tools, formally called employment benefits and measures, were designed as a highly flexible set of instruments to help unemployed Canadians get and keep work and thereby reduce further financial draws on the EI account. These measures, available to individuals receiving EI income benefits (i.e., 'existing claimants' or 'reachback claimants,' those who had received EI benefits in the last three years), were funded entirely from the EI account and involved significant expenditures, beginning from a base of $1.9 billion in 1996–97 and rising, through new incremental funding, to over $2.2 billion by 2000–

2001. At the very time that all programs were being dramatically cut or eliminated, this, along with the new Transitional Jobs Fund, was the only area of new activity with an increasing budget.

The employment benefits and measures included wage subsidies, earnings supplements, self-employment assistance, job creation partnerships, and skills loans and grants. The department's program evaluations had provided some reliable evidence about what worked and what did not work when it came to employment programs. While there was no single formula, one conclusion, which was universally shared, was the need for flexibility at the local level. Therefore, rather than applying national program rules and guidelines across the country, local HRCCs were given the authority and were expected to design the mix of these programs that best fit their client and community needs. For example, wage subsidies could be provided to employers to hire new workers, and earnings supplements could be provided to eligible workers to top up wages, depending on the particular circumstances. The terms and conditions for these employment benefits and measures were intentionally broad to support local flexibility and innovations in delivery. They also enabled innovative service delivery through the creation of single-window co-locations ('guichets uniques') with provinces and municipalities at the local level.

The legislation, regulations, design, and delivery parameters for these Part 11 programs were developed against the backdrop of the Prime Minister's commitment in the final days of the 1995 Quebec referendum on sovereignty-association to transfer labour market training programs to the provinces. Because this commitment was the centrepiece of the government's efforts to renew the federation through non-constitutional means, finishing touches were made to the EI legislation to ensure that the Part 11 provisions would be 'provincially friendly.' The overall approach was decidedly asymmetrical, with the clear expectation that different arrangements would emerge in each province, depending upon its desire to enter into a labour market agreement and its own unique labour market requirements. On the one hand, this meant an emphasis on program results, in the form of measuring the extent to which the initiatives encouraged EI recipients to return to work and stay in work, and the consequent savings to the EI account. On the other, it meant there would be no 'one-size fits all' national operational guidelines and no overall program-input controls and rules. The program guidelines were flexible so that different program terms and conditions could be tailor-made to address the varying local needs across different provinces.

Over the next two years, Ottawa and the provinces and territories negotiated a number of high-profile Labour Market Development Agreements (LMDAs), which involved, in varying degrees, a significant shift in responsibilities from the federal to provincial governments in the area of results, programs, accountability, and financial and human resources. In the space of a few years, HRDC moved to four separate and distinct asymmetrical arrangements. At the one end of the spectrum there were seven provinces and territories, led by Alberta and Quebec, and including New Brunswick, Manitoba, Saskatchewan, the Northwest Territories, and Nunavut, which moved to a full devolution of labour market training, including the full transfer of programs, financial and human resources, and accountability. At the other end there was Ontario where HRDC, under an environment of great uncertainty, continued full responsibility for the delivery of labour market training, despite over five years of 'on again-off again' LMDA negotiations.

In between were two distinct arrangements under which LMDAs had been negotiated. One was the 'co-management arrangement' which had been negotiated in Newfoundland, Prince Edward Island, British Columbia, and the Yukon and which involved joint federal and provincial labour market planning and accountability, but with responsibility for delivery and resources retained by the federal government. In the case of British Columbia, some viewed this as an interim arrangement and as a first step towards an eventual full devolution. The other arrangement was the 'strategic alliance,' negotiated in Nova Scotia and involving a greater role for the federal government in the determination of planning and priorities than was the case in the co-management arrangement. As result of these four separate and distinct arrangements HRDC transferred nearly 2,000 of is service delivery and support employees to provincial and territorial governments. Once again corporate memory was lost to the department.

Four separate and distinct regimes for the delivery of labour market training programs added immeasurably to the complexity faced by the department. Those regions that devolved responsibilities to provinces also transferred program delivery and administrative support personnel. This resulted in an imbalance of administrative support across regions and between the regions and headquarters.

As the department devolved its labour market training programs to the provinces, it reduced its investment in management information systems for its grants and contributions programs. In the face of limited resources, the need for a program information systems that operated at the national level was less important. As a result, the department focused on developing regional information systems to meet the specific needs of the regions. Some had strong links to national headquarters and others did not. In the face of extraordinarily large, one-time costs to ensure safe passage through the Y2K problem, the department's scarce information systems resources were diverted away from grants and contributions programs and towards addressing legacy systems in support of statutory programs. There was disinvestment in those regions that devolved programs, underinvestment in the Ontario region, and little or no new investment in a national information system for grants and contributions. As a consequence, for example in Ontario, important information about the design and objectives of projects and services was located only in paper files that were located in many different offices. Computer systems no longer tracked project descriptions and target group details. This meant that when questions were raised in Parliament or in the media about individual grants and contributions projects, the department and the minister were often unable to provide immediate, accurate, and reliable answers.

Looking Ahead: A New Vision for the Department

As HRDC devolved a significant part of its discretionary program responsibility to provincial and territorial governments, the deputy minister launched a major effort to integrate the remaining pieces of the department and to provide a future vision for the new HRDC. This would preoccupy the senior executive and many of the program delivery managers in the department. The focus of this exercise, which would guide the department into what was called 'the post-LMDA world,' was the development of a new departmental vision through extensive consultation with employees. The vision was decidedly ambitious and expansionist. It set out a mission statement of 'enabling Canadians to participate fully in the workplace and the community,'[31] which was based on three concepts: enabling Canadians to help themselves by building upon the traditional role of the department as 'provider' and 'guardian'; encouraging full participation of all Canadians in the economy and society; and integrating the 'workplace' and the 'community' to capture the social and economic aspects of human development.

The vision also set out five important directions for HRDC policies and programs that would have immediate implications for staff. First, the department would provide 'the highest quality services' in its core programs of public pensions, employment insurance income benefits, labour regulation in federally regulated sectors, and the Canada student loans program. Second, it would 'emphasize preventative measures' and thereby reduce the risk of someone having to rely upon the department's remedial programs. Third, it would place new priority on the provision of information products and services to help Canadians make informed learning and employment choices. Fourth, it would focus on 'community capacity building' by using local offices as community resources centres and supporting staff as community catalysts and information partners. Fifth, it would 'act as leader in policies and programs' by making greater use of headquarters' policy analytical capacity at the regional and community levels.

As if this was not enough, two other elements were included in the vision statement, both of which would be important in shaping its implementation. The first was 'supporting people,' which was closely linked to the major initiative by the Clerk of the Privy Council to renew and revitalize the public service through the widely publicized 'La Relève' exercise.[32] HRDC, like most other departments, was especially concerned about it ability to recruit young, highly skilled, and promising professionals into its ranks. It also worried about the high number of its most experienced and skilled employees leaving for jobs in the private sector or retiring. Recruitment and retention, or 'R & R' as it came to be known to many in government, became the watchword for the department. Significant efforts were made to recruit university graduates, provide meaningful summer employment opportunities for students, and ensure greater training and development opportunities for existing staff. It was increasingly recognized that attending to the needs of employees, particularly in difficult times, was an important ingredient in ensuring a motivated and productive workforce.

The second was the launching of a major values and ethics initiative, which was built upon and extended the seminal work undertaken by the Deputy Minister Taskforce on Public Service Values and Ethics, headed by John Tait, as well as on earlier work by academics.[33] In its vision statement, HRDC emphasized that its core values, which had guided the actions of the department and staff over some time, had not changed but remained the foundation of the vision. After what the Auditor General referred to as 'an extensive dialogue with all staff,'[34] the department published a *Handbook on Values and Ethics in HRDC*[35] in 2000. The department also encouraged its managers to engage employees in openly discussing actual ethical dilemmas that they faced in their day-today work. The core values, which drew directly from the work of the Deputy Minister Task Force, included:

- democratic values, based on serving the public interest while respecting the legitimate authority of the ministers,
- people values, based on respecting, helping, and supporting the Canadian public, our partners, all employees of HRDC, and ourselves,
- professional values, based on carrying out our duties in the best manner possible, striving to continuously improve on the past traditions of Canada's public service, and
- ethical values, based on continually earning the public trust that comes form putting the common good ahead of personal advantage while abiding by our legal framework.

The *Handbook* emphasized that it had 'not developed any new values that (were) not already part of our culture at HRDC.' The values were intended to provide 'a context for values-based decision making,' recognizing that 'our system of laws and regulations provides the basis for many of our specific decisions.' While the document did not explicitly speak of the need to balance these values, it clearly indicated that 'democratic values provide the context for our professional, ethical and people values,' which was consistent with the John Tait Task Force.

The value and ethical dilemmas that HRDC officials, and indeed all public servants, were increasingly facing were found beneath the public sector reforms that were underway. Some of these dilemmas were less obvious and were deeply buried, whereas others could be uncovered by scratching the surface. New requirements for quality service to clients and traditional notions of accountability were placing public servants in difficult situations. Striking the proper balance between flexibility and responsiveness in programs to meet the specific needs of citizens on the one hand and accountability and control in programs and expenditures on the other, was not at all obvious. It represented a major new challenge for employees directing programs in the field and for employees managing programs and expenditures at headquarters. To meet that challenge, HRCC directors in the field increasingly sought the direct input of Members of Parliament and political staff at the local and national levels in an effort to better serve citizens.

Yet issues of political neutrality and political sensitivity were lurking just under the surface and dilemmas began to emerge. Public servants were being asked not only to develop partnerships with voluntary organizations in the delivery of public services but also to help build capacity within communities by strengthening such organizations. New dilemmas for public servants around public duties and private (voluntary) interests were also beginning to appear. Issues of confidentiality of government information in an environment of greater openness, stakeholder consultation, and citizen engagement raised perplexing ethical dilemmas that went well beyond the rules and regulations associated with access to information and the Official Secrets Act. Employees faced critical privacy of information issues in a department that relied heavily on large integrated personal data banks not only to ensure program integrity and minimize fraud in major benefit programs, such as employment insurance and income security, but also for the purposes of undertaking sound policy analysis and effective program design.

Throughout this period, the old values of traditional public administration – accountability, political neutrality, anonymity, and consistency – were rubbing up against the new values of the new public management – client (for some, customer) service, responsiveness, innovation, performance, and results. If the old values were the product of history reinforced through decades or even centuries of the traditions and practice of public administration, then the new values were the mantra of the private sector and were being adopted by the public service and very rapidly spreading throughout its ranks. That the two values could lead in different directions was generally recognized by most public servants, whether at the top of the organization, managing the departmental relationship with the minister, or at the bottom, managing the service delivery relationship to the citizen. What was not at all clear was how to deal with the undeniable tension between the two and in so doing synthesize or integrate them into the department.

There can be little doubt that the work of John Tait and the Deputy Mininster Task Force and the ensuing dialogue on values and ethics within HRDC was helpful in sensitizing employees to some of the fundamental value and ethical dilemmas that they faced. This dialogue was, however, only the beginning of an effort to reconcile the new values with the old in an organization under great pressure and fraught with its own contradictions.

Looking Behind: Making Grants and Contributions Auditable

As HRDC focused its attention on looking ahead to the challenges it faced, it occasionally glanced over its shoulder to see what was behind.

In 1998, in response to concerns about the management of The Atlantic Groundfish Management Strategy (TAGS), the House of Commons Standing Committee on Fisheries and Oceans asked the Office of the Auditor General to undertake an audit of the TAGS projects administered by HRDC. The Office of the Auditor General did not do this work itself. Instead, it asked the Internal Audit Bureau of HRDC to undertake this audit on its behalf. The audit was not a financial audit of the projects. Instead, it was a review of the paper documentation contained in individual project files. It concluded that there were 'a number of weaknesses in the management, control and monitoring of TAGS contribution projects.'[36] These results were included as a small part of the 1998 Auditor-General's report to Parliament, made without any opposition or public reaction. In recognition of these concerns about the administration of TAGS, HRDC executives asked its Internal Audit Bureau to undertake an audit of the administration of all other grants and contributions in the department in order to get a clear sense of the risks involved and whether any corrective action was required. This was the genesis of the 2000 internal administrative audit that was to shake the department and rock the entire government.

The internal audit of the HRDC grants and contributions programs was undertaken against the backdrop of a decade of dramatic change in public management. In the words of the audit report itself, it was undertaken in a 'new context for program administration.' It emphasized that 'the context for the administration of all of the department's programs, but especially for the Human Resources Investment Grants and Contributions programs (had been) considerably modified'[37] by the significant changes in most HRDC programs from the government-wide program review, the major downsizing of HRDC workforce and the disproportionate loss of those with experience, the new modes of service delivery, and the negotiation of LMDA agreements with the provinces. It went on to observe that 'conscious of the risk created by the increased complexity in program delivery, the changes to the environment and the impact of declining resources, HRDC management asked that the review of grant and contribution programs be given higher priority.'[38]

The new public management with its emphasis on increasing the autonomy of public sector managers to better serve citizens intensified the demands for financial and non-financial flows of information, be it information for program managers, senior executive, ministers, Members of Parliament, or the public. As Michael Power astutely explains:

> The 'hollowing out of the state' by the [new public management] gener-
> ates a demand for audit and other forms of evaluation and inspection to fill
> in the hole ... This is a deliberate erosion of central capacity in favour of
> the long distant mechanics of auditing and accounting ... The disaggrega-
> tion and devolution of public service provision require the specific tech-
> nologies or reaggregation and recentralization which accounting and
> auditing promise.[39]

The HRDC managers wanted a review of how the department was
administering its grants and contributions in a period of significant
change. By turning to their Internal Audit Bureau they were, by definition, asking for a static audit and not a dynamic review. The challenge
for auditors was to 'make things auditable' in the face of wholesale
changes in *what* was being audited (i.e., the grants and contributions
programs) and the dramatic changes in the *standard* to which the programs and management were to conform. This was a formidable challenge for auditors. How could they audit changing programs against
changing standards? If the new public management was asking a lot
from the audit, so were the senior HRDC managers of their own Internal Audit Bureau. What was the capacity of auditors to deliver? Were the
managers of the new public management asking too much? Or put
slightly differently, could an audit adequately fill in 'the hole' that the
new public management had created?

The concept of an audit has been evolving, some would say explod-
ing,[40] in Canada and elsewhere in the past thirty years. The commitment
to value for money (VFM) audits is internationally widespread and has
predated the development of new public management in many countries. These VFM audits can be broadly defined as 'audits' concerning
the adequacy of the development and management of programs to
ensure economy, efficiency, and effectiveness in the manner that an
organization pursues its goals and objectives. These audits go well
beyond traditional financial audits, which central audit authorities in
many countries have increasingly offloaded to internal audit organizations within government departments. In Canada, by far the most fundamental and far-reaching change in audit was the passage of legislation in
1977 which, for the first time, based the activities of the Auditor General
in law. Under this new mandate, in addition to the traditional 'financial
audit,' the Auditor General had important new responsibilities for VFM
audits to address 'the three E's' of government – economy, efficiency,
and effectiveness.

The new public management was fundamentally changing the way in which public servants were actually going about developing, managing, and delivering government programs. In short, the focus was on outputs and results and not inputs and administrative processes. The VFM audit was focusing on 'the three E's' through the development and application of supportive tools and techniques – such as results measurement, risk assessment, risk management, and wide-scale sampling – and by doing so offered the promise, perhaps more the hope, of reliable and timely feedback information for managers to ensure proper management and control. The focus of auditing changed fundamentally – from auditing the transaction, which was the underpinning of traditional financial audit, to auditing the management and control systems. As Power explains in cautionary language, 'the abstract system tends to become the primary external auditable object, rather than the output of the organization itself, and this adds to the obscurity of the audit as a process which provides assurance about systems elements and little else.'[41]

If new public management was fundamentally changing what managers and public administrators were focusing on, it was not changing the way in which internal auditors were undertaking their responsibilities. If we view the audit function as one component of accountability, it is easy to understand why. As Christopher Pollitt and Geert Bouckaert explain: 'The additional pressures which (new public management) reforms have put on accountability have not been met with any clear and coherent new doctrine to cope with the new circumstances.'[42] In the absence of clarity about how an audit should best be conducted in the world of the new public management, auditors continued with their existing practices. In short, they audited changing programs against old standards. While new public management has given public administrators the means to 'push things out' to better deliver programs and to achieve results, it has not yet provided them with the information to 'pull things in' to ensure sound management.

The Internal Audit Bureau did not view its task of auditing grants and contributions as new and thereby requiring a tailor-made methodology. Auditors simply viewed the audit as an extension of the way they did similar audits in the past. While the programs might have been changing, the audit standards were not.[43] In addition to the HRDC audit, the Bureau had previously undertaken two other management audits of grants and contributions programs – one in 1991 of the Canada Employment and Immigration Commission, and the other in 1994 shortly after the creation of HRDC.[44] The purpose of all three of these management audits was to review the documentation as contained in project files and to verify the presence or absence of special purpose forms which, to the auditors, would indicate the quality of the management and administrative controls. The completion of the forms containing information about the project inputs would be the measure of the quality of the management of the program. More specifically, the auditors reviewed paper forms in four management areas: selection and approval of projects, contracting for projects, overseeing projects, and disbursement of funds. These three audits were based almost exclusively on information contained in the individual project files. There was little or no information from site visits with sponsors or recipients where the projects actually took place or from interviews with officers directly responsible for the administration of the programs.

The 1991 audit found that many of the project files reviewed did not contain completed forms required by the relevant administrative manual. On this basis, auditors concluded that management control was deficient. The auditors concluded that poor documentation meant poor management, conjecturing that 'present monitoring does not offer adequate protection against possible misuse of public funds.' The 1994 audit found that none of the 1991 recommendations were satisfactorily implemented. The 2000 audit found that the state of documentation contained in the project files was deficient. Of the 459 project files reviewed, 15 per cent did not have applications from the sponsors. Of the remaining files 'missing documentation' included:

- cash flow forecasts, 72%
- estimates of the number of participants, 46%
- descriptions of the activities supported, 25%
- budget proposals, 11%
- descriptions of expected results, 11%[45]

Over the summer and fall of 1999, senior departmental officials[46] reviewed the preliminary findings and recommendations of the internal administrative audit that pointed out significant shortcomings in the adequacy of documentation contained in the project files. While they probed the audit results and questioned the internal auditors, they did not engage in a series of hard-nosed discussions and intense negotiations over the accuracy, reliability and, most important, the meaning and interpretation of the audit findings. The officials accepted the audit findings for what they said and focused their efforts almost exclusively on preparing an action plan to address the recorded deficiencies. This was dramatically different than the normal practice between departments and the external auditor (i.e., the Auditor General) where lengthy, difficult, and detailed negotiations over facts and interpretations take place often at the highest levels. Why was this case different? Why was there not a greater dispute over the audit findings and what they meant? Why did the department focus on addressing the problems that the auditors gave them and not on challenging their validity? In part, it goes to the essence of the distinction between internal and external audits.

The client for the internal audit is the department, including its managers and its deputy minister. The client for the external audit is Parliament and by extension the taxpayer. The head of the Internal Audit Bureau reports functionally to the deputy minister, usually through an assistant deputy minister. The external auditor – the Auditor General – is an agent of Parliament and more specifically of the Public Accounts Committee. He or she does not report to the government. Internal audit reports are provided to departmental managers (usually with copies to the Treasury Board Secretariat) and are normally made available publicly in a low-key manner on request or placed on the department's Web site. External audit reports are tabled quarterly in the House of Commons through the Speaker of the House in a high-profile manner, just as the Minister of Finance tables a budget, complete with an advanced 'lock-up' of the media. The Auditor General gives interviews to all media and his or her external audit is widely reported by the media. The internal audit has been the victim of significant departmental downsizing; the external audit has not been reduced as dramatically. The internal audit sometimes undertakes 'systems under development audits,' which provide immediate and ongoing results to managers so that programs can be changed and adjusted as they are implemented. The external audit normally produces final audits that identify areas for improvement after the program has been implemented.

While internal and external audits are different, they are related. There is varying, but limited, coordination between the two. In the case of HRDC, a senior member of the Office of the Auditor General is a member of the departmental audit and evaluation committee that provides broad guidance for undertaking audits and for their follow-up.

Looking Outward through an Internal Action Plan

HRDC officials focused less on challenging their internal auditors about the problems they had unearthed and what they meant for the organization and more on developing an action plan to correct the problems and gaining support from departmental employees for its implementation. A senior HRDC regional executive was assigned responsibility and an implementation team was put in place. The action plan that emerged was not complicated, but it did require moving quickly and sustaining the effort, and included a series of department-wide initiatives:

- the establishment of a new grants and contributions directorate to track and report on improvements in the management of grants and contributions,
- clear direction to all employees on proper management procedures,
- supplemental training sessions for staff,
- holding managers accountable for ensuring proper procedures are followed, and
- the development of new management information systems.

The department invested heavily in preparing the action plan. The need for a strong and credible plan was apparent to all. During the early summer and fall, the Minister and the Prime Minister were often on their feet in the House of Commons in response to opposition questions, fuelled by media reports about specific Transitional Jobs Fund projects in the Prime Minister's riding. Some Members of Parliament were calling on the Auditor General to undertake a review of these grants and contributions projects.

Following a briefing of the Minister by officials on the audit on 17 November 1999, the action plan was further strengthened. A week before the public release of the audit in January, the deputy minister spoke to 2,000 departmental employees via closed circuit television, briefing them on the results of the audit, securing their support in implementing the action plan and stressing the need 'to secure the right balance' between achieving results and ensuring accountability in the delivery of grants and contributions programs.

The department prepared a communications plan with options for the release of the audit against the backdrop of mounting criticism from the opposition and the media, particularly the *National Post*, about the Transitional Jobs Fund.[47] Essentially, there were two options: treat the internal audit in the standard low-key manner for such audits by posting it on the department's intranet Web site; or give the audit a higher profile and greater context by releasing it publicly. The HRDC Minister selected the latter option, which included a press release, a technical briefing of the media by officials, and a follow-up media scrum by the Minister.

Managing under New Public Management

It was against the backdrop of the new public management philosophy that HRDC went about addressing the significant challenges that it faced over the 1990s. The HRDC approach was a part of the approach taken by the federal public service in Canada to public management reform. Canada did not undertake a radical reform, but instead adapted elements of new public management to suit its own unique circumstances and requirements through a gradual and incremental approach. Some have viewed this as a prudent approach, others as 'half-measures';[48] others have seen it as a unique 'Canadian model';[49] others as lacking in 'strategic focus' and 'consistency,' with 'the results' having 'fallen well short of expectations';[50] others as 'a bewildering series of over-lapping and only loosely coordinated initiatives,' and still others as 'impressive, by any international standards.'[51]

HRDC similarly took a middle of the road approach to these management reforms as befits a social and human development department with a large decentralized service delivery function and significant policy responsibilities. Unlike the departments with responsibilities for agriculture, heritage, and customs and revenue, HRDC did not create new independent operating agencies with special authorities for its separate 'business lines' of employment insurance, income security, labour regulation, labour market training, student loans, and social development. Unlike Transport Canada, it did not privatize its insurance function or its student loans program. Like Transport Canada that transferred its airport responsibilities to local airport authorities, HRDC did transfer its labour market development responsibilities to various provinces in various ways. When it came to public management reform, HRDC took an approach that stressed quality service, flexibility in program delivery at the local level, partnership arrangements, eliminating unnecessary administrative barriers, accountability for program results, and a supported and empowered workforce.

Throughout the 1990s, HRDC had been seen as a leader within the public service in its efforts to reform and change public management. It received a number of significant awards and recognition for it innovations in quality service delivery, use of technology, innovative human resources practices, and reporting of results. A recent book, *The New*

Public Organization, which provides a comprehensive analysis of the 'post-bureaucratic organizational model' with an emphasis on innovation in public sector management, cites with approval many of the HRDC practices. For example,

> innovations at HRDC Quebec demonstrate many aspects of the post-bureaucratic model: a focus on clients and citizens; a people-focus; collective action; a change orientation; a results orientation; leadership; empowerment; and decentralization. On the other hand, HRDC Quebec's organizational form has not changed significantly, and there has been no significant movement to competition or revenue generation. The results achieved suggest that, over a period of several years, adopting key features of the post-bureaucratic model can help organizations to improve their performance significantly, even during times of great turbulence and change.[52]

Significant and far-reaching public sector management improvements and innovations have been achieved at HRDC during a period of enormous change and turbulence, which involved a fundamental re-examination of the role of government in society through the program review; a dramatic reduction in government expenditures that significantly affected programs and perhaps more importantly the administrative support for these programs; and a significant realignment of federal and provincial responsibilities for labour market programming. It is not surprising that at the very same time as these great external pressures for fundamental social and economic change were taking place, the internal pressures for administrative reform were becoming more focused. The very forces that brought about the need for public management reforms in the first place – program change, restraint, and redefinition of responsibilities – were the same forces that constrained and shaped how the reforms were conceived and subsequently implemented.

Up to this point, I have focused on the 1990s and how public officials went about administering grants and contributions and undertaking an internal administrative audit in the context of implementing elements of the new public management reforms. I have examined what was being done inside government by the public service in response to and in anticipation of a rapid set of fundamental external pressures. I now turn to outside government to examine the media's reporting of the public release of HRDC's audit of its grants and contributions in January 2000.

CHAPTER THREE

Outside Looking In

The Media's First Impressions Become Lasting Impressions

This chapter moves outside government and focuses on the media. It describes how the media viewed and, more importantly, shaped the events that emerged from the public release of the internal HRDC audit. Theories and models about news-making are used to explain how the media reported the grants and contributions audit; the story they reported is described using the media's own words and is compared with the reality experienced by the department and by citizens. If the release of the grants and contributions audit was about anything it was about news and how it is created. This chapter is therefore about news-making in public administration.

Overviewing the Media

The volume of media reporting about the grants and contributions audit, in both electronic and print format, was enormous. Never before had an audit of any type, yet alone an internal audit about the administration of programs, evoked such significant and sustained media reaction and overreaction. The media selectively reported and commented on what they heard primarily from opposition critics and Members of Parliament, the Minister and her office, departmental officials, and the Prime Minister and his office. They also reported on, although much less so, on what others outside the government said, project sponsors, former public servants, and academics. But not only did the media report on what they heard, they also reported on what they read in the 100,000 pages of information in government memoranda, reports, and e-mail exchanges released under the Access to Information Act through a barrage of requests undertaken by the opposition parties and the media. This information became a key source for the media's ongoing stories.

The reporting was built around the ongoing series of daily media events, including question period in the House of Commons; testimony before Parliamentary Committees; scrums with ministers and opposition MPs; media interviews with ministers and their aides, departmental spokespersons, and opposition MPs and their assistants; technical and media briefings; formal press conferences; and the usual informal flows of information between journalists and politicians, their aides and public servants. The media coverage took all forms. It included headlines in the print media and lead stories in the electronic media; video coverage of hearings, scrums, and media briefings; editorials and commentaries; and panel discussions with journalists and other commentators. Not surprisingly almost all the electronic coverage was based on the five-second 'sound bite,' and most of the print coverage reported on the reaction to what was said either by the government or the opposition.

The media reporting began with their storyline of '$1 billion lost,' which was viewed as a 'stunning revelation about government mismanagement on a monumental scale.' This first impression would continue as the media spotlight moved from issue to issue over the course of the next six months. The release of more information invariably led to more questions and to more reporting, with little of it on the substance of the audit and the programs themselves. There was practically no media coverage of the measures being put in place through the six-point action plan to correct the problems. The limited reporting that was done on the action plan criticized it for containing little that was new and expressed scepticism that the problems would be fixed. Although the reports of the parliamentary committee focused on the minority reports by the opposition parties and the commentary by opposition MPs, the media reporting did not focus on the substance of the committee's reports, findings, and recommendations.

The audit was released at a time of low interest in government in the quiet, dreary days of a mid-January morning in Ottawa. The threat of collapse to the country's computer systems as a result of the Y2K crisis in government had failed to materialize. Government computers were churning out the regular batches of cheques and information without a hitch. Members of Parliament were not in town; they were in their ridings across the country or on much needed vacations south of the border. The House of Commons was not in session. January 2000 was a slow time for the government and hence a slow time for the media.

But if the media interest in government was at a low, the competition among the media was not. This was, in fact, a time of high-stakes competition within the print media. The newly established *National Post* and the long-standing *Globe and Mail* were in the midst of an intense and vigorous battle to capture readership for their national newspapers. The owner of the *National Post*, Conrad Black, was in an open and highly visible feud with Prime Minister Chrétien, over the failure of the federal government to support his peerage appointment to the House of Lords in the United Kingdom. The majority Liberal government, which for six years had been the beneficiary of a deeply divided and ineffective opposition in the House of Commons, was the target of a ballooning number of access to information requests from the *National Post* and the opposition Reform Party concerning the awarding of some seventeen TJF job-creation projects in the Prime Minister's riding. The *National Post*, in particular, had launched a series of regular reports on the handling of TJF projects in the Prime Minister's riding with allegations of jobs not being created, financial mismanagement, inappropriate use of trust funds, and political interference in the approval of projects.

While the media's reports on 20 January would begin with a bang – the 'billion dollar boondoggle' – they would eventually end with a whimper when HRDC claimed that it had made overpayments to organizations amounting to $85,000. It seems unimaginable that what started as 'the biggest scandal in Canadian history,'[1] and preoccupied the government and the opposition for six months until June 2000, did not become an issue in the November general election and did not affect the election outcome. How could an issue become so big so fast and last for so long, yet not become an election issue?

Theories, Models, and Techniques about News-making[2]

At one time the principal theory for explaining news-making was the 'mirror theory.' It took the view that the news mirrored reality and that it reflected the events, issues and personalities as they really were and as they really happened. According to this theory, journalists held up a clean mirror to the world and the mirror reflected back the reality of the events, issues, and people. This was the 'I-am-the-camera'[3] school of journalism. News was not twisted, adjusted, and distorted but rather seen as an objective reflection of reality where fact and opinion were clearly separated. The mirror theory was popular in the 1950s and 1960s, with David Brinkley asserting, 'What television did in the sixties was to show the

American people to the American people ... It did show them people, places and things they had not seen before. Some they liked and some they didn't. It wasn't that television produced or created any of it.'[4]

Today, the principal theory is not the 'mirror' but the 'distorted mirror' theory, which is particularly useful in explaining how the media formed and shaped the news about the grants and contributions audit. According to this theory, journalists and news organizations are not passive, neutral, and objective reflectors of reality but active agents that change the reflection in various ways. Events are transformed to fit the schedule and requirements of journalists. News stories are chosen according to the needs of owners, news organizations, and journalists. With the pressure of time and the reality of space most events are ignored, others downplayed, and only a few highlighted. Veteran Canadian journalist Peter Desbarats writes that the loss of faith in the objectivity of journalism 'has been the single most important development of our time in journalism, and its effects are still not fully understood or appreciated by many journalists.'[5]

There are different but complementary views about the ways in which the mirror is distorted and, hence, different models of the 'distorted mirror' theory. Four of these models can be applied, in varying degrees, to explain how the media reported on the grants and contributions audit. The first model emphasizes that what is reflected in the mirror is the predispositions of the owners of the news organizations. In the second, the need to secure large audiences and readership and attract advertising dollar is so overwhelming that news is driven by audience demand. The third model sees the news being shaped by the 'organizational dynamics' of news organizations and the 'pulling and hauling' imposed by the constraints and standard operating procedures of these organizations. And the fourth sees the news being shaped by the subtle interplay between journalists and their sources, such as politicians, officials, interest groups, and business representatives.

The first model, or the 'corporate or owners model,' is based on the view that the news is significantly shaped by the large corporate interests that own significant parts of the Canadian media. This is thought to be particularly the case in newspapers where family-owned chains have carved up the market into their separate empires. For example, there are or have been significant ownership blocks represented by the Thomson Corporation, Conrad Black's Hollinger Inc., Maclean Hunter, Quebecor Inc. founded by Pierre Peladeau, the Irving family in Atlantic Canada, and the Aspers in Western Canada. The key question, of course, is the extent to which the owners determine the editorial content.[6] As David Taras points out, 'While there is little evidence to suggest that Canadian owners exercise direct control, there is wide suspicion that power is wielded subtly and indirectly. It is argued that owners invariably hire media managers who share their values, beliefs, and priorities; managers presumably use the same criteria in hiring journalists.'[7]

The second or 'audience model' is based on the hypothesis that 'news is selected and packaged according to audience demand and that entertainment values have come to predominate.'[8] The need to appeal to audiences stems from the perspective that advertisers do not so much buy the programs as they purchase certain audiences having characteristics that watch these programs. Journalists, then, do not tell audiences what they should know but tell them what they want to hear. The 'audience model' suggests that the news tends to mirror what the audiences demand. Competition within the media for readership and viewership is an important element of this model, which can therefore serve as a counterbalance to what some might see as the tyranny of the 'corporate or owners model.'

The 'organizational model' argues that the institution through which news is reported acts as a prism to refract and filter events, issues, and personalities. In this third model, the news is 'recontextualized to fit the product needs of the institution presenting it.'[9] The constraints of the medium (750 words for newspapers, sixty seconds for television, and the twenty-second radio bite) and the tight deadlines within which journalists work serve to condense and determine the news. The organizational deadlines of space and time impose closure on what is news and how it is reported.

The 'political model' is based on the premise that both journalists and their sources (politicians and officials, for example) are the products of news. Journalists prepare the stories and speak through their sources, who confer legitimacy on what is being reported. News is the result of intense negotiation between journalists and their sources, often over conflicting versions of the same story. There is competition both within and between journalists and their sources, with some sources favouring particular journalists over others. Sometimes, as in this case of the grants and contributions audit, the media can take on the role of opposition to the government. Sometimes linkages, cooperation, and even close collaboration can develop between certain news media and certain political parties. This fourth model is played out on a daily basis on the 'media-political battlefield,'[10] a battlefield that not only involves wars between the media and the politicians but also within the media and across and within political parties.

These four complementary models are associated with similar techniques that shape what becomes newsworthy and how the news gets reported. An important study[11] of the behaviour of journalists suggests that there are five techniques journalists use to determine newsworthiness and to shape news stories:

1 Simplicity. For an event to be newsworthy it must be simple, close to home, and relatively unambiguous in meaning.
2 Dramatization. Newsworthiness is based on recognizing how the event can be visualized through dramatic development and dramatic effects. Important elements of drama include conflict, surprise, and juxtaposition.
3 Personalization. News events are portrayed and developed in relation to the personalities involved. Politicians and increasingly public servants are considered newsworthy personalities. Complex events are explained in terms of their impact on the average individual.
4 Preformed storylines. Stories are expected to be consonant with the preformed storylines of journalists. Journalists usually prejudge significant events, visualize what is going to happen, and then prepare stories to make that outcome apparent.
5 The unexpected. Unexpected events with negative aspects enhance newsworthiness. This is especially the case when mistakes are made. These unexpected incidents are often framed as part of a preformed story line so that the media presents these 'surprises' as seemingly 'expected events.'

These five techniques, in combination with the four models of the 'distorted mirror' theory, are especially useful in describing how the media viewed and shaped the events emerging from the public release of the grants and contributions audit. These techniques and models are also helpful in understanding why the reporting by the media was in many cases a distortion of the reality experienced by the department.

As indicated in chapter 1, the fundamental issues around which the news would revolve over the course of 2000 were largely foreshadowed in the media reports within the first twenty-four hours of the release of the audit on 19 January 2000. These first impressions reported by the media, whether fully accurate or not, became the preformed storyline around which subsequent events would unfold.

Because this chapter focuses on the media and not on individual reporters, columnists, and editorialists, and because the actual language used by the media in their reporting is critical to understanding their perspective on the story and because the media coverage was extensive, this chapter contains a large number of direct quotes from the media. Detailed citations for these direct quotes are not linked to specific individuals within the media. Instead, the quotes are attributable to the particular media, whether print or electronic, and the time in which they occurred. I begin the media's story of the 'lost billion dollars' with the release of the audit on 19 January and conclude with the Auditor General's report on the 'imbalance between fast service and good control' on 17 October.

'One Billion Dollars Lost'

After the immediate release of the HRDC grants and contributions audit on 19 January, and for the rest of that week, the media used a simple and dramatic storyline: 'One billion dollars lost.' The expression, however distorted, was dramatic and the image vivid. A seemingly dull internal administrative audit was 'recontextualized' into a newsworthy sound-bite and a catchy headline. In fact, no money was lost. After months of individually reviewing 17,000 grants and contributions files across all programs in the department, representing some $1.6 billion, HRDC officials concluded that the amount of outstanding debts owing the government was $85,000.

The editorial in the *National Post* declared that 'the money was just shoveled out the door ... no questions asked: free money – no red tape.' This dramatic effect was increased through the imagery used by the *Ottawa Citizen*: 'HRDC job fund was a bank machine that required no card or PIN – just line up and get your withdrawal.' Bringing the issues closer to the average citizen, a *Globe and Mail* columnist created the impression that the long list of grants all went to frivolous projects: 'funeral monument manufacturing, a museum of farm artifacts, a story-telling event, caribou hunting, and a dancer transition resource centre.' There was no mention of projects to help disabled persons find jobs, to help textile workers upgrade their skills, or to help youth-at-risk secure meaningful work experience.

Based on claims by the Reform Party, the media developed a pre-formed storyline that the grants were used for political purposes and, as a consequence, corruption was inevitable. This began with the HRDC

Reform Party critic stating that, 'the only reason these moneys went out the door was for political purposes.' The *National Post* asserted that, 'it is painfully obvious that these job grant programs have always been thinly disguised political slush funds whose purpose is to aid Liberal ridings, and in particular ministerial ridings.' A *Toronto Star* columnist reinforced the storyline by linking it to past practices: 'The frantic dishing out of money to create instant, short-term jobs for various appropriately worthy groups is an exact replica of the governing style of two decades ago.' An editorial in *The Edmonton Journal* extended political purposes to possible corruption. It suggested that the Reform Party had been 'too kind' in labelling it a 'slush fund' and concluded that 'a program run so loosely can breed corruption, or at least the appearance of corruption.' In yet a further extension, *The Globe and Mail* focused the corruption theme not just on politicians but on the public service, arguing that the audit 'justifies the public's worst preconceptions about the federal bureaucracy,' that there is 'favouritism at work or pork-barrel patronage or laziness or rank incompetence.' In fact, there was no corruption in the public service. Nine months later, in October, the Auditor General reported to the media that 'we did not in our audit find any cases of malfeasance by public servants,' and, at the same time, the Clerk of the Privy Council observed in the media that 'there has never been an allegation of malfeasance or impropriety against any public servant.'

The media personalized the issue and searched for who was responsible. They highlighted the demands of Reform MP John Williams that 'heads have to roll because the condemnation of this audit is so severe and pervasive across the department that it's hard to believe this could happen overnight.' Reform MP and HRDC Critic Diane Ablonczy found it 'unbelievable' that 'nobody is going to suffer the slightest consequences' and called on Minister Jane Stewart to resign. The Hollinger-owned media reported surprising and unexpected news that managers responsible for 'badly kept records' would receive bonuses to 'clean up the sloppy paperwork.' In fact, when appraisals were completed later that year, HRDC officials involved with the grants and contributions programs did not receive any performance pay because they did not meet their ongoing commitments as required in their performance agreements.

From 'Cover Up' to 'Tiger Tails'

During week two, beginning 24 January, the media barrage escalated, the issue expanded, new allegations were made, and the Minister fought back. Curiously, despite five days of similar media stories, the week began with a significantly different perspective taken by one *Globe and Mail* columnist. He downplayed critics' demands for 'body bags' and emphasized that the internal audit drew attention to improper management and accounting practices, which did not mean that 'the money was stolen or lined some lobbyist's pocket or was stuffed under the mattress.' He objected to the demand that the Minister step down, attributing the internal audit findings to a 'systematic screw-up' that is not 'the responsibility of any particular politician or civil servant.'

The principal approach, however, taken by the media was to reinforce the original storyline that $1 billion dollars was lost, to attribute blame to individuals, and to personalize the story. The media actively sought out the views of backbench Members of Parliament, and widely reported the sensationally worded demands of a Reform MP that the Clerk of the Privy Council, who was the former deputy minister of HRDC, should resign: 'He should be dropped kicked right out of his role as the top bureaucrat.' *The Toronto Star* argued in an editorial that 'in a strange confluence of circumstances and political forces, Liberal backbenchers are emerging as this government's real opposition,' pointing out that 'an outspoken critic of the government's controversial TJF program' had made an 'aggressive request' that Minister Stewart appear before a special committee of the House of Commons.

Other media presented their own variations on the preformed storylines, interspersed with unexpected events that told slightly different stories of why the Minister publicly released an internal audit. One *Globe and Mail* columnist praised the Minister for 'taking the unusual step of publicizing' the audit in the name of 'openness and transparency.' Another journalist noted correctly, however, that there was an access to information request for the audit. Yet another journalist cautioned that the 'surprise' release of the audit should be 'tempered' by the knowledge that the Auditor General was releasing a report in the fall. She went on to explain that TJF was designed to address the 'painful restructuring' of EI reform and that although TJF did 'push some worthwhile initiatives,' it usually supported 'white elephants that will one day stand as testimony to the enduring cult of political expediency.'

A new and unexpected development, complete with dramatic visuals, provided yet a new story for the media. In what the media described as a 'stunning revelation,' Progressive Conservative MP Jean Dubé alleged 'a massive cover-up' by the Minister and the department. He explained that the cover page on the audit released at the technical briefing the previous week was undated. He showed the media a fax copy of the cover page of the audit dated 5 October, which he had just received from HRDC. The MP claimed that Minister Stewart 'was kept in the dark for six weeks' because her press secretary had indicated the Minister was briefed on the audit findings by departmental officials on 17 November. The media across the country immediately picked up on this surprising new development with CBC-TV's *The National* reporting that 'in the midst of damage control comes another allegation: that even while (the Minister) stood in the House to defend the jobs program, she knew the results of the audit.'

The media did not report that it was normal practice for internal audits to be finalized only after the department had completed a management response to address the problems identified. Only a few media reported Liberal MP Tony Ianno's seemingly bureaucratic, yet straightforward, explanation that the internal audit findings were completed on 5 October, a management response was subsequently prepared, and then Minister Stewart was briefed on both the findings and response on 17 November. *The Globe and Mail*, however, cast the story around the drama of officials withholding information from the Minister. It quoted from a source in the Minister's Office who 'defended the bureaucrats up to a point saying they were "right" to come up with a plan to solve the administrative mess before informing the Minister.' According to the report, the source went on to explain that 'when you talk to a minister and you have something negative to tell her, you have to be ready to offer solutions.'

The media noted that the Minister 'broke her week-long silence,' and reported briefly on her 27 January statement to 'set the record straight.' The statement emphasized three points: first, that 'money is not missing' and 'the audit did not indicate any political interference'; second, 'best practices regarding audit dictate that an audit is only finalized when the auditors produce their findings and departmental management responds as to how it will rectify any weaknesses identified'; and third, 'a six-point action plan' had been 'adopted to address the administrative deficiencies.'

What was more important for the media than the statement were the series of interviews with the Minister that personalized the issue and provided two new dramatic images, which were used to reinforce the seriousness of the audit results and the overall importance of the audit itself. One image was of the Minister holding the audit 'tiger by the tail' and her determination to wrestle it to the ground. The other was a ministerial perception that accounting procedures were 'in the Dark Ages.'

In one of the interviews, Minister Stewart emphasized that she was not obligated to make the audit public:

> There's nobody that forced me to do this. This is me and there's a lot of people looking askance and saying you've got to be crazy. But I can't do it any other way. The idea that it's standard practice, that it gets swept under the carpet until the opposition decides it's going to make an issue of it, that's not the way I do business.

She went on to ask:

> Is the system we've created such that if you identify problems from the inside, you're a bum, but if you identify them from the outside, you're a hero? How does that encourage a minister to stand up and say, 'I've got problems,' because then all the critics are saying: 'Ooh, she'll never be able to survive in her department, they'll brown envelope her to death.' I don't believe that, because if I did I might as well pack up and go.

Would she resign?

> No way. Quitters quit. This isn't the time to quit. I tell you, I've got a tiger by the tail here and I'm going to bring this one to the ground.

In an interview with a journalist of the Hollinger media, the Minister pointed to outdated bookkeeping procedures for explaining the findings of the audit. 'We have got people making decisions at the local level but we didn't give them a credible accounting process. We were still in the Dark Ages.'

As if to foreshadow the upcoming week, the media concluded week two with an article quoting the Prime Minister's director of communications: 'The Prime Minister has absolute confidence in Jane Stewart. She walked into the department, saw a problem, made an audit public, and is now addressing the issue.'

'It's Not a Billion Dollars, It's Thirty-seven Cases'

Prime Minister Chrétien spoke out publicly on the controversy for the first time at a scrum after the Liberal caucus meeting on 2 February. The media interpreted the Prime Minister's strong support for Minister

Stewart and senior officials as an indication that he was blaming lower-level public servants. The national print media reported that the Prime Minister 'gave his support to the two ministers and his top bureaucrat, downplaying' the mismanagement by 'blaming it on staff cuts, decentralization and sloppy work by volunteer groups.' Yet another reporter concluded that the Prime Minister had given a 'strong endorsement to Minister Stewart and senior bureaucrats' by 'attempting to shift the blame from national headquarters to lower-level public servants in the regions.' This led to a report in *The Toronto Star* that included a 'warning' from the Public Service Alliance of Canada (PSAC) 'not to lay the blame at the feet of public servants who were following government instructions.' The media's report of the Prime Minister provided an opening for the HRDC opposition critic to extend the story by declaring that 'to blame the lower levels of the department is absolutely unacceptable ... I think this kind of scapegoating should be beneath elected people.'

The Prime Minister downplayed the issues, telling reporters that 'the audit uncovered only routine problems' and that 'administrative problems of this nature always exist.' The *Ottawa Citizen* reported that the Prime Minister 'tried to turn the scandal ... into a minor administrative foul-up involving as little as $30 million.' 'It's not $1 billion, it's thirty-seven cases,' said the Prime Minister. The media did not accept the Prime Minister's explanation and continued with their preformed storyline. A *Globe and Mail* editorial viewed the Prime Minister's defence as an act of 'absolution' from 'shocking carelessness with the public's money.' It concluded that the audit pointed to 'scattershot and ill-considered job creation programs' that are 'ripe for political abuse' and should be 'abolished altogether.'

The media dismissed explanations and briefings by departmental officials as too complicated, confusing, and simply designed to support the Prime Minister. The *Ottawa Citizen* reported on a technical media briefing by two senior HRDC officials,[12] claiming that they were 'dispatched by the Prime Minister's Office to clear up some of the "factual misunderstandings" and to back up Mr Chrétien's interpretation of it.' The *Citizen* story noted that, 'like Mr Chrétien, (the official) suggested the vast majority of the 459 projects involved no improper expenditures, just sloppy paper work and poor record keeping. Only 37 projects, worth a total of $30 million, were found to contain enough irregularities, including possible overpayments that further investigation was recommended.' The story went on further to say that '(officials) insisted the department has names and addresses for all grant recipients and knows where every penny has gone. Moreover, they argued that performance evaluations have demonstrated that the programs are working well, even if the paperwork has been sloppy,' and that '(officials) tried to disentangle the audit story from the controversy surrounding the Transitional Jobs Fund,' which 'accounts for only $125 million of the $1 billion.' The *Ottawa Citizen*, concluded that 'opposition parties did not buy the concerted attempt to minimize the import of the audit, nor did reporters, who sometimes betrayed open hostility during the briefing by officials and earlier grilled the Human Resources (Development) Minister so mercilessly that Mr Chrétien came to her rescue.'

A *Globe and Mail* columnist tried to explain why the media relentlessly held on to the initial story. He observed that explanations by HRDC officials at the media briefing 'resulted in more confusion, especially since the department, as incredible as it seems, is still unable to assemble a list of the 459 grants and contributions that its internal auditors spot-checked and on which it then based its devastating conclusions.' He added that the Minister 'doesn't seem to be able to explain what is really at stake, in part because her department does not yet know what is at stake.' As will be explained in more detail in chapter 4, the internal auditors were unable to compile a list quickly because the codes they used to record the files at the time of their audit were different from the registry codes used in the local and regional offices where the files were then located.

On 3 February, *The Globe and Mail* reported on the national caucus meeting in which the Prime Minister told his caucus that the story would 'evaporate in weeks' and attributed the crisis to 'highly competitive media.' The *Globe and Mail* story also reported that some Liberals expressed 'fear that the government's credibility on fiscal matters has been tarnished.' That night on the *CBC National*, a political correspondent attempted to explain the distortions in the media, observing that 'this is really a communications problem; the word got out early through many media outlets that this was about a billion dollars lost and the government insists that's not the case, this is a matter of accounting procedures for a part of a billion dollars and the feeling is, over time, they will succeed in getting that message out.' On *CBC Newsworld*, a reporter concluded that 'the Liberals have mounted a campaign of damage control, blaming the media for overplaying how much money is involved, but the opposition parties aren't buying it.'

The close linkage between the media (particularly the *National Post*) and political parties (particularly the Reform Party) was reported as journalists became part of the story and were making their own news. The *Hill Times* carried an interview with a *National Post* investigative journalist who had been pursuing the TJF story for many months. The journalist, who objected to being asked about obtaining documents from the Reform Party, observed that

> people are going to say '(the *National Post*) coverage is some Reform Party driven, ideological agenda' – that is a piece of cr-p. Did I work on stories involving the job creation funds – Yes. There's probably been over a hundred written under my byline. Some were based on documents I obtained. Some were based on documents the Reform Party obtained (under access to information) that were authenticated by myself (and) that were checked over by officials ... stories that included their comments.

The media reported what they viewed as a surprising new development in the Transitional Jobs Fund story. A *Globe and Mail* columnist wrote about 'maverick' Liberal MP Roger Galloway's 'discovery' of the Minister's 'special representations' and 'fiddling of criteria' and the subsequent $1 million grant to attract an American-owned telephone call centre to her riding in Brant, Ontario, which was originally slated for Galloway's riding in Sarnia, Ontario. The journalist concluded that if Brant was not unique, then 'Mr Galloway is certainly on to something here – it's called greasing the system with political favours.' There was no reporting of the broad guidelines used by officials and the Minister to permit projects to proceed in specific parts of regions with high levels of unemployment.

The print media put context around the dramatic images reported by the electronic media. A *Globe and Mail* reporter reconstructed the events behind 'that embarrassing scene on Tuesday (the Prime Minister stepping into the Minister's scrum) ... emblematic of the government's confused handling of the HRDC mess.' He concluded that 'throughout, the government's approach has been uncertain, or more accurately, divided ... the Minister, her department, and the Prime Minister have had different objectives and different strategies ... three distinct, largely self-interested streams of explanation.' The reporter claimed that no one had foreseen the 'media frenzy,' reporting that the Prime Minister had privately 'blamed the tempest on the newspaper wars.'

Once the media had framed the issues surrounding the audit, they made little effort to search out and report other views other than those from the opposition. One exception was the CBC Radio program *The House,* which interviewed Arthur Kroeger, a former deputy minister, on 5 February. Kroeger explained that

> in program review, the department was cut by 20 per cent, or 5,000 people. At the same time, there was an emphasis on greater service to the client, along with greater devolution. The 5,000 people you took out were the overseers and the managers. The emphasis was to get the program delivery working and not to worry too much about the paperwork ... And this has now come back to haunt the department.

He reminded listeners that there was a conflict between financial oversight and leaner government. 'There is a price to be paid for that. People say, "Oh, we'll eliminate red tape, you don't need all those bureaucrats." Well, it turns out you do.'

In preparing for the return of Parliament the following week, the Prime Minister's communication director once again foreshadowed the upcoming events with a quote in the *Ottawa Citizen*: 'This is quickly going to become a philosophical debate, Liberal versus Reform, over the value of job creation programs.' In the same article, the HRDC Reform critic explained that 'the Liberals would like to do a bait-and-switch, as I call it, and get the issue away from their own unprecedented level of incompetence and on to the worthiness of their goals. You know, kind and compassionate Liberals versus mean, nasty Conservatives. But that isn't the issue at all.'

From 'Binder Boy' to 'No Master List'

The media reported on the Prime Minister's performance in light of the expectations set out by his communications director. Reporting on question period in the House of Commons on 7 February, a *Globe and Mail* columnist concluded that the Prime Minister, by 'swinging his rhetorical bat and hitting the job-creation grants scandal out of the park,' has saved his government and his Minister and 'successfully used the bait-and-switch tactic to divert attention from a bad audit to the merits of the job-creation grants program.' The journalist credited the Prime Minister for reading out loud in the House of Commons letters, handed to him by 'binder boy' (the Government House Leader Don Boudria), from opposition Members of Parliament 'praising the impact of TJF in their ridings.' Another columnist expressed surprise that the opposition 'made no use of the hundreds of pages of audit documents that were released (through access to information) by HRDC yesterday (Monday) morning,' but concentrated instead on when the Minister knew about the problem in her department.

Despite efforts by the department to highlight the corrective action it was taking through implementing its action plan, there was almost no reporting of this effort. The media saw the plan as complicated, routine, impersonal, and bureaucratic. But most significantly, they were inconsistent with the preformed storyline that $1 billion dollars was lost. Therefore, it was not newsworthy. The limited reporting belittled the plan and expressed 'scepticism' about its effectiveness. For example, an *Ottawa Citizen* editorial declared that the six-point action plan 'seems to be nothing more than the basic management practices required under the Financial Administration Act.' The plan also provided the opportunity for the media to create a new story about more administrative problems throughout government. For example, the same *Ottawa Citizen* article went on to criticize the Treasury Board for 'allowing government record keeping to deteriorate to a point where departments simply do not know what information they have or where it is kept.' The *Citizen* concluded that the 'serious' problems at HRDC were 'just one element of the much wider administrative and management problems plaguing the federal government.'

While the media largely ignored the plan, they did speculate that the centre of government was reluctant to highlight the plan for fear that it would overemphasize the seriousness of the problems. For example, a Hollinger-media journalist reported a 'senior strategist' as saying that 'the government is trying to walk a fine line: insisting the controversy is not as serious as the opposition contends, while appearing to be serious about cleaning up the management.'

The media extended stories by searching out explanations for events that were dramatic and unexpected. They then presented these 'unexpected events' as 'expected' since they reinforced the public's generally held views about government. For example, the media dramatized the divisions between politicians and public servants. A *National Post* journalist alleged that 'in a bid to contain the political uproar, the government was quietly pointing the finger' at a former HRDC deputy minister who had instructed departmental managers in 1995 to focus on 'service to clients' even if that sometimes meant 'breaking bureaucratic rules.' The journalist claimed to have found 'clear signs (that) HRDC's accommodating spirit went overboard.' Another journalist reporting on an interview with the Reform Party's chief strategist observed that the Party hopes to 'establish a conspiratorial link ... that the Prime Minister's Office was manipulating HRDC bureaucrats to do their political handiwork.'

Minister Stewart's appearance before the Standing Committee on Human Resources Development on Thursday, 10 February, was reported in stories that reinforced and further developed the original storyline of the lost money. Lost money meant corruption, which in turn meant cover up. A *National Post* editorial concluded that 'unlike the APEC scandal, the corruption at HRDC is not rooted in one single event' and 'the Liberals have compounded their original misdeeds by trying to cover their tracks.' The editorial considered that 'the cover-up is now an issue itself,' and predicted that once 'the camouflage is cleared away, massive politicization of the civil service (will be) revealed.' A columnist in the *Post* concluded that MP Diane Ablonzcy had proved a 'formidable interrogator' in Committee: 'soft-spoken, unpretentious, and devastating in her ability to pose short questions from which there is no escape.' *CBC Newsworld* that evening carried several of her questions, including 'I'm asking the Minister how much. I'm asking the Minister how much ... how much of the one billion dollars of spending represented by the audited programs was not supported by proper evidence? How much is a number?' The *National Post* concluded that the Minister had given the Committee 'unclear answers about how much money was mismanaged.'

The media did not focus on the factual information that the Minister presented to the Standing Committee. This information was downplayed and largely ignored because it was significantly different from the original storyline that $1 billion dollars had been lost. In her 'powerpoint' presentation, Minister Stewart gave a progress report on the thirty-seven 'problem files,' amounting to $33 million, that the auditors had identified as requiring further review. She indicated that to date, ten of the thirty-seven file reviews were complete and overpayments of $251.50 had been identified. She noted that the money would be recovered and the review of the remaining files completed by 18 February. The $251.50 figure was not picked up in the national press, only in the regional press, buried under headlines in the *Times Colonist* (Victoria) and *The Sault Star* (Sault Ste. Marie): 'MPs charge Liberals of "twisting" the facts.'

The media received documents from opposition Members of Parliament obtained under access to information requests and produced new and unexpected stories containing dramatic charges about the department's conduct. The lead story on CBC Radio's *World Report* began with:

> CBC News had learned that Jane Stewart's Human Resources Department altered government documents with the effect of concealing the way Ottawa tracked millions of dollars in job creation grants.

Later that same day, *CBC Newsworld* on its program 'Dayside' quoted from the Minister's explanatory testimony at the Parliamentary Committee:

> The honourable member talks about lists being altered ... We receive requests for information through access to information and other means all the time. And the lists that we then compile, are done so to respond to the specific requests of the person asking for the information ... the list can be different depending on what's being looked for.

In fact, documents were not altered. The documentation provided by the department was in response to a large number of separate requests under access to information on TJF projects over the course of many months. The information provided in response to each individual request varied because over time projects changed as did the status of each project in the approval process. Also, in each access to information request the information requested was different. For example, some requested information on the approved and planned or actual expenditures of a project, and others requested information on the number of bankruptcies, number of jobs created, or private sector contributions.

The media, thirsty for more information to feed their story, called on the opposition parties to make more use of access to information requests. The *Ottawa Citizen* advocated that opposition parties 'insist the government make public all the relevant information' on all grants. The article observed that the existence of the briefing binder (used by the Prime Minister) and the briefing documents carried to the Committee by the Minister and officials showed that 'the government has a lot more information than it is willing to share.' A *National Post* editorial concluded that opposition MPs 'have a duty to bombard ministers with access to information requests.'

The report by a Hollinger-media journalist, reflecting on the events since 19 January, indicated how a well-crafted preformed storyline not only leads to a number of additional substories but also becomes more entrenched and hence more difficult to change with the passage of time. He wrote: 'So many attack avenues have opened up for opponents that there is little chance of (the scandal) being struck down soon.' Moreover, 'the main theme of the story – Ottawa's misuse of taxpayer dollars – is so broad that any number of stories can be made to fit,' while 'the sub-theme of patronage and porkbarrelling' is 'so broad that it invites any number of possibilities.' He added that the issue had reawakened interest in allegations of 'shady dealings' in the Prime Minister's own riding. He questioned whether 'bureaucrats were operating under the pressure of the political arm of government,' and concluded that a finding that no money has gone missing would not be enough to 'shut down all the windows of opportunity that have opened' for the opposition.

The media looked to opposition Members of Parliament to provide context and to set the agenda for the coming week. A commentary by Diane Ablonczy carried in the *Ottawa Citizen* reflected on the apparent contradictions and defined the outstanding questions:

> The Liberals claim to take responsibility while avoiding consequences. They blame bureaucrats while claiming the buck stops with the Minister. They claim this was a problem that pre-dated Jane Stewart, while declaring that the former minister, Pierre Pettigrew, cannot be questioned. They claim to be transparent, while hiding behind the Access to Information Act. Most outrageous, they claim there is no riding-by-riding list of grants, while Government House Leader Don Boudria, now known as 'Binder Boy,' hands Prime Minister Jean Chrétien riding-by-riding lists of grants during question period.

From Action Plans to 'Pockets'

Not all journalists filed mainstream reports. A few took a different tack. For example, one *Globe and Mail* columnist downplayed calling the audit 'a scandal.' He argued that there was 'not a clear pattern of political favouritism ... nobody subverted justice, no criminal acts were involved. Instead, some perfectly defensible programs for the disabled and those needing additional training, and others lacking a sensible policy rationale such as the Transitional Jobs Fund, got botched in their administration.' The media also sought out comments from sources outside government. For example, Hollinger papers carried graphic commentary from political scientist Donald Savoie, who indicated that the administration of TJF had 'blurred the lines' of ministerial responsibility and had 'become an ever-widening circle of accountability' where no one could be held accountable. The article quoted the professor as saying: 'If there are twenty-five hands in the soup, it's hard to figure out who is truly accountable ... we have diluted accountability to the point that trying to hold somebody to account is like grabbing smoke.'

The media did their own analysis to draw their own conclusions. In a *National Post* story, a journalist questioned, but did not refute, the government-released report indicating that opposition ridings got more TJF money than government ridings. Instead, he noted that the *Post*'s own 'computer-assisted analysis' of the same 1,082 TJF grants provides 'clear evidence of election-style pork-barrelling,' particularly in Quebec ridings where the strategy appears to have involved luring voters away from the Bloc Party. The *Ottawa Citizen* carried detailed accusations by opposition MPs that TJF and its successor, the Canada Jobs Fund (CJF), contained 'qualification loopholes' such as 'pockets of unemployment regulations.' The article went on to state that these details were 'kept secret' and were 'custom-made for ministers' for their benefit. The article contrasted MP Pat Martin's riding of Winnipeg Centre with Minister Stewart's Brant riding.

Open conflict between the Minister and Members of Parliament in question period provided the media with a personalized story, complete with accusations of lying, expulsion, backtracking, and subtle nuance. A *National Post* journalist reported that the Speaker of the House 'almost lost control of the proceedings' when Reform MP Jim Abbott was expelled from the House. The Reform MP had called the Minister 'a liar' for telling the House that he and two other MPs had personally telephoned her office to seek speedy approval of grants for their ridings. Journalists explained that the Minister's strategy of accusing three Reform MPs who had denounced TJF and then sought job-creation grants for their own constituencies had 'backfired.' The journalists explained that the Minister subsequently clarified her statement that one of the three Members of Parliament 'did not personally' call her, but that his office did.

The media amplified and magnified the dichotomies and contradictions that were inherent in the six-point action plan that public servants were attempting to implement. For example, a journalist in the *Ottawa Citizen* concluded that the action plan would effectively 'rebureaucratize government and undo a decade of reforms to cut red tape.' The feature article observed that, 'within days of the furor, departments reverted to their old ways and brought back the rule books and red tape,' and that the action plan 'took a page out of the old command-and-control management style the government has been trying to shed for more than a decade.' If the pendulum of administrative reform was beginning to swing within government, the weight of the media was giving it added momentum.

A *Globe and Mail* columnist focused on the newsworthiness of political personalities. He sharply criticized the Minister by saying that 'she has failed to understand a general convention in Parliament that the specific overpowers the general.' The columnist went on to observe that the Ms Stewart had attempted to answer specific questions under a 'general mantra, which has two parts. The first is "a six-point action plan ... approved by the Auditor General" and the second, which is given to questions about grants in her riding is about "how people in her riding have benefited from the jobs programs."' The columnist went on to observe that 'this may well be true, but it doesn't answer the specific question of how ... Brantford qualified for money under TJF when most of the statistical evidence seems to be against her. That leaves the inference of special treatment.' On CBO TV, an *Ottawa Citizen* reporter argued that 'she (the minister) cannot defend why a number of grants went into her riding that has so called "high pockets of unemployment," and why it didn't go into other ridings of MPs who are not cabinet ministers, who might be in the opposition, who had equally high amounts of unemployment in their ridings.'

As if to foreshadow events of the week ahead, a Hollinger-media reporter observed that 'neither (the minister) nor her aides or HRDC officials have yet produced any documents explaining how such pockets were determined.'

'The Paper Dump'

The release of the largest amount of information on grants and contributions programs by any government was a dramatic and newsworthy event widely reported in the media. On 22 February, *The Toronto Star* reported that the Minister 'unleashed a paper blizzard yesterday, dumping more than 10,000 pages of job grant documents on the opposition, with the minister all but daring MPs to "read the documents" before they make any more allegations about mismanagement and pork-barrelling of taxpayers' money.'

A journalist, speaking on *CBC Newsworld*, openly explained how the media would use this information to develop new stories:

[Releasing the information] is a smart move on the part of government, in order to kill the accusations that Stewart is hiding information, that's absolutely certain. However, I think that by giving lists of grants going out to various companies across the country, researchers will be pouring over those; journalists like myself are going to start doing corporate searches on names of these companies and seeing the linkages to politicians and people in power and we're going to be finding ... lots of stories. I can guarantee it.

The media started first by reporting on grants received by 'numbered companies,' which raised a natural curiosity in the average citizen. Global TV's *First National* reported that the government 'seem(s) perplexed that opposition parties and journalists keep hammering away at the billion dollar controversy. But the case of a numbered company (339 3062) alone should be enough to have all Canadians demanding plausible answers.' The *National Post* reported 'in an attempt to explain why a numbered company that received a $165,984 grant to build a textile plant in Montreal had the business transferred to a village near the Prime Minister's hometown ... Ms Stewart told MPs yesterday the decision was made because officials were unable to find an appropriate location for the plant in the intended riding.'

What Budget?

The most unexpected event happened on 29 February, when the Minister of Finance tabled his much-anticipated budget, which the opposition ignored. The media made this simple but important 'non-event' newsworthy. The lead story of CBC's *The National* began with '(Minister of Finance) Paul Martin certainly didn't expect question period to turn out the way it did ... The opposition all but ignored his new budget, and concentrated on alleged misspending at Human Resources.' A columnist for the Sun media wrote that 'you'd hardly know Minister Martin delivered a budget Monday promising $58 billion in tax reductions.'

The media reported on a new story that reinforced the original story-line of lost money and extended it to the likelihood of corruption. *The Globe and Mail* reported that 'there are now three different RCMP probes into allegations that HRDC grants were misused.' CTV *Newsnet* noted that 'today we learned that there's not one, not two, but seven different RCMP investigations underway as well as two forensic audits.' Hollinger media reported that the Minister acknowledged that '"out of tens of thousands" of projects, I am currently aware of seven active RCMP investigations and two active local police investigations.' CBC Radio Ottawa reported that 'a New Brunswick company received a $70,000 grant from HRDC four months after another government agency alerted the RCMP of concerns about the now bankrupt firm. ... A spokesman for HRDC said he could not comment on the situation because of the (police) investigation.' In the end, a dozen of the 60,000 grants and contributions projects were referred to the police for investigation, not relating to the impropriety of public servants but to a few private sector sponsors and proponents. Almost all investigations were dropped without charges.

Under an access to information request by the Reform Party, HRDC released a draft communications plan that provided the basis for the media to recast an old story of 'who knew what when' as an entirely new and surprising development reinforcing the preformed storyline. A *CTV National News* anchor reported that

> for weeks they've had her on the defensive over the government grants fiasco. But tonight the opposition believes it's caught HR Minister Jane Stewart in a lie. An internal document suggests the Minister knew of the bookkeeping disaster in her department months before the Minister claims she was told about the multi-million dollar problem.

CBC TV's *The National* reported,

> When did the Minister know about the mess in her department? The (departmental communications planning) document obtained by Reform through access to information warns a political furor could erupt over the findings of an internal audit and a separate audit by the Auditor General. It says the release of these reports will individually and collectively provide critics with two new opportunities to criticize and attack the integrity of the program and the government.

It is common practice for communication planning documents to be prepared within departments in advance of officials briefing ministers on an issue. Carried in the same report on *The National* was a concluding explanatory statement:

> An official with the Minister's office said it is perfectly normal for departmental officials to work on an issue before they brief the Minister. The rule is, don't go to the Minister with a problem if you can't offer up a solution.

As Members of Parliament prepared for the upcoming one-week recess of the House of Commons in early March, a journalist of the *CTV National News* summed up the previous week's activities: 'This is a very difficult story to cover, because there is a lot of insinuation and innuendo and yes, there may be some murky business going on, but some of the allegations are proving fairly hard to prove.'

'Everyone Loses'

With the House of Commons in recess, no news became news itself. On 7 March, *The Toronto Star* reported that 'for the first time in five weeks, nothing happened here at 2:00 pm yesterday. There were no accusations of a billion dollar bungle ... Not once did Jane Stewart wearily rise in the daily question period to praise the program or her six-point action plan to fix what the government insists are niggling administrative problems.'

The earlier foreshadowing by the media that the release of 10,000 pages of project-specific information would lead to a series of stories on the distribution of funding by constituency became a reality. On 16 March, the *National Post* headlined its major story with 'PM's riding got more cash than Alberta: First comprehensive survey of job-creation programs: Quebec received more than twice as much grant money as any government.' The article, in an effort to demonstrate a scientific basis, indicated that these multi-year findings 'emerged from a *National Post* computer-assisted examination of $7.2 billion worth of HRDC grants handed out in 301 ridings across Canada.'

Other stories were developed from the 10,000 pages of information released by HRDC, although not all of these stories were accurate. For example, on 20 March, the *Ottawa Citizen* ran a story with a headline that read '$200 million in cheques gets lost in the mail: HRDC grants sent to wrong addresses.' The article, in fact, said just the opposite. As the Deputy Minister of HRDC explained in a letter, subsequently published in the *Citizen*, 'this information is not used for the purposes of issuing cheques ... a financial information system is used for financial payments.' Over the course of eight weeks, the Deputy Minister found it necessary to write six times to various editors protesting distorted reports, false assertions in editorials, and misleading headlines.[13] In contrast, a much different story was carried in the 'op-ed' page of *The Globe and Mail* on 23 March under the heading: 'Everyone loses, one of Canada's most respected former civil servants decries the widespread damage caused by the HRDC scandal.'

The media focused on personalities and reported widely on the unusual appearance of the former deputy minister of HRDC and the Clerk of the Privy Council before the Standing Committee on Human Resources Development on 21 March. The *National Post* reported that the clerk testified that 'HRDC went through an intense period of change that left the department vulnerable,' although 'none of this is an excuse for allowing bad bookkeeping and bad record-keeping.' The stqry reported that the clerk 'allowed that better bookkeeping measures are necessary but said the department should not return to past practices "of significant red tape."' The story went on to note that 'making political hay' out of the unusual appearance before the Committee was 'exactly what some public administration experts feared.' The report quoted indirectly from political scientist Donald Savoie, who indicated that 'public servants are supposed to be impartial and non-partisan, but MPs can't resist their "partisan instincts" to use them to "score political points."' The article included an important warning from Savoie: 'If we want public servants engaged in political and partisan debates with the opposition and cabinet, and to unleash the consequences of that world, then we will have a very different public service and a different system.'

The media also looked for contradictions. The *Ottawa Citizen*, reporting on the appearance of the former deputy minister, headlined its story with 'Cappe testimony contradicts Stewart: No "explicit guidelines" defined "poverty pockets."' The story reported that Mr Cappe indicated 'there were "no explicit guidelines" spelling out "poverty pockets" for the controversial Transitional Jobs Fund. TJF ... was meant to be flexible and designed to reflect local variations and local differences so that it could take into account the supply and demand within the local (labour) market.' The story also quoted Reform MP Deborah Grey as saying 'Mel Cappe today blew the lid off her (the Minister's) excuses. People say that if you ask the guilty the same question long enough and often enough the truth is bound to slip out. So, we'd like to know today, Who is telling the truth?' In the end there were no contradictions between the Minister and the former HRDC deputy minister.

The media widely reported on the Auditor General's appearance before the Standing Committee on 23 March. The *Hamilton Spectator* headlined its article as 'Auditor blasts job grant controls: "Unacceptable way to spend public funds."' The Montreal *Gazette* reported that the Auditor General told MPs that 'his audit will never get to the bottom of whether the grants were subject to political meddling or influence.' The story reported that the Auditor General testified to the committee that 'political influence in a file is hard to find ... we keep our eyes and ears open all the time, but going to the bottom ... requires a police investigation every time.' A Canadian Press report noted that the Auditor General 'complimented' the department on its action plan.

The Search for Balance

In early April the media reinforced their original story and reported extensively on the steps being taken by the Treasury Board to strengthen management controls across the government. On 3 April the *Ottawa Citizen* ran a story under the headline 'Treasury Board cracks down on sloppy record-keeping.' It reported on the new management framework that the president of the Treasury Board, Lucienne Robillard, unveiled under the title 'Results for Canadians.' The article described the actions by the Treasury Board as a 'significant shift and departure' for a central agency that has been sharply criticized for its hands-off management and lax enforcement of its own guidelines. The report indicated that the Minister 'agree(s) that we should have a more active monitoring role of control practices.' She cautioned, however that 'I will not go back to the old formula of command-and-control and (re-bureaucratize) the public service so much that clients will suffer. ... You can have good control of spending and due diligence, on the one side, and offer good services to clients on the other.'

The media reported new and unexpected negative events that reinforced the original storyline, and ignored those that did not. On 7 April, the *National Post* ran a front-page story under the distorted headline 'HRDC "tampering" with files, union says.' The story, based on a response by the president of an employees' union to a question during a Standing Committee meeting, reported that 'employees at HRDC were ordered to review their job-creation grant project files, fill in any blanks, and backdate documents so records would appear to be in order.' The article also indicated that 'the union's leaders also alleged that HRDC workers are often subjected to political interference, either by ministers and MPs or by senior government bureaucrats acting at their behest.' The newspaper did not print a 12 April letter to the editor from the Deputy Minister of HRDC objecting to the 'one-sided reporting' and indicating that 'written instructions, provided to the staff for the purposes of reviewing the files ... state: "documents currently on file are not to be altered."'

The media did, however, correct one story but not others. The *Ottawa Citizen* carried a letter from the Deputy Minister of HRDC, regretting the newspaper had used a 'misleading headline' ('HRDC workers abusing fund') to accompany an otherwise 'factual report' on the interim review of financial management. On 3 May, the *Ottawa Citizen* ran an inaccurate story under the headline 'Stewart fell short with HRDC plan,' claiming that the six-point action plan was flawed because outside experts (Deloitte-Touché) had judged it to be insufficient. A further report the next day reinforced the storyline with the headline 'Remarks come back to haunt Stewart: Minister said HRDC crises under control while consultant's report disagreed.' The media did not correct the story even though the Deputy Minister of HRDC wrote a letter on 4 May to the newspaper pointing out that a principal of Deloitte-Touché had testified to the Parliamentary Committee that 'the department has taken our advice, the advice of others, and revised the action plan.'

On 14 April, when the Commons Committee on Human Resources Development released its interim report, the media focused on the minority report prepared by the opposition members that foresaw more problems. The media largely ignored the majority report prepared by the government members that suggested solutions. Hollinger newspapers noted that opposition members were 'unanimous in accusing the government of not wanting the full extent of the problem known.' The *Globe and Mail* headlined their story with 'Opposition MPs reject report backing HRDC clean up plan.' It went on to say that: 'the opposition MPs who released a dissenting report called on the government to launch an independent inquiry ... pass a law protecting civil servants who blow the whistle on mismanagement or the abuse of public funds.'

The majority interim report posed a series of questions that the Committee hoped to answer over the next several months. The report concluded with a quote from the Auditor General, who told the Committee that 'it would not make sense for necessary changes to lead to excessive tightening of the system and unnecessary red tape. HRDC has a varied set of programs to deliver. A balance will need to be established to meet the needs of recipients, ensure adequate controls, assess risk, and deliver results to taxpayers.' The report indicated it will 'search for that balance.' In contrast, an editorial in the *Ottawa Citizen* found the Committee's conclusions 'laughable' for suggesting that 'nothing is really wrong, it has been fixed.'

Divide HRDC and Eliminate CJF

The media reported on tougher grants and contributions guidelines.

On 1 June, the *Ottawa Citizen* reported that the Treasury Board was putting in place 'a new set of tougher rules for departments dishing out grants and contributions to head off another jobs grant fiasco.' The article noted that 'the Treasury Board will keep closer tabs on the terms and conditions of grant programs and review them every five years to ensure they are effective and achieve promised results.' It also stated that 'critics argue' that the 'loose and broad flexibility of grants ... opens the door for political interference' while others worry the 'tougher rules will pile more work on departments ... but won't root out the potential for political meddling or influence.' In conclusion, it noted that the Auditor General 'has argued that Treasury Board bears some responsibility for the HRDC fiasco,' having raised 'serious questions about Treasury Board's role in policing departments to ensure they comply with rules and guidelines.'

On 1 June, the Parliamentary Committee released its final report entitled *Seeking a Balance*. Once again the media did not concentrate on the report, which 'commended the government's six-point action plan' and called on the government to 'divide HRDC into several more homogeneous and focused structures.' Instead the *Ottawa Citizen* ran the front-page headline 'Liberals "just spreading cancer": Opposition mocks plan to break up HRDC as defensive move to duck public inquiry.' The *National Post* story on the Committee report focused on the TJF program under the headline 'HRDC jobs fund run unfairly, Liberals say: Report on scandal: Program seemed devoid of "well-defined criteria."' This story indicated that the Liberals on the Commons Committee 'criticized their own government's showcase job creation program, saying TJF was plagued by problems and the bureaucrats ... didn't apply the rules equitably across Canada.'

The media focused on the controversy surrounding the role of Members of Parliament in the TJF approval process. On 7 June, a more detailed follow-up story ran in the Moncton *Times & Transcript* under the headline 'Liberals admit caucus had fingers in grant pockets.' According to the article, 'the committee reported that "the bureaucrats running the program were unable to point to any official pockets policy"' and cited the recommendation in the committee report that 'HRDC should ensure that eligibility criteria governing access to all its programs are clearly identified and adequately communicated and applied equitably across the country.' The article also reported on the involvement of MPs in the review of TJF projects, indicating that 'the majority (on the Committee) suggested that the direct involvement that currently exists (MPs are asked for their opinion on proposals but they do not have the authority to veto or approve them) should be replaced with a local committee system that would ask the opinions of other community leaders.' It concluded with a quote from Andy Scott, Liberal MP and a member of the Committee who said, 'I always sought outside advice whenever I developed an opinion on any proposal.'

Five months after the release of the audit, the media reported on the termination of CJF. On 22 June the *Ottawa Citizen* ran this headline on its front page: 'Liberals kill controversial jobs fund: Program at heart of HRDC scandal scrapped, $110M budget handed to regional agencies.' The accompanying article observed that 'the Canada Jobs Fund (CJF) is being scrapped, in part, to prevent the ongoing controversy surrounding it from discrediting the good work of the other programs, for which more stringent administrative guidelines have been issued.' *The Globe and Mail*, reporting on the same subject, quoted the Minister of Industry as saying that under the federal government's four regional development agencies the 'emphasis would be on innovation and the new economy ... different from the old program.' The *National Post* headlined its story with 'It's over, Stewart says: Critics unimpressed,' writing that 'opposition MPs and the Canadian Taxpayers Federation dismissed the changes as "a snow job,"' although it reported that the Minister insisted the program is being scrapped because 'the national unemployment rate dropped to 6.6% from 9.4% in 1995, when TJF, the predecessor to CJF, was being devised.' Southam Press headlined its story 'Alliance slams shovelgate "shell game": "Slush fund" not eliminated, just renamed, opposition says.'

On 28 June, the *Ottawa Citizen* ran this headline: 'PM to unveil $700M Atlantic plan: Chrétien woos region with strategy for long-term growth.' The article noted that 'the government is expected to pump roughly $375 million in new money into the region and re-target about $325 million in existing job-creation and economic development funds.'

An Imbalance between Fast Service and Good Control

When Parliament recessed for the summer, media interest in the story waned. It was reignited in the fall with the release of the long-awaited report of the Auditor General. On 17 October, *CBC Newsworld* reported that the Auditor General had confirmed the accusations of 'financial mismanagement' by HRDC, although he also indicated that 'steps had been taken to turn things around.' One reporter described the Auditor

General's report as 'a regular second look at the government's books,' and summed it up as 'scolding government for not checking to see if money was well spent.' He noted it had been far less critical than the report of the Information Commissioner and speculated that the Auditor General's report might be 'the final word on the uproar that engulfed the Commons earlier this year.' The CBC's *The National* also ran the Auditor General's report as its top story, outlining the main criticisms of the four HRDC programs under review and emphasizing the difficulty in estimating overpayments and the Auditor General's disagreement with HRDC's job-creation figures. The *National Post*, in response to the findings of the Auditor General, observed that TJF was not 'out of control (but) in fact operating precisely as intended: TJF was expressly designed to be political, its every contribution requiring the approval not merely of the Minister, but of the local MP.'

The Auditor General's press conference and follow-up interviews were widely reported. He referred to the 'quite extraordinary corrective action' already taken by HRDC, and that few departments 'have the financial management capabilities they need today, let alone for the future,' nor did they have the 'solid framework of values and ethics' that would be needed as the private sector and the government came to work more closely together. In response to the question, Did you find evidence of political interference? the Auditor General answered, 'We identified a certain number of situations in which standard procedures were not followed.' He added that 'political interference is hard to prove' and noted that a minister has 'a right to make certain decisions and deviate from certain standards,' but 'the process must be transparent.' In response to the question, 'What would happen to a CEO in the private sector in a similar situation?' the Auditor General noted that the problems found at HRDC were not specific to that organization, nor did the report single out any individual for blame. Rather, he viewed it as 'a shared responsibility.' He concluded that there was 'an imbalance between the desire for fast service and the need for good control over spending of public funds.'

The media widely reported the reactions of the opposition and the Minister. The leader of the Canadian Alliance called the Auditor General's report 'the most atrocious record of mismanagement of public funds.' The Canadian Alliance HRDC critic stated that 'the government has grossly exaggerated, even fabricated the number of jobs created (through TJF).' In response to the comment that 'the Auditor General has said nothing about a "billion dollar boondoggle,"' the MP responded that the original audit involved a one-billion dollar program, and that 80 per cent of the grants and contributions had lacked financial tracking or supervision, adding that 'you can't say that this is not a boondoggle.' The Minister said that the headline of the Auditor General's press release indicated that 'a long-standing problem is finally being fixed'; one that had persisted through three auditors general and five separate governments. She said the report was 'all about administrative practices' and that it was 'not about absconding with the funds.' Furthermore, the Auditor General had 'given us unqualified support, and asked us to sustain our efforts.' The Prime Minister was quoted in *The Globe and Mail* as saying, 'When you are in public administration, there are problems that occur.'

The Perception of Citizens

The initial perception of citizens about the grants and contributions audit reflected what they had learned from the media. Immediately following the release of the audit on 19 January 2000, more than fifty citizens dashed off quick e-mail messages to Minister Stewart. The views contained in these messages reflected what they had seen on their evening television screens and read in their morning newspapers. It also reflected their predispositions to government in general and the governing Liberal party in particular. They found the issues to be simple, clear, and dramatic, and their language echoed the media. They were 'truly shocked at the bungling'; 'mind-boggled that it was allowed to happen'; astonished by 'the huge amount of money that was handled inappropriately' and that 'a billion dollars was missing.' They referred to it as 'a political slush fund' and exclaimed that 'giving bonuses to staff to correct the problems was unbelievable.' It was 'incredulous that no one would be reprimanded or even demoted or fired for their incompetence'; they told the Minister 'you should resign' and 'every assistant deputy minister should be removed from office.'

Not surprisingly many citizens expressed their concerns as taxpayers. One citizen from Saskatoon wrote, 'Three billion dollars may not seem like much once you reach the levels of the federal government, it does mean a lot to me who has to pay a large amount of his pay cheque in federal taxes.' Another wrote, 'In reading some of the action you plan on implementing to correct the problem, I find it unbelievable that it was not thought of before spending our tax dollars.' 'Those "wasted funds,"' wrote another, 'could have been put to better use – for example, on health care, Western farmers, and the children living below the poverty level.' An accountant provided this advice to the Minister: 'You should lower our taxes, dump the GST, fold up the senate and the Governor General, cut your pensions to a third, and quit bowing to every special interest group.'

Three and half months later, the results of public opinion polling[14] and focus group discussions[15] (undertaken in late April and early May 2000) suggested that citizens had only a slightly different view of the grants and contributions audit than the first impression created in mid-January. Citizens' awareness of the issues associated with the audit was not high, but one in ten citizens polled indicated they had followed the issue very closely. Few focus group participants identified the audit when asked to identify the biggest news story out of Ottawa in the past three or four months. Participants did not see the issue as 'top of mind' compared with other pressing priorities such as health, education, taxes, jobs, and fiscal transfers. If awareness of the issue was relatively low, awareness of government's efforts to rectify the situation was non-existent. No one in the focus groups had heard of the department's six-point action plan to address the issue or of any other plans to remedy the problem.

The poll and focus groups indicated that citizens were sceptical of the government, the opposition, public servants, and the media, believing that they all had agendas that could lead them to exaggerate or downplay the seriousness of the issue. Citizens, however, viewed the Auditor General as very credible. When it came to the level of 'believability in discussing the problem at HRDC,' 70 per cent of those polled saw the Auditor General as 'highly believable' compared with slightly more than 42 per cent, 36 per cent, and 35 per cent respectively, for the media, opposition parties, and senior public servants, and only 26 per cent for cabinet ministers. Three-quarters of those polled believed that the government was more interested in making the issue disappear than in seriously addressing the problem. Seven out of ten believed that opposition parties were exploiting the situation for political gain. Fifty per cent believed that the media were exaggerating the issue to create sensational news stories. Half of those polled believed that HRDC was doing something about the problem and should be given time to fix it.

The majority of those in the focus group felt that 'the lost or unaccounted-for money' was the result of poor paper work, poor accounting, or mismanagement, rather than the result of corruption, fraud, or political favouritism. While most participants agreed that it was a lot of money, most suspected that it was not actually lost. Not surprisingly, there was confusion about the actual amount of money involved, ranging from a couple of million to tens of billions of dollars.

None of the participants in the focus groups were surprised about what they had heard about government; they were predisposed to believe that there is some mismanagement of money in government. The reporting of the events by the media, however, did serve to reinforce an increasing view of many citizens that governments, at all levels and of all political stripes, are inefficient, waste money, and prone to political interference. Asked if they would pay much attention to the issue if it were raised in the upcoming election, most participants said 'no' on the grounds that elections were times to look ahead and that the issue could just as easily happened to any government.

The Distorted Mirror

These models of the 'distorted mirror' theory help us to understand how the media conceived of the audit the way they did and why the first impressions of the media would become lasting impressions for the public. They also help us understand the difficult challenges faced by HRDC and the government in attempting to provide an explanation different from the preformed storyline of the media. The 'political model' is most useful in understanding how the media, in the face of fragmented opposition parties, took on the role of the opposition to the government. It helps to explain the close collaboration between the *National Post* and the Reform Party. The 'organizational model' helps us to understand how the news was recontextualized to fit the requirements for print headlines and the electronic sound bites.

We have seen how the media made extensive and skillful use of the techniques associated with the distorted mirror – preformed storylines, personalization, dramatization, simplicity, and the unexpected – to create the initial story and to sustain it over an extended period of time. Simplicity and dramatization of message, personalized into terms and images easily understood by the public, made it a compelling story. These techniques allowed new and unexpected events to be cast with great drama and yet explained and incorporated into the initial storyline. By reinforcing new stories, the original story became increasingly entrenched.

We also see how the dichotomies and contradictions underlying much of public management reform can become amplified and intensified through the scrutiny of the media. What may appear to public servants inside government to be a reconcilable dichotomy is cast by the media outside government as an irreconcilable contradiction. All this points to the increasing challenges for governments, and particularly public servants, as they attempt to undertake both the routines as well as the reforms of public administration in the fishbowl world in which they live.

This chapter has viewed the grants and contributions audit from the outside looking in. The perspective has been that of the media and what makes news. In the next chapter, I focus on the inside looking out to examine how the public service reacted to the events that it faced.

CHAPTER FOUR

Inside Looking Out

Crisis Management in HRDC

This chapter describes how HRDC reacted to the steady stream of events that were unleashed with the public release of its internal audit. It describes how the department assessed the public reaction to the audit and the immediate actions it took in an effort to address the concerns that were raised by the Minister, the government, the opposition, and the media. If the public management reforms had moved the department in one direction over the course of the previous decade, then the reactions of the media, the opposition, and the public to the findings of the audit moved it in an opposite direction in a matter of weeks. Although the pendulum of public administration had moved slowly towards decentralization, flexibility, and autonomy, the political and media reaction to the events accelerated its swing in the direction of centralization and standardization. These actions and reactions are described in terms of what the department faced – a crisis of major proportions.

A Framework for Crisis Management in Public Administration

Over the past fifteen years, a large selection of literature on the management of crises within the private sector has been developed, but there has been surprising little developed on crisis management in the public sector.[1] There are many definitions of organizational crisis, but this recent and comprehensive definition summarizes it well:

> An organizational crisis is a low-probability, high impact situation that is perceived by critical stakeholders to threaten the viability of the organization and that is subjectively experienced by these individuals as personally

and socially threatening. Ambiguity of cause, effect, and means of resolution of the organizational crisis will lead to disillusionment or loss of psychic and shared meaning, as well as to the shattering of commonly held beliefs and values and individuals' basic assumptions. During crisis, decision making is pressed by perceived time constraints and colored by cognitive limitations.[2]

One of the common features of crisis management literature is the extent to which it defines a crisis as a situation created by a rapid or sudden loss of control and alleviated by a set of reactive forces that can stabilize the situation.

In describing the HRDC grants and contributions crisis, I draw upon a framework developed by Peter Meyboom, a former deputy minister of the Department of Fisheries and Oceans.[3] Simply put, a crisis in government can be viewed as a time of danger when the stakes are high and the ability to influence the events is small. A crisis in public administration invariably relates to a lack of *confidence* in elected officials or administrators, or both. We can capture this on a horizontal confidence scale, ranging from 100 per cent (full confidence) to 0 per cent (no confidence). Similarly, a crisis is related to a lack of *control* of events on the part of government. We can capture this on a vertical control scale, ranging from 100 per cent (full control) to 0 per cent (no control). If we combine the two scales, we have four quadrants with varying portions of confidence and control as set out in figure 1.

Quadrant A can be described as 'Business as Usual.' Both confidence and control are high. Whatever situations arise are handled through existing processes and the standard operating procedures of the organization. Quadrant B has high confidence, but reduced control. Those affected may believe that the legislation or the programs have been poorly administered, although there is no loss of confidence in the legislation, the programs, the department, the minister, or the government. This quadrant is called 'Daily Panics.' Quadrant C is characterized by high control but reduced confidence. Whatever the issue, it will involve the minister and his or her authority will be challenged. This, therefore, is called the domain of 'Ministerial Concern.' Quadrant D is characterized by both diminished confidence and diminished control. Whatever the issue, it is a matter of 'Government Concern' and a 'Crisis.' When there is extreme lack of confidence and loss of control, the minister resigns.

For each of these quadrants there are media and communication

Figure 1: The Four Quadrants of Confidence and Control

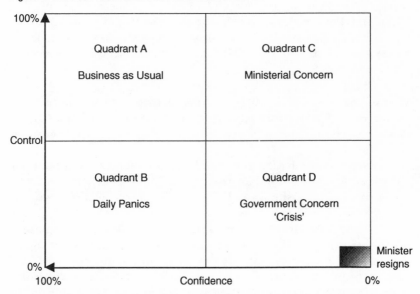

Note: The reader should observe that in this and subsequent figures the horizontal confidence scale is displayed as 100 per cent on the extreme left along the vertical axis and 0 per cent on the extreme right.
Source: Adapted from Peter Meyboom, 'Crisis Management in Government' (Ottawa, 1988).

characteristics that indicate how the public concerns are communicated to the department, the minister, and the government. These characteristics are set out by quadrant in figure 2.

In Quadrant A, there is 'no news' or perhaps the occasional piece of 'good news.' It also contains follow-up stories on previous crises. Quadrant B is characterized primarily by concerns about the department. It includes anecdotal stories in the regional press, specific one-time stories in the national press, letters to the minister, questions in caucus, and, on occasion, 'bureaucrat bashing.' Quadrant C involves criticism in local and regional press and letters to the editor. The minister's name is mentioned and linked to the issues. There are questions addressed to the minister and officials in Parliamentary Committees. Quadrant D is characterized by full coverage of the national media and extensive questioning in the House of Commons. There are questions to several ministers,

Figure 2: Media and Communication Characteristics of the Four Quadrants of
Confidence and Control

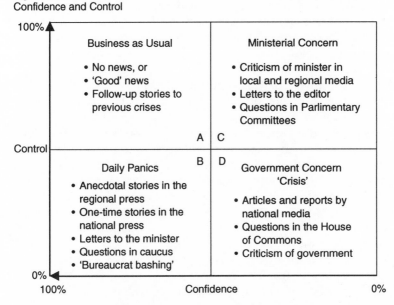

Source: Adapted from Peter Meyboom, 'Crisis Management in Government' (Ottawa, 1988).

the Prime Minister, and government officials. Contradictions between ministers and between ministers and officials are reported. The legitimacy of the institutions of government and the integrity of politicians and public servants is under attack. Under the worst circumstances, the minister resigns, or in the extreme, a government falls. This quadrant is the true crisis.

Whether a crisis is short or long, it changes shape as it grows. There are two opposing forces: the forces of non-confidence and the forces of restoration. Depending upon the particular situation, the crisis will lead either to collapse (i.e., the minister or the government resign) or to a restoration of confidence and a return to 'business as usual.' As we will see, however, the business may be 'usual,' but it will not be the same. After the crisis there is a need for considerable readjustment within the organization to compensate for initial reactions and overreactions.

The forces of non-confidence are the opposition parties to the government (whose task it is 'to unmake the government') and the taxpayers or citizens who feel aggrieved by the situation. The media organizations, which are increasingly in competition with one another and have positioned themselves as an opposition to a majority government in the face of fragmented political parties, are also a force of non-confidence.

The forces of restoration have two components: organization and information. The first is concerned with how the government is organized to handle the crisis. This includes the quality of its crisis management team, the resiliency of its employees, and its ability to quickly connect to and work with central agencies, especially the Privy Council Office and, depending upon the crisis, the Prime Minister's Office. The second component is the capacity of the organization to provide rapid and reliable information to the media, the general public, and outside interests who are highly attentive to the crisis and its outcome.

The media are viewed as a force of non-confidence particularly in the early stages of a crisis, where they can be instrumental in influencing whether and how a crisis will emerge and how it is reported. Once a crisis is underway, however, they can be a force of restoration. As we will see, their role in 'creating' the crisis is important and so, too, is their role in helping to 'defuse' it. By reporting accurately on the actions being taken by government, the media can contribute to the forces of restoration and to the rebuilding of public confidence.

In examining the course of a crisis over time, it is useful to think in terms of three distinct phases: pre-crisis, acute crisis, and post-crisis (see figure 3). In the pre-crisis phase, before the actual crisis strikes, there are usually signs of a potential crisis. In government this can take many forms – letters to the minister, a flood of access to information requests, questions in a standing committee, questions in the House of Commons, a pending report, or a series of articles and reports in the media. Whatever the symptoms, they are often hidden in the steady and constant flow of other information, and, as a consequence, the pre-crisis symptoms are often overlooked in government. Once the symptoms are recognized, there is sometimes a period of denial before the final stage of the pre-crisis phase that is usually characterized by fear and sometimes anger.

The acute crisis phase begins when the failure becomes visible. This is often a period of panic – events are unstructured, chaos sets in, and people are trying to get a handle on a situation that is running out of control. During this phase, which can last a short time or a very long time, as was the case in the HRDC audit, the crisis eventually moves to a climax. If the organization does not deal with the ambiguity and the par-

Figure 3: The Stages of a Crisis

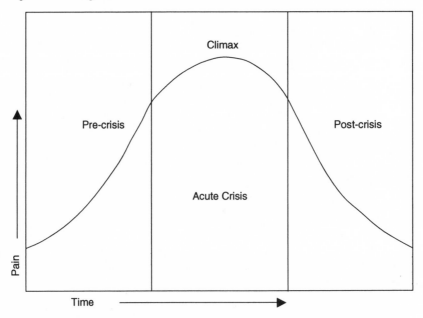

Source: Adapted from Peter Meyboom, 'Crisis Management in Government' (Ottawa, 1988).

adox of the acute crisis phase, the crisis can lead to collapse. If the organization can develop and implement a sustained strategy for addressing the crisis, it can move beyond the acute crisis and into the post-crisis phase. This last phase is a period of restoration, rebuilding, and readjustment. It is a period of gradually increasing confidence and control, and it is typically a period of significant, sometimes radical, change in the organization.

Charting the Crisis

We can chart the course of events in the crisis that emerged with the release of the HRDC grants and contributions audit. This is illustrated in figure 4, which maps the overall events from the pre-crisis phase beginning with the audit of The Atlantic Groundfish Strategy (TAGS) projects in 1998, to the post-crisis phase with the release and reaction of the Auditor General's report in October 2000 and the federal election

Figure 4: The Dynamics of the HRDC Grants and Contributions Audit Crisis

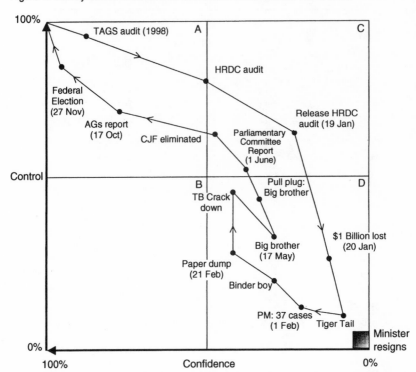

in November 2000. Figure 5 charts the acute crisis phase and sets out in detail the events in Quadrant D, 'Crisis,' as well as Quadrant C, 'Ministerial Concern.' This figure traces the events from the release of the internal grants and contributions audit in January to the elimination of Canada Jobs Fund (CJF) in June.

These charts illustrate several important findings. The department viewed the internal TAGs audit as 'business as usual,' a corrective action plan was put in place and the wider grants and contributions audit was initiated. In one sense, the grants and contributions audit, like all internal audits, was seen as 'business as usual.' In another sense, however, it was viewed as a 'ministerial concern' because of its link to the Transitional Jobs Fund (TJF), for which Minister Stewart was under pressure in the House of Commons throughout the fall of 1999 and also because of the deficiencies in administration that had been found. With the pub-

Figure 5: The Detailed Dynamics of the HRDC Grants and Contributions Audit Crisis

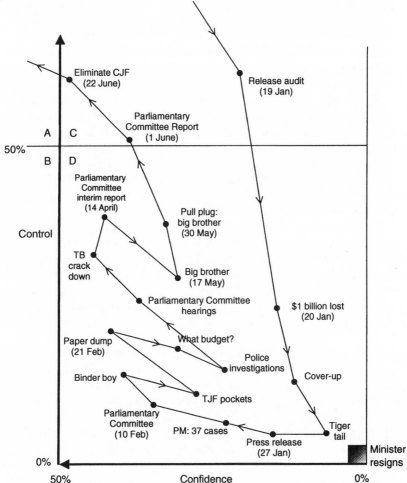

lic release of the HRDC grants and contributions audit, control by the department was immediately reduced and confidence in the Minister and government plummeted as the media reported '$1 billion lost.' The Minister and the department, and then the government were in acute crisis. Confidence was further reduced with allegations of a 'cover-up' and of an 'altered' cover page to the audit report. Confidence and control were eroded still further when the Minister compared the issue to a 'tiger,' of which the government only had a grasp of its 'tail.' In the absence of reliable factual information being made available to the media, the increasing determination of the Minister 'to fix the problem' only added to the perception that this was a major crisis that likely involved lost money.

The first, small forces of restoration were the Minister's press release on 27 January, along with the Prime Minister's attempt to contain and reduce the issue to thirty-seven 'problem cases.' The Minister's appearance at the Standing Committee on 10 February and the release of the department's comprehensive action plan added to the stabilization efforts. The Prime Minister's performance in the House of Commons with the assistance of the Government House Leader or 'binder boy,' who passed him sheets of information on the grants received by opposition members, added temporarily to the forces of restoration. However, allegations that liberal ministers had benefited significantly from the TJF 'pockets' of high unemployment and commentary by Liberal caucus members reduced confidence. The public release of an unprecedented amount of information by the department through the 'paper dump' on 21 February helped to restore some limited confidence and control. This was, however, short-lived as the opposition skillfully ignored the Minister of Finance's budget and kept its focus on the crisis.

Confidence was eroded still further with the allegations and some confirmations of the police investigations of a handful of individual projects. The unusual appearance of the former HRDC deputy minister and Clerk of the Privy Council before the Standing Committee on 21 March provided some measure of increased confidence. The Treasury Board's 'crack-down on sloppy record keeping' helped, but the erroneous allegations by a union head that HRDC employees had 'tampered with files' did not. The Parliamentary Committee's interim report on 14 April added somewhat to the restoration of confidence, but this was undercut by the widespread media reporting of the unanimous minority report of opposition MPs.

Just as the government and HRDC were slowly creeping out of crisis from Quadrant D and were moving towards Quadrant C, the 17 May national news announced that the department had a 'big brother database' of personal information on every Canadian that plunged the department ever deeper into crisis. By quickly 'pulling the plug on big brother' thirteen days later on 30 May, the department restored some confidence and control. The final report of the Standing Committee the next day also added to the confidence, but anxiety increased for HRDC employees because of the report's recommendation that the department be broken up. Finally on 22 June, after many months of uncertainty, the elimination of CJF marked the beginning of the post-crisis phase. Both confidence and control began to gradually increase. The announcement of the 'Atlantic Plan' by the Prime Minister on 28 June was reinforcing. With the Auditor General's report on 17 October, confidence momentarily dipped, but shortly thereafter increased with the realization that the Auditor General endorsed the HRDC action plan and the steps being taken to correct the administrative problems. After the election in November, the department returned to the 'business as usual' quadrant, but as we shall see, it was a very different kind of business for the department.

How a crisis is managed depends not just on the organization's management skills but also on the organization's underlying values and beliefs. A crisis usually starts with the natural human reactions of denial, anger, and fear. How the organization copes with these emotions may well determine how the organization deals with the crisis itself. The immediate pre-crisis period normally evokes the 'fight or flight' syndrome. The quick acknowledgment that there is a crisis sets the stage for a firm resolve to 'fight.' If, on the other hand, the organization suffers from internal mistrust, the stage is set for 'flight,' with associated recrimination and panic. Internal trust is the essential ingredient for the fight. Within government this means trust at three levels. There is the essential requirement for a network of trust within and between the political and the public service domains. This means trust between the minister and the deputy minister, and by extension the minister's office and departmental officials. Within the political level there is the requirement for trust between the minister and his or her office and the Prime Minister and his or her office. Within the public service there is a requirement for trust between the deputy minister and the staff in the department and between the deputy minister and the Clerk of the Privy Council and other central agencies, and by extension the officials in these offices.

All of these relationships contain elements of faith and elements of fear, and their interplay determines to a large extent the position the organization takes at the beginning of the crisis and how its positions are developed throughout the crisis. Therefore, depending on the interactions across these elements, the government's stance on any crisis can be fearful but courageous, fearful and fainthearted, or fearless but cautious. (It is assumed that government will not want to be both fearless and reckless in the handling of a crisis.)

This overall framework provides a useful analytical tool for better understanding the interplay of the forces of non-confidence and the forces of restoration during a time of crisis in public administration. It can help us understand why administrative change is often a reaction to the perceived failings of the previous reforms, why reactions in public administration are likely to be overreactions, particularly at a time of crisis, and why balance in public administration is so hard to maintain. We now turn to a closer examination of how public servants and politicians operated during the period of the crisis as they went about trying to react to and marshal these forces in the face of a sceptical and, oftentimes, hostile media.

Grappling with the Media's Overreaction

If there was any relief on 19 January for HRDC officials after the technical briefing of the media and for the Minister after the scrum and media interviews, it was short-lived. With the lead news stories that evening on national television and the headlines in the newspapers the next morning that 'the department had lost $1 billion' it was apparent that a problem, perhaps a significant one, was in the making. What the department viewed as a 'daily panic,' or more likely a 'ministerial concern,' was now beginning to be seen as a possible 'government concern.'

The department immediately tried to focus in two directions at the same time. It looked inward at its fifteen-page, six-point action plan. It quickly concluded, in the rapidly deteriorating environment, that the current action plan was an inadequate basis for convincing parliamentarians, the public, and the media that the department was actually taking corrective action. At the same time, it looked outward with a great sense of uncertainty and confusion. It attempted to assess what it viewed as a surprising overreaction by the media and to figure out how to respond. In the inevitable confusion, the department did not instantaneously appreciate that the media and the public had interpreted the audit as indicating that the government had actually 'lost' one billion dollars and that they saw the entire billion dollars as money destined for job-creation projects.

On 20 January, the day after the release of the audit, in an effort to demonstrate control over grants and contributions, two assistant deputy ministers – one for Finance and the other for Programs[4] – scrambled to issue a directive within the department. The directive was 'effective immediately' and instructed that there were to be 'no payments issued under HRDC grants and contributions programs unless [five] conditions [were] met.' In summary, these conditions were a signed agreement consistent with approved Treasury Board terms and conditions; adherence to delegated signing authorities; meeting policies and guidelines on advance payments; receiving claims forms and supporting documentation from third party sponsors; and reviewing expense claims and certifying that expenses were allowable. While this was not a freeze on spending, it did require that all executives provide certification to the senior financial officer that managers and staff administering grants and contributions understood and adhered to these conditions. Did this action by HRDC management contribute to a sense of crisis? Not likely, primarily because it was one component of the action plan and was a continuation of the efforts by the department to put in place additional program controls over the course of the several months preceding the release of the audit.[5]

The Six-point Action Plan

The department began in earnest to develop a revised action plan that could gain the confidence of outside experts and authorities. Officials reasoned that external support and validation were necessary in order for the department's corrective plan to be credible. This meant revising and strengthening the existing plan, and most important, consulting with key external authorities to receive 'the best advice available' and to secure their endorsement for the plan. The new plan that emerged, like the old one, had six points:

1 Ensure payments meet financial and program requirements.
2 Check and correct problem files.
3 Equip and support staff.
4 Ensure accountability for results.
5 Get the best advice available.
6 Report progress to the public and to staff.

The department began implementing the first two points of the plan immediately. This required the complete mobilization of most of the department. The first point entailed a dramatic and immediate tightening up of the administration of all grants and contribution files. As a result,

- no payment would be made until senior managers certified a project file met the five criteria,
- no new agreements approved until certification of certain elements,
- departmental staff would individually review 17,000 active files and by 1 April certify their completeness, and
- performance would be reviewed by a Performance Tracking Directorate based on a sampling of files and field visits with reports starting in February.

The second point of the plan, to 'check and correct problem files' found in the audit was developed to define and limit the problems and thereby demonstrate that things were being brought under control. This involved the investigation of the thirty-seven 'problem files' the auditors had identified from the 459 cases they had included in the audit sample. An interim report was to be provided on 4 February and a final report on 18 February. The plan indicated that a screening method would be developed with an independent accounting firm to identify other files that could be at risk and to resolve these issues by 31 August. As well, the results of the screening would be assessed externally, recovery of any overpayments would be made, and cases of suspected fraud would be referred to the police.

The department indicated that points three and four were longer term. For the third point, staff would be equipped and supported through directives, tools, training, and additional resources. Staff workload, which was ballooning, would be reassessed and additional resources temporarily provided. For the fourth point, managers would be appraised on their success in implementing the action plan. In addition, progress on the plan would be reported to the Minister and the Parliamentary Committee, the department would review its accountability and management structures, and external reviews of progress would be undertaken in June and January.

Points five and six, which the department called 'supporting actions,' were developed to restore credibility and public support. The fifth point required the department to 'get the best advice available' from outside experts. The plan included securing advice from and providing progress reports to the Treasury Board Standards Advisory Board, consisting of highly respected private sector accounting experts. An independent assessment of the action plan would be obtained from a senior private sector financial expert at Deloitte-Touché by 4 February. The Auditor General received and subsequently endorsed the action plan in a letter of 2 February to the deputy minister. Monthly meetings with the Assistant Auditor General were established to chart progress. Exchanges of information and best practices with other departments were undertaken.

The final point of the plan involved 'reporting progress to the public and staff.' This was to consist of information to third-party sponsors and partners concerning plans, progress, and requirements; briefing of the media on progress; and correction of misinformation. It also included a presentation to several thousand departmental delivery staff by the Minister and Deputy Minister using closed circuit TV on 4 February and regular communication with staff through briefings, bulletins, Web sites, teleconferences, and round-table discussions.

The Inadequacies of Information

Restoring control and confidence was made much more difficult because of the significant inadequacies of the internal audit as outlined in chapter 2.[6] In short, the auditors were unable to quickly retrieve individual project files and the audit was not a random sample of project files. When the internal audit was undertaken, the department did not expect that it would be released publicly. When the audit was released the auditors in the Internal Audit Bureau in Ottawa did not have in their hands the 459 project files on which the audit was based.[7] Instead, these 459 files were scattered throughout several hundred regional and local offices across the country. It took the auditors many days and considerable difficulty to retrieve the documentation, because the codes used to record the files at the time of the audit were different from the registry codes in the local and regional offices. The 'audit comments' for each of the projects were, in a number of cases, incomplete and had to be reconstructed by auditors from working documents and, in some cases, directly from the project files themselves. This took many days of around-the-clock effort.

All this became a major problem for the department and the minister. The department was unable to quickly assemble reliable information on each of the 459 projects and the thirty-seven 'problem cases.' It took several weeks just to obtain basic, reliable information on the thirty-seven projects – for example, project names, locations, descriptions, contract values, audit comments, status of the follow-up. This meant that three weeks after the public release of the audit, at the third technical briefing of reporters at the national press theatre on 7 February, HRDC officials were unable to produce the factual evidence base for the audit. In short, the department could not respond quickly and authoritatively to even simple questions or report on the positive outcomes for each project, which would have helped to contain the rapidly ballooning crisis.

Despite the requirement for random sampling in audits as a basis for drawing meaningful conclusions,[8] the grants and contributions audit was not a random sampling. It contained sixty-three projects that were selected not randomly but on the basis of the availability of project officers or sponsors for site visits or telephone interviews with the auditors. This led to enormous confusion and suspicion on the part of the media which immediately attempted to extrapolate from the 462 projects and the thirty-seven problem cases. Throughout, HRDC officials insisted that the sampling was not random and therefore it was inappropriate to extrapolate to the entire population of some 60,000 projects and $1 billion in expenditures. They also insisted that one could not extrapolate from the thirty-seven problem cases that represented $30 million in expenditures. This only raised the suspicion of the media even more – the media expected that an audit would only be done if the sampling were random so that reliable conclusions could be drawn about the entire population. It was not until 16 March, when the Director-General for the Internal Audit at HRDC testified before the House of Commons Standing Committee, that the non-random nature of the sampling in the audit became fully known.[9]

As the department looked outward it saw an overreaction by the media that, on Wednesday evening, 19 January, and Thursday morning, 20 January, reported the story as '$1 billion lost.' The department was unable to correct the story through the media by the weekend. There are likely many possible explanations. First, it is very difficult to change a story once it is in the media, primarily because the media go on to report on further developments to the initial story (e.g., 'bonuses for cleaning up the mess' and a 'political slush fund') and report on reactions to the initial story (e.g., 'heads have to roll' and 'audit released because of access to information request'). The department had to focus on these new stories and on the reactions to them. Second, the media have no interest in modifying or adjusting the initial story even if they were not fully sure of its accuracy, since it was the basis for the generation of new developments and reactions, on which the media was busy reporting.

Third, the department was not prepared for the magnitude of the reaction. The department and the Minister had focused their attention on developing a strategy to respond to and correct the problems identified in the administrative audit. Both the department and the Minister shared the same view on the problem. 'Administrative deficiencies' was the language of the department and 'sloppy administration,' the words of the Minister. Both the department and the Minister were confident that the problems could be readily fixed. Fourth, while the department attempted to report its side of the story, for a number of reasons it was not always successful. For example, *CBC National News* did not report the department's challenge to the media story on its important Friday evening newscast, three days after the release of the audit, since it claimed it had lost the tape of an interview that afternoon with a senior HRDC official.[10]

During week two, as the media attention escalated, it became immediately clear that the department and the Minister could not fully answer the barrage of questions posed by the media. As one journalist reported, there were 'foggy ministerial explanations that led to more questions than answers.' The department prepared a more detailed chronology of the audit and a lengthier set of the 'dirtiest questions' and answers: When was the Minister informed of the audit? Why was the audit withheld from the Minister? Why did the Minister say in the House that there were no problems with the TJF projects when she had an audit that indicated otherwise? The chronology and the questions and answers were required so that Minister Stewart, her office, and departmental media spokespersons could provide consistent, reliable, and immediate responses to media questions. They were also necessary to show to the Privy Council Office and the Prime Minister's Office that the department was 'on top' of the crisis and had a workable strategy for its resolution.

Making Mistakes

It is during periods of crisis that organizations are most prone to error, and these questions did not anticipate the major error that would take place later that week. On 25 January, Progressive Conservative MP Jean Dubé telephoned the department to request a copy of the audit. He received a fax copy with a cover page dated 5 October, the date the auditors completed their draft findings, not the date of the completed audit with the management response by the department. Upon discovering the error a short time later, an official in the department immediately called the MP's office to correct it. A major news story broke out across the country's media: 'A massive cover-up by the Minister and the department.' This not only extended the 'lost billion dollar' story but led to a fresh line of attack by the opposition and vigorous questioning from the media as to 'when did the Minister know what.'

On Friday of that week, the Minister made a significant effort to 'set the record straight' by issuing a press release and holding media interviews, but it was not effective. The Minister's comments that she had a 'tiger by the tail' and was going to 'bring it to the ground' were not interpreted by the media to mean that the government could fix the problem, but that the government was facing a large and somewhat terrifying situation on which it had only a limited grasp. The additional comments by the Minister that accounting procedures in the department were 'still in the Dark Ages' reduced confidence even further and infuriated many professional and union staff in HRDC and throughout government who worked in the area of finance and administration. The efforts of the department to contain the grants and contributions audit were not working. The media story was not only getting bigger, it was also spinning off new stories.

Minimizing the Problem

Across the Ottawa River, the Privy Council Office (PCO) and the Prime Minister's Office (PMO) had been closely watching the unfolding of events. An internal audit report, which had been expected to be a 'one-day wonder' and then disappear from public attention through the normal rush of ongoing events, was still in news and still on the front pages. It was now time for 'the centre' to step in and play a more active role. Getting 'a safe pair of hands' from the PCO on the crisis is not unusual. As Donald Savoie describes it, 'a great deal of time' is spent by PCO officials 'managing what they label as visible and invisible errors.'[11] If this is 'governing from the centre,' it is easy to understand why it was necessary. A minister who enjoyed the strong support of the Prime Minister was under unexpectedly sharp attack, there were calls for her resignation and that of the Prime Minister's 'deputy minister,' the Clerk of the Privy Council. The Prime Minister believed in the merits of direct job creation projects in areas of high unemployment. In his own riding, there were some seventeen TJF and CJF projects that he had vigorously defended under mounting pressure from the opposition and the media over the last six months.

Whereas the Minister and the department had focused on maximizing their efforts to fix the problem, the Prime Minister focused on minimizing the problem itself. As he said, 'It's thirty-seven cases ... routine problems ... administrative problems of this nature always exist.' While the Minister and the department had 'played the issue up,' the Prime Minister tried to 'play it down.' This deliberate strategy of minimization had some limited, initial success in slowing down the further development of the issue. It did not, however, lead to the issue 'evaporating within weeks,' as the Prime Minister thought it might. There were several reasons for this. First, the department and, hence the Minister, did not have information readily available on the details of all the projects in the audit and all the grants and contributions projects in the department. The department was not, for example, able to release a detailed list of the 459 projects because the auditors could not quickly link their findings to the project files. Second, many Liberal caucus members did not understand how eligibility for TJF projects worked under the so-called pockets of unemployment, and their comments to the media reinforced opposition allegations of political influence. Third, the question of 'when did the Minister know what' was still in the air in the aftermath of the alleged 'cover-up' associated with the incorrect cover page on the audit report. Fourth, it appeared at least to some, that the Prime Minister, the Minister and the department were pursuing 'different strategies.' Fifth, and perhaps most important, the Official Opposition and the increasingly competitive media had the government 'on the run' for the first time in many years on an issue that they had cast as gross mismanagement of public money, and neither was going to give up.

By Monday, 7 February, at the third technical briefing by officials for the media, the department was able to provide some information on the audited projects. It provided a status report on the thirty-seven projects, including detailed information about them. It indicated that documentation in three of the thirty-seven project files, representing about one-third of the $33 million, was now complete and no overpayments had been made to the recipients. The department provided a list of the other 424 projects that did not require follow-up, but it did not yet have detailed information for these projects. Again, this created deep scepticism in the media – how could they trust that the problems uncovered in the audit did not extend to 'hundreds of more projects'? This scepticism undercut the officials' statements that these were not problem cases.

That afternoon in the House of Commons, Prime Minister Chrétien responded to specific questions with the aid of Government House Leader Don Boudria acting as his 'binder boy,' passing him notes from a large black binder. The Prime Minister successfully deflected opposition questions by reading out letters of support from opposition MPs on specific grants and contributions projects in their ridings. The tactic lasted a few days and served to instill a sense of momentary confidence and control. However, it was recognized and reported in the media that the strategy of restoring confidence required walking a fine line by 'insisting that the controversy is not as serious as the opposition contends, while appearing to be serious about cleaning up the management.' On Thursday, in an appearance before the Standing Committee, Minister Stewart reinforced this strategy of restoration. She explained that ten of the thirty-seven file reviews were completed and only $251.50 in overpayments had been identified. She presented her detailed six-point action plan, and emphasized the Auditor General's endorsement of the plan as 'a thorough plan for corrective action to address the immediate control problems.' Despite her forceful attempt to use factual information to show that the financial risks were very small and were well in hand, her critics were not convinced. 'One billion dollars lost,' not $251.50 in overpayments, remained etched in the media's mind.

One side-effect of the Prime Minister's strategy and the use of the black binder was to create the perception that the department had a 'master list' of all its grants and contributions projects and that it managed these programs on the basis of political constituencies. Neither was the case. This preoccupation with lists is reflected in the exchange among Members of Parliament at the Standing Committee on 10 February:

> *Mr. Maurice Vellacott:* In December 1999 one of your top officials denied three times emphatically that the TJF funds were tracked by riding. Now we know that in fact they were tracked by riding and they were in fact at a point earlier tracked by name of the member of Parliament. (Names an HRDC official), I happen to know you have in your briefcase the fuller seven-column list. My telepathic powers and telescopic vision indicate that to me. I would want to know through the minister, can you provide that TJF seven-column list to me today?
>
> *Hon. Jane Stewart:* Again the question of lists is an interesting one because we received requests from many different sources for particular. pieces of

information. That's what we respond to. I would recognize that the Reform Party has identified our department as being one of the best in terms of responding to access to information.

Mr. Vellacott: If I might just interject, my question was simply may I have today that seven-column list that is in (names an HRDC official) briefcase? As a member of Parliament attempting to do my duty, can I have that list today?

Hon. Stewart: I'm not as clairvoyant as the member, Mr. Chair. I don't know that he has it in his briefcase.

Mr. Vellacott: He has it in his briefcase. It has been spied.

The Chair: Point of order.[12]

Once a crisis in government takes on a momentum of its own, the avenues for attack are seemingly endless.

Explaining TJF, Keeping CJF

By week five in mid-February, much of the controversy continued to revolve around the one program that was a source of considerable criticism by the media and the opposition: the Transitional Jobs Fund (TJF). Although the three-year, $100-million dollar program had terminated nearly one year earlier in March 1999, the government was unable to put the program behind it. The continuation of a similar program, the Canada Jobs Fund (CJF), contributed to the perception that TJF was still operating. In fact, the differences between TJF and CJF were not significant from the point of view of the opposition, the media, and the backbench Liberal MPs.

From the outset it was clear to the department that drawing distinctions between TJF and CJF would not change the public perception about the program. The department immediately put in place further administrative changes for CJF and, at the same time, explored options for significant reform or possible termination of the program. The department tightened up program assessments and program approvals by requiring that all projects be recommended to the Minister for approval by the national headquarters, rather than directly by the regional executive heads in the field. It also implemented a thorough system of checklists and forms for project approval and monitoring. More significant changes were considered but not implemented. These included eliminating subregions or 'pockets' as a basis for eligibility; a more transparent method for calculating the number of jobs created; and eliminating the advisory role of local Members of Parliament in the decision-making process. Officials explored various alternative program rationales for eliminating the program entirely. One rationale was that the unemployment rate had dropped significantly since TJF was first announced in 1995 and there had also been significant time for adjustment by unemployed workers living in regions that had experienced the negative effects of EI reform.

From the point of view of crisis management, it could be argued that immediately terminating CJF would have been a significant first step by the government in restoring confidence and control. Such an announcement would have eliminated the target for much of the opposition's and the media's attack. However, some argued it would have been seen as 'caving in to pressure' and admitting that the program was ineffective at a time when the Minister, with the support of the Prime Minister, was vigorously defending it. Furthermore, there was a sense within government at the time that this crisis, like others, would 'blow over.' In the absence of an appetite on the part of ministers to immediately change the program, HRDC attempted to explain the program in a written document that was released along with 10,000 pages of public information on the department's grants and contributions programs.

Explaining publicly the administration of a job-creation program that is at the centre of a governmental crisis is not an easy task. There were no outside third parties such as academics, professional organizations, or sponsors of the projects themselves, prepared to publicly defend the program, especially when it was under attack. In fact, some academics were publicly critical of the advisory role of Members of Parliament in the approval process that they saw as undermining ministerial accountability and placing undue influence on public servants.[13] Throughout the crisis, the Minister and the HRDC officials attempted to explain why some Members of Parliament, including some ministers, were eligible for TJF and CJF projects and why others were not. In particular, attention was drawn to Minister Stewart's riding of Brant. In 1995 the City of Brantford was eligible for projects under TJF because the unemployment rate in the Brantford subregion or 'pocket' was 11.8 per cent, with peaks of up to 14.5 per cent. In 1997, Brantford was eligible for projects under CJF because it was located in the EI region of Niagara, which had an unemployment rate of 10.3 per cent. It was especially difficult to explain publicly how subregions of high unemployment permitted eligibility to the program. In the case of TJF alone, about one-third of the projects were approved on the basis of subregions. The administrative flexibility, which had been a source of strength to efficiently target the areas of highest unemployment for these programs, was a significant source of weakness when it came to matters of public accountability.

Explaining the Limits of Administrative Information

HRDC recognized the urgent need to provide the media with accurate and reliable information on its grants and contributions, especially since it had had such difficulty in providing immediate follow-up information on its internal audit. While the department focused all its energies on the crisis, it was not until mid-February that a dedicated quick-response team was established under the leadership of an assistant deputy minister to systematically anticipate media stories, review access to information requests, to coordinate their responses, and to ensure quick follow-up to the media's questions.

At the meeting of the Standing Committee on 10 February, opposition members demanded that the Minister release a 'master list' of all the grants and contributions projects. There were high expectations on the part of the media, the opposition, and the public for more information; it was not surprising, however, that the department did not have a master list. In total, there were eight separate grants and contributions programs, twenty-seven subprograms, and nearly 60,000 individual projects that were delivered to the public from headquarters and from hundreds of local offices across the country. The information was gathered and organized on the basis of the programs, and given the size of some of the programs, on the basis of subprograms.

On 21 February, HRDC officials released over 10,000 pages of information on the grants and contributions programs at a national media briefing. The amount of information was staggering, consisting of data on some 60,000 projects compiled in 4 metres of binders that officials wheeled into the briefing room on a dolly. The information was also available on HRDC's Web site. Both in the briefing of the media and in releasing the materials, officials attempted to emphasize the significant limitations of the information. The approach taken by the department was to be as comprehensive and transparent as possible in providing to the media all the project-specific information that was used in the administration of the programs. Officials attempted to explain that some lists were more comprehensive and more reliable than others, and that all lists had significant limitations. HRDC believed that it was better to provide all the information and explain the significant inconsistencies and limitations than to adjust and simplify the presentation, which would run the risk of being seen to selectively withhold information.

In an introductory 'Notes to the Reader' section, the department cautioned that HRDC did not keep a 'master list' of all its grants and contributions programs, and that the information had been assembled from numerous records used for internal management of the programs. It noted that the information was not comparable across programs serving different clients and having different program terms and conditions. Officials indicated that HRDC did not manage programs on the basis of political constituencies; however, the data base for some programs like TJF, CJF, and social development programs did permit retrieval of project information by constituency. The 'Notes to the Reader' cautioned that constituencies were identified on the basis of the sponsor's mailing address and did not necessarily reflect the constituency where the activity actually occurred. This was especially the case for contributions made to national and provincial organizations located in Ottawa or in other large cities and whose work was undertaken across the country or across a province.

Officials drew attention to a seemingly obscure report entitled 'Constituency Codes not Available,' which included information on projects that could not be associated with a particular constituency because of missing postal codes, invalid, or non-designated postal codes. They cautioned that the TJF information included projects which were approved but which never took place, or for which no expenditures were incurred, as well as fifty-one projects that went bankrupt. Officials went so far as to instruct the media on which three of four columns of annual expenditure information should be added together in order to reach the most accurate estimate of expenditures on a project over the three-year life of the program. They pointed out that TJF and CJF projects were included in two separate project lists and identified which was the more reliable list for the purposes of analysing the projects. HRDC set up a 1-800 number and an e-mail address to respond to the follow-up questions from the media, Members of Parliament, and the public.

Why was the department so concerned about stressing the limitations of the information on individual grants and contributions projects? There were some good reasons, especially given the way in which the media had used, and in some cases misused, information released under access to information requests. For example, over the course of several days in early February, the national print media carried a number of major stories which concluded that an employment wage-subsidy contribution program had been used for 'political purposes' in the 1997 general election. This immediately prompted a barrage of questions in the House of Commons. Complete with detailed graphs of extensive data, the media stories alleged that for 'election purposes' the government had dramatically increased its expenditures on the program in April 1997, with the number of individual project approvals spiking to 600 in that month.

The program in question was Targeted Wage Subsidies (TWS), which offered temporary wage subsidies to employers if they hired people who were unemployed and would otherwise be collecting employment insurance benefits. The data, obtained through an access to information request for another purpose, were inaccurate and incomplete for the purposes used by the media. Two-thirds of the TWS projects were not included in the information, since the media's published graph included only those projects over $5,000. The data did not include provincial projects that were undertaken by several provinces under the new labour market development agreements. The peak number of project approvals in April also occurred in 1998 and in 1999 when there was no election. The April peak marked the beginning of the fiscal year when new funds became available and also marked the time when employers hired the majority of their seasonal workers.

Tightening Administration with Checklists and Forms

At the same time the department was releasing to the media and the public unprecedented amounts of project information, it was also reviewing individual projects and putting in place new and more stringent requirements for the assessment and approval of projects. HRDC moved quickly to strengthen the administration of its grants and contributions programs and launched a major reform of its administrative procedures throughout the department, putting into place a comprehensive and elaborate set of administrative checklists and forms that officials would use across all grants and contributions programs in the consideration, review, and approval of projects. The emphasis was decidedly on ensuring that complete and comprehensive information would be included in each project file. The effort was thorough, professional, comprehensive, and bureaucratic.

The development and implementation of checklists for individual project approvals was nothing short of major administrative reform. The focus of the effort was not on the program level but on the level of each individual project. Separate administrative procedures that applied to the twenty-seven different subprograms were replaced with a single master set of checklists and forms that would be applied to each and every project. These new checklists and forms were designed to standardize file content across the department; provide generic rules to meet standards for documentation and compliance; ensure consistency across regions and programs; support staff in the file documentation process; and support a process of quality assurance for the maintenance of complete files. The checklists and forms did not replace but were put on top of the detailed guidelines that were required for all programs in the existing 'Contributions Operations Manual.'

The new procedures required that prescribed forms and checklist be used in the review and approval of each project in six major areas, reflecting the stages of the 'project's life cycle.' These areas included application; assessment, recommendation, and approval; agreement; payment and advances; monitoring; and close out. Each of these areas in turn contained individual forms and checklists. In total, there were twenty-four separate forms and checklists that were required to be completed for each project. For example, the area of 'application' included five forms and checklists for completion:

1 A file content checklist (EMP5210E) consisted of a list of the documents contained in the project file at any time.
2 An application for funding form (EMP5209E), to be completed and signed by the applicant providing basic information about the applicant and financial information about the proposed project. It also included a section on 'Declaration – Lobbyist' to be completed for all applicants requesting more than $25,000. Also included was a section for 'Official Use Only' to record data required for 'tracking system purposes,' and should the applicant withdraw the proposal, an instruction to support such a decision by 'notes to file EP5224B.'
3 A declaration of amounts owing to the government (EMP5225E), in compliance with the Treasury Board policy on transfer payments. If the applicant had an outstanding amount owing to the department, a printout of the Departmental Accounts Receivable System (DARS) was also to be included.
4 A sponsor information sheet (EMP5214E), to be completed by the

applicant, which included information such as the business number, the GST registration number, and the individuals who had signing authority within the recipient organization.

5 An environmental assessment pre-screening decision (EMP5213E), which was a form to determine whether or not an environmental assessment of the project was required under the Canadian Environmental Protection Act. The applicant could also be asked to complete an 'Environmental Assessment Questionnaire' to assist with the pre-screening decision.

Each of the twenty-four forms that had to be completed for each project required that officials fill in a series of separate and detailed information fields. For example, one of the twenty-four forms, 'Proposal, Assessment, Recommendation and Approval' (EMP5211(11-00)E), contained seventy-three separate information fields to be completed. These information fields ranged from answering questions such as 'does the proposal avoid any appearance or reality of unfair competition' or 'if applicable, has union concurrence been received in writing?' to more elaborate descriptions such as a 'summary of proposed project,' including items such as 'expected results, capacity and expertise of applicant to achieve expected results, conditions for approval.' One of the three monitoring forms, entitled 'Monitoring Checklist,' contained ninety-three information fields, including such items as confirming 'appropriate visibility for HRDC, balancing of petty cash, and approval of capital assets by HRDC.' When taken together, the approval procedures for any single project were staggering. Each project required the completion of twenty-four individual forms and checklists, which in some cases required the filling in of as many as 1,800 individual fields of information.

Not all of this extensive form-filling work had to be completed by HRDC officials. Some of it was the responsibility of the proponents and sponsors of the proposals. For example, this included such organizations as the Council of Canadians with Disabilities in Winnipeg; the Literacy Coordinators of Alberta; Labrador Inuit Association; College Communautaire of Campbellton, New Brunswick; CAMO fonds d'integration, Montreal; and the Canadian Mental Health Association of Kitchener. The form entitled 'Application for Funding,' which had to be completed by the applicant, included 145 separate fields of information. Most of these organizations were small and had limited administrative capacity and resources to engage in extensive, costly, and time-consuming activities associated with applications and monitoring.

At the same time that HRDC employees were implementing this major administrative reform to significantly tighten the management of grants and contributions, they were also reviewing the 17,000 active project files, as required by the six-point action plan. The 17,000 active files reviewed represented nearly $1.6 billion in expenditures. According to the department, they found that the outstanding debt owing to the government from these projects was $85,000. In other words, even in the absence of the new administrative checklists and forms, the amount of overpayments made to project sponsors was only 0.004 per cent of the total grants and contributions expenditures. One has to wonder how much smaller that number would become with the new procedures in place.

Community Sponsors React

When HRDC began to put these new administrative procedures into place, it began to receive sharp criticism from its community sponsors and partners about the high cost associated with increased paperwork and record keeping and the delays in project funding. Not surprisingly, until that point, recipients of grants and contributions had been reluctant to speak out publicly on the issue. Al Hatton, Executive Director of the Coalition of National Voluntary Organizations, explained in testimony before the Standing Committee:

> We remained relatively silent on this issue because for us, this has become a major political problem ... A lot of (voluntary) groups said we don't want to go near that. We are based in the community. We don't want to be in the front pages of the *National Post*, the *Globe and Mail* or the local newspaper ... The way the story has been so often reported – very seldom has the good work of HRDC and the government been highlighted.[14]

However, in testimony at a number of the Standing Committee hearings, academics, former public servants, and community sponsors expressed deep concerns about the need to ensure that the corrective action did not go too far. For example, Arthur Kroeger cautioned against 're-bureaucratizing' the process:

> As a result of four months of controversy in the House, daily media headlines, there is ... the strongest possible incentive to play it safe and do it by the book. That incentive is not limited to officials engaging in what is

thought to be normal bureaucratic behaviour. That incentive extends to ministers because no minister wants to take any chances of being pilloried in the House week after week and, therefore you play it safe and try for maximum error-free government, and error-free government is bureaucratic government.[15]

Sean Moore, a public policy adviser with a major law firm, lamented, 'I couldn't tell you how many organizations ... now find the reporting requirements attached by funding from various levels of government hardly worth the hassle.'[16] Al Hatton noted that organizations 'are seeing more and more detailed requests for information ... a lot of new projects being put on hold, delays in payments on existing projects, and hours and hours spent on justifying what we consider to be pretty normal expenses: traveling to a place to monitor, meeting with groups, and trying to make sure that the money is being well spent.'[17] Delays in and, in some cases, suspension of project funding were creating a cash crunch for a number of voluntary sector organizations, which were having difficulties in sustaining their operations and in meeting their payrolls. Diane Richler, Executive Director of the Canadian Association of Community Living, expressed the frustration of her own organization with the new procedures being put into place: 'We managed to make the May 15th payroll (but) I honestly don't know what is going to happen by the end of the month if more [money] is not forthcoming.'[18]

Dispensing Quickly with a New Crisis

As HRDC was gradually beginning to regain some control of its grants and contributions, a new and different government crisis rocked the department, threatening to severely undermine its confidence and credibility and plunge it ever deeper into a state of severe crisis. On 17 May, front-page national newspaper stories, triggered by the report of the Privacy Commissioner, alerted the public to what the media described as 'an Orwellian style big brother' database held by HRDC. The database contained up to 2,000 different pieces of information on the lives of nearly every Canadian. For the next thirteen days this dramatic story would dominate the press with headlines such as these:

• MPs say Canadians should ask to see their Big Brother file: Stewart attacked: Bloc, Western media want people to flood Ottawa with requests.

- HRDC's original SIN: Worried about what Jane Stewart's database says about you? The federal government had your number a long time ago.
- Big Sister is watching, Jane Stewart outrages civil rights advocates after database revealed.

Initially, the Minister and the department defended the database as required for the purposes of reliable policy analysis, but less than two weeks later, the Minister announced that it was being dismantled. Why, after three years of battles between the department and the Privacy Commission, did this issue get resolved so quickly? Why did the department agree to organize its important time series and longitudinal information into more costly and less efficient 'silos,' thereby reducing its ability to quickly and reliably assess the impact of existing and proposed policies and programs?

On 4 June, William Watson, a columnist for the *Ottawa Citizen* who had been described as a 'ferocious critic' of the department, wrote a story under the headline 'A few kind words about Big Brother and his data file.' As an editor of a policy journal and economics professor at McGill University, he reported on a conference he had recently attended where an economist presented new statistical results on the growth of income inequality in Canada in the 1990s. The economist said that his estimates were practically free of sampling error, and also noted that these latest results indicated that his earlier conclusions, based on a much smaller data set, had been wrong. As Watson 'realized,' the economist's results were drawn from the 'longitudinal labour force file' that had just been dismantled. He went on to write in the *Ottawa Citizen*:

> If you're doing any kind of social science research, detailed longitudinal data is usually what you need. Who moves to the U.S. and why do they go? How many return? How many Canadians are permanently poor? How many are poor for a year or two and then climb back out of poverty? How many people who pay capital gains taxes are really rich and how many are rich only because in the year they sold their capital, their income was as a result much higher than usual? Are today's young people really poorer than their parents were at the same stage of life, or are they just facing a steeper 'age-earnings profile'? What's the financial payoff to more years of education? To answer these and hundreds of other policy-relevant questions, detailed information on how given individuals are doing year after year is exactly what you need. Nothing else will do.

The longitudinal labour force file was a large data bank made up of several smaller data banks that were linked together for the purposes of research and policy analysis. It was not a universal file on every Canadian. It included time series information on some 34 million individuals (living and deceased) containing some 2,000 data elements. The information came from HRDC employment insurance data, Canada Customs and Revenue Agency taxation and income data, and social assistance data from several provinces. The data was provided to HRDC pursuant to federal and provincial legislation and under federal-provincial data sharing agreements.

Although the longitudinal labour force file was not a universal file, the Privacy Commissioner called it 'a citizen profile in all but name.' He acknowledged, however, that there had never been a known breach of security and that the department had operated within the Privacy Act. In his report,[19] he raised four concerns with the file. It was too comprehensive: 'continually centralizing and integrating so much personal data on almost every person in Canada poses significant risks to our privacy.' It was relatively invisible: 'HRDC is not trying to hide its existence ... (but) Canadians don't know how much information is being collected about them or the extent to which it is being integrated and shared with others.' It was permanent: 'this database is never purged.' There was no legal protective framework: 'the government's pre-eminent statistical agency, Statistics Canada, operates under very strict legislation ... no such walls protect the HRDC research databases.'

In the context of the grants and contributions controversy, the 'big brother' file escalated immediately with a flood of questions in the House, extensive negative media coverage, expressions of deep concern by interest groups concerned with privacy, and fears about an all-pervasive government intruding into the private lives of Canadians. Perhaps the most significant event for HRDC was the avalanche of requests from Canadians, triggered by radio talk shows, to have access to their personal data held by the government in the longitudinal file. Over the course of two months, this amounted to over 65,000 individual requests to which the department had to respond.

To the applause of the Privacy Commissioner, the Minister promptly dismantled the file, eliminated the computer link, put in place a new governance structure for the file modeled on Statistics Canada practices, and increased transparency and accountability through external advisory committees, a legal protective framework, and annual reports. The long-term additional costs and inefficiencies for the department of having to undertake its longitudinal policy analysis under a more restrictive procedural regime was less than the immediate costs of a prolonged battle with the Commissioner, the opposition, the media, and, most important, the public over the privacy of information.

Seeking a Balance

The final report of the Standing Committee of the House of Commons, entitled *Seeking a Balance*,[20] was released on 1 June. The report was prepared and endorsed by the Liberal majority Members of Parliament on the Committee, with individual dissenting reports filed by the Opposition Members on the Committee. The report assisted the department and the government in restoring some measure of confidence and control, and attempted to answer a number of questions posed in the majority interim report in April that go to the heart of public administration and the new public management. These questions included:

1 Do the new governance arrangements that involve HRDC partners enhance or impede good administration? What is the appropriate role of the private sector in partnerships with government?
2 What is the appropriate balance between decentralization, flexibility, and control?
3 What is the appropriate role of Members of Parliament in the approval of grants and contributions?

The majority report concluded that a number of factors contributed to the shortcomings in the administrative management of grants and contributions. They included 'a substantial and seemingly incongruous departmental restructuring, new modes of service delivery, insufficient resources, and the absence of a senior managerial commitment to sound project management and clear direction.' According to the report, 'these circumstances contributed to a situation where the primary focus became the delivery of funds, while the importance of sound file management slipped away.'

The Committee report called for 'a better balance' of many competing requirements:

• a better balance between serving those who are supposed to benefit from this spending and the need for proper accountability,

- a balance between the requirements for sound financial administration and the need for responsiveness to local circumstances, and
- better balance [of these] risks by continuing to provide quality service within a framework that guarantees adequate accountability and transparency.

The report was especially balanced in its caution concerning the possible re-bureaucratization of the administration of grants and contributions. It concluded that, in achieving the balance, 'there is no need to enlarge the bureaucratic processes underlying the delivery of HRDC grants and contributions.' It went on to note that 'this only serves to bog down the system [and] moreover, this approach would not guarantee results nor would it eliminate the risks associated with delivering these funds.' The report did not indicate how this balance could be achieved without reinstituting some bureaucratic procedures. Its suggestions for improvement were at a high level of generality, and included 'better management, enough well-trained project officers aided by modern-day tools capable of working within a flexible delivery system, and an overall structure that ensures that the policies and guidelines in place to administer these funds minimize risks and provide the level of accountability that Canadians have come to expect.'

The report viewed the HRDC problem as one of lack of balance and believed that it could be addressed through a rebalancing of service to citizens and accountability to taxpayers. It did not see the need for any hard choices in public administration, since it believed that this could be accomplished 'without a retroactive return to red tape.' At the same time the report was also destabilizing for the department since it recommended that 'the government should divide HRDC into several more homogeneous and focused structures.'[21]

Taking Tylenol Off the Shelf

In late June, two closely related announcements allowed HRDC and the government to finally extract themselves from the glare of the media spotlight. One was the announcement on 22 June by Minister Stewart that CJF was being closed down and that all the associated CJF funding was being redirected to the regional economic development agencies. The other was the announcement by the Prime Minister on 28 June that $700 million, including all these funds from CJF, would be provided for an Atlantic development strategy. The strategy included an 'innovation fund' to help startup high-tech enterprises get underway and to help existing companies expand. There was also additional money for the National Research Council to help boost research capacity and encourage high-tech industrial clusters. In a departure from traditional regional development funding, the government set up an advisory board of academic and private sector representatives. In the words of the former premier of New Brunswick, the board was designed to help ensure that funding decisions would be more 'market and community responsive,' less political, and more arm's length from the government.

Why did it take so long (five months since the release of the audit) to terminate CJF? Why did the government not operate like the private sector and immediately 'take the Tylenol off the shelf?' In a recent action-research round table of senior public servants on risk assessment, Johnson & Johnson's immediate handling of the Tylenol poisoning scare was cited as 'a model' for the effective management of mistakes in the private sector. The report notes that Johnson & Johnson 'quickly recognized the problem and took significant action to correct it (i.e., removed all bottles from stores voluntarily), followed by measures to prevent it from happening again (i.e., designed plastic seals on bottles).'[22]

There is no single or simple answer to why it took so long for the government to terminate CJF. The timing of specific decisions in public affairs invariably comes down to a multiplicity of factors that begin with 'It depends.' It depends on the predispositions of the Minister and, much more important, on the Prime Minister. It depends on the Prime Minister's insistence to link the termination of one program with the announcement of a new program. It depends on the extent to which the decision would be seen as 'caving into the opposition.' It depends on the political importance of the programs to the government. It depends on early perceptions about the nature of the crisis and expectations about whether and when it will 'blow over.' It depends on the capacity and determination of the government to sustain opposition, media, and public attack. It depends on the credibility of the public explanation for terminating the program. It depends on upcoming events in the mandate of a government.

Although the reasons for the delay in terminating CJF were not entirely clear to the department, there was one thing that was. The continuation of the CJF made the department's management of the crisis all the more difficult.

The Auditor General Reports an Imbalance

The much-awaited report of the Auditor General on 17 October confirmed the extent of the administrative shortcomings and suggested that they were more significant than contained in the previous internal audit. The report did, however, serve to restore some confidence because it provided assurance that the corrective action plan was in place and beginning to work. The Auditor General's report indicated that HRDC had responded positively to the report's findings and would continue to sustain the progress in meeting the commitments in its six-point action plan. The report noted that 'the department had made good progress toward meeting the commitments,' and in an interview, the Auditor General referred to the 'quite extraordinary corrective action' already taken by the department. The report emphasized that the department 'needs to make today's extraordinary effort tomorrow's routine and fundamentally change its day-to-day approach to the delivery of grants and contributions.'

Returning to 'Business as Usual,' But Not the Same Business

The 27 November 2000 election marked the turning of the page in the HRDC grants and contributions saga. The Liberal government was returned to power with a majority of 172 seats in the House of Commons, and the Minister of HRDC was re-elected in the riding of Brant, increasing her share of the vote from 53 per cent in 1997 to 58 per cent in 2000. For HRDC, the election signalled the completion of the first stage of rebuilding and recovery, a stage which began in earnest in June with the termination of CJF and the report of the Standing Committee, and continued throughout the fall with the release of the Auditor General's report in October.

While the department was over the acute crisis and had returned to Quadrant A, the 'Business as Usual' quadrant, it was far from dealing with the same business that it had previously undertaken. Over the course of 2000, the department put in place a large number of structural, organizational, and procedural reforms that significantly changed the way it administered its programs.

To be sure, HRDC undertook extensive follow-up action to the grants and contributions audit. Most, but not all, of the corrective action was centred on the implementation of the six-point action plan. In his report of October 2000, the Auditor General assessed the department's progress against the action plan and noted that 'the department has made good progress toward meeting the commitments.' The Performance Tracking Directorate was immediately made fully operational with a staff of twenty-three and a budget of $2.7 million. In the words of the Auditor General, the Directorate 'has become an important means for continuous monitoring of the extent and impact of corrective action.'

The department regularly reported on the progress of its action plan. For example, the *Third Progress Report*[23] made in December 2000, which was ninety-nine pages long, indicated that twenty-two of the thirty-eight elements in the action plan were complete, fourteen were ongoing and on schedule, and two would be reported in the next report. A Web site containing comprehensive information for sponsors on grants and contributions programs was launched. The progress report was unprecedented in its comprehensiveness and level of detail. For example, a random sample of 219 files indicated that an 'environmental assessment was addressed adequately in the file' in 98.2 per cent of the files, compared with 29.6 per cent in the original internal audit of the 459 cases, and for the four cases where evidence was not in the file, corrective action had been taken. A random sample of 219 files indicated that in 99.1 per cent of the cases an 'application for funding from the sponsor was on file,' compared with 85.2 per cent in the original audit. For the two files where an application was not in the file, corrective action was taken; the other case did not require an application under the terms and conditions of the Aboriginal human resources development program. Not only were the public servants attending to the details, they were publicly reporting on their detailed attention.

In anticipation of the October 2000 audit by the Auditor General, HRDC undertook a comprehensive program analysis of all its grants and contributions programs. If the termination of CJF was designed to finally 'take Tylenol off the shelf,' then this analysis was designed to put tamper-proof caps on the remaining programs. The program-by-program review of the twenty-seven individual programs was intended to clarify program objectives and ensure that results measures were in place, information on performance was available, and corporate and program roles and responsibilities were understood. The department also provided extensive training to over 5,000 employees in modern comptrollership, financial control, and program management, and it published on its Web site descriptions of all its grants and contributions programs, including terms and conditions, eligibility requirements, and information on how organizations could apply.

It is probably not an exaggeration to say that HRDC put into place one of the most extensive and elaborate project review and monitoring systems ever before implemented in the federal government. This major administrative reform effort was undertaken throughout the department by implementing a comprehensive standardized set of checklists and forms that officials would use to consider, review, recommend, and approve projects. As indicated earlier, this involved the use of twenty-four separate forms and checklists and requiring the completion of as many as 1,800 individual information fields in the review of each project through six stages of the 'project life cycle' – from application to approval, to payment and project close out.

In the wake of many crises in government there is invariably organizational change. HRDC was no exception. The Standing Committee, in its June 2000 final report, called on the government to 'divide HRDC into several more homogeneous and focused structures.'[24] The Prime Minister, with the responsibility for the machinery of government and little inclination for organizational change, did not restructure the department. Instead, in March 2000, in advance of the Committee's report, the department reorganized itself by dividing its large and diverse grants and contributions branch – the Human Resources Investment Branch – into two separate units, each headed by a separate assistant deputy minister. One was for nationally delivered programs, including social development, human resource partnerships, and learning and literacy, and the other for regionally delivered programs, including labour market, Aboriginal human resources development programs, and youth employment. Two assistant deputy minister positions were also created – one for homelessness and one for planning and coordination. Under the leadership of the deputy minister, the roles and responsibilities of the deputy minister and associate deputy minister were clarified, a more formalized structure of departmental committees was put into place, and the accountabilities of program and corporate assistant deputy ministers and regional executive heads were more clearly articulated. The department took steps to strengthen and enhance its Internal Audit Bureau and the role of its Audit and Evaluation Committee.

Crisis Management: Reaction, Reform, and Readjustment

Crisis management in government can be linked to administrative reform. We have seen how the crisis triggered by the release of the audit involved a sudden loss of control for the department, the alleviation of which required a set or reactive forces in order to stabilize the situation. We have seen how new administrative and management reforms are often the reaction to the shortcomings of the old reforms. Not every crisis in government leads to administrative reform, but when administrative changes are used as a principle means to regain stability, such changes are likely to be an overreaction. This is not surprising. Dramatic and immediate administrative change – in this case, the significant tightening of administrative procedures in the awarding of grants and contributions – was required in order to regain a sense of control and to begin the process of restoring confidence in HRDC. Regaining control required losing flexibility and reducing responsiveness. Because change had to be made quickly, there was no time for fine-tuning and tailoring the response, even though the programs were significantly different from one another. Since there was no appetite on the part of ministers, and especially the Prime Minister, to immediately terminate a program like CJF, there was greater pressure on the public service to ensure that the administrative reforms across all programs were not only dramatic but were seen to be so.

It is not surprising that different people had different perspectives on the new administrative reforms undertaken during the crisis. Those at the centre of the crisis, the most senior officials in the department and the Minister, who lived through the crisis day after day and had to endure the eye of the storm, invariably saw these tough measures as essential for survival. Tough actions were juxtaposed against soft attitudes and justified in terms of getting the balance right. Those who experienced the storm, but only around its edges, supported the tough administrative actions but expressed a hope that they would not go too far, wrapping the department and possibly the government in unnecessary red tape and becoming less responsive to citizens. Those who were not directly involved in the crisis and did not experience firsthand the force of the storm but did have the benefit of distance, expressed the fear that the actions would lead to a return of 'command and control' and 're-bureaucratization' in the department and throughout the government.

If we think of administrative reform as a single unified initiative emerging from a single event, it is difficult to reconcile these different perspectives. Who is right? Where one stands on the issue invariably depends on where one sits. If, however, we think of administrative reform as a complex set of dichotomies and even contradictions undertaken in response to many events, then explanation, if not reconciliation, is possible. From the point of view of public administrative reform, it is useful to think of crisis management as involving three distinct stages: reaction, reform, and readjustment. First, HRDC reacted to the crisis it faced (although very slowly) in order to get control of the situation and regain confidence. Second, it reformed its administrative processes and put into place a common set of restrictive procedures to increase control (and the perception of control) across all of its grants and contributions. Third, it slowly began the process of re-examining those across-the-board administrative procedures to see where adjustments might be required. The first two stages are high-profile and are essential for crisis management; the third, if it happens at all, is low-profile and is essential for good public administrative reform.

In most cases of administrative reform the third stage is either missing or poorly and invisibly executed. There are many reasons for this. First, external critics will seek assurance from seemingly reliable internal and external auditors that the 'crisis-ridden' department continues to be on track in implementing its action plan long after the initial action plan has served its purpose. Second, internal departmental administrators, not wanting to face the prospects of another bad audit, will continue with the overly restrictive measures that have been prescribed to them by the central controllers within the department. Third, voluntary sector organizations which receive grants and contributions and which suffer the burdened of excessive administrative controls might raise their concerns, but without a concerted external voice and sympathetic internal ear, which they do not have, there is not likely be any change.

A deliberate readjustment strategy and plan, therefore, should be an essential feature of administrative reform undertaken during periods of crisis. While the crisis will soon pass, the impact of the reforms will not. Through a program-by-program monitoring of the implementation of the new administrative procedures, public servants should be in a better position to readjust and tailor these measures in light of specific program requirements. It makes little sense to continue with the same level of detailed administrative scrutiny for very small and less risky projects as it does for larger and more risky ones. Because the reforms undertaken in response to the crisis are often an overreaction, some procedures will need to be reduced and eliminated.

In the case of HRDC, more visibility of its readjustment strategy is required. Reporting publicly on the readjustment strategy both by the department and by Treasury Board should be an ongoing feature. For example, the department could report regularly on the readjustments through its reports on the status of the HRDC grants and contributions action plan and directly to the Parliamentary Committee. This reporting will be critical to ensure that politicians better understand that there is no single, one-time fix in public administration and that grant recipients understand why procedures need to be different across programs. In the absence of a deliberate readjustment strategy, the fears of re-bureaucratization and red tape are likely to become entrenched, or alternatively, the potential benefits of administrative reform will simply slip away as public servants are compelled to undertake ad-hoc and inconsistent adjustments to the restrictive across-the-board procedures in an effort to properly serve individual citizens.

These administrative reforms covered all the programs included in the audit. Some have argued, however, that the source of the 'billion dollar boondoggle' was not the 90 per cent spent on programs for unemployed people, youth, Aboriginals, persons with disabilities, and the illiterate. Instead, it was the 10 per cent spent on the direct employment program – TJF and CJF. Indeed, the media focus was almost exclusively on this program with the result that many came to believe incorrectly in the existence of a '$1 billion job fund.' In the next chapter, I focus on the TJF and CJF direct employment program. A closer look at this program is important for understanding the complete story of the HRDC grants and contributions audit and to illustrate the dichotomies and contradictions that underlie the development and implementation of this program.

CHAPTER FIVE

Looking Closer
'The Billion Dollar Job Fund'

At the centre of the HRDC audit crisis was a direct employment program, the Transitional Jobs Fund (TJF), and its successor the Canada Jobs Fund (CJF).[1] The attacks from opposition Members of Parliament and the media coverage immediately following the release of the internal audit gave the impression that the department was running a $1 to $3 billion jobs fund. Among opposition and government Members of Parliament, there was also confusion and misunderstanding about the size and scope of this job-creation program. In reality, the jobs fund program amounted to about $110 million annually, with slightly more than 1,000 projects undertaken over a three-year period.

Differing Perspectives on Direct Employment Programs

It is easy to understand why there was confusion about the most elementary features of the program. There are deep philosophical differences among, and even within, political parties about the merits of governments undertaking direct job-creation programs. This reflects fundamental differences across the country about the role of government in the economy and in society. There are those who argue that it is the role of the private, and not the public sector to create jobs in a free-market economy. Public sector involvement in private activity invariably leads to economic distortions, inefficiencies, and barriers to effective labour market adjustment. At the other extreme are those who argue that government must play an active role in direct job creation. There are regions, labour markets, and sectors of the economy where the private sector on its own has little or no incentive to undertake economic activity, thereby resulting in sustained unemployment, joblessness, and unacceptable social conditions.

In between there is a wide range of views. One view proposes that government involvement, if any, should limit itself to creating the proper fiscal, investment, economic, and social environment to encourage business investment in a particular region of the country. This view argues, not for implementing new government programs, but for ensuring that the 'fundamentals' are in place – low interest rates, adequate financial capital, education and skills development for workers, and investment in research and development. Another view calls on government to recognize that there are particular areas in the country which, because of geography, history, natural resource dependence, or changing economic conditions, lack the private sector investment necessary to secure acceptable levels of employment. Proponents of this view advocate targeted and limited government programs. These take the form of training and skills development for workers; regional development through strategic public and private investment; various forms of leveraged partnerships; and selective direct job creation in areas of the country with the highest unemployment.

Over the last century, at one time or another, all Canadian political parties have adopted one or more of these perspectives. Governments, once elected however, have generally taken actions that have tended to favour more public sector intervention in dealing with the needs of the unemployed in areas of chronic high unemployment. This has been the case for both Liberal and, to a lesser extent, Conservative governments. Parties in opposition, for example, the Reform Party, have favoured private sector initiatives.

Whatever the perspective, the record of accomplishment has not been a good one, in large part, because of the complexity of the economic and social problems surrounding regional economic development. What is perhaps more surprising is that whatever the government and whatever the perspective adopted, there has always been some element of direct job-creation programs by the public sector. Over the years this has ranged from public works schemes in the Depression of the thirties, government procurement projects during the Second World War in the forties, winter works projects in the post-war period of the fifties, 'make-work' and other unemployment insurance–related projects in the sixties and seventies, employment programs to deal with wrenching adjustments in resources sectors and single-industry communities in the eighties, and public–private direct employment partnerships in the nineties. While the design and emphasis of direct employment programs has changed and their size and relative importance as part of regional economic development has diminished, the existence of such programs has not.

Partnerships and Their Limits

Employment programs are usually developed and implemented through partnerships between the public, private, and voluntary sectors. What are the practical boundaries to these partnerships in the area of employment programs? What is the capacity of government and the private and voluntary sectors to actually do partnerships in employment programs? Why have these programs been so difficult to deliver? Why has there been so much interest in these programs by Members of Parliament, the government, the opposition, and the media? What is the appropriate role for Members of Parliament in the delivery of these programs?

There clearly are limits in the private sector concerning what jobs are created, where and for how long, and who is trained and with what results. There are limits in the voluntary sector, especially when the overextended delivery capacity of its diverse organizations is compared with the increasing expectations from government and the private sector. There are limits in the public sector associated with where employment activities take place, who is helped and how much, and how public money is spent.

There are benefits to be achieved through public, private, and voluntary sector partnerships in the delivery of employment programs. No one sector can do it all, especially in addressing chronic unemployment. The private sector creates the jobs and, in the knowledge-based economy, has an increasing demand for a skilled, innovative, and adaptable workforce. The voluntary sector, with its diverse and autonomous organizations, can provide a level of flexibility and on-the-ground responsiveness that governments can rarely match.[2] Governments have the capacity to redistribute public resources and to help ensure that the needs of the unemployed and the excluded are addressed.

One way, but not the only way to get answers to these questions is to ask what happens when things go wrong. To do so, I examine TJF and its successor CJF in the context of the public sector reform in the 1990s, the release of the HRDC internal audit, and the events that subsequently unfolded.

Most new programs are designed and implemented against the backdrop of the prevailing public management philosophy of the day, and most are developed in response to external pressure. On both counts,

TJF was no exception. TJF was developed by HRDC in the context of its public management reforms and as an integral part of the employment insurance (EI) reform in December 1995. In the face of long-standing concerns about the impact of unemployment insurance in undermining incentives to work, especially in Atlantic Canada, program eligibility to EI benefits for seasonal workers and repeat users was significantly tightened. As a consequence, there were large income losses to both workers and unemployed individuals in Atlantic Canada and in significant parts of Quebec. Pressure mounted from government caucus members and some Members of Parliament and provincial premiers in Atlantic Canada to provide assistance in those regions of the country where individuals would be losing benefits as a result of EI reform.

At the same time, many members of the Liberal caucus were concerned that the federal government was becoming more distanced from Canadians and losing its ability to directly touch citizens as it downsized government, eliminated programs, transferred training programs to the provinces, and privatized a number of its functions. At yet another level, both government and opposition Members of Parliament were searching for a stronger role for individual Members of Parliament, including greater independence for individual members and more direct influence on policy and program decisions.

It was in this context of the need to balance these competing concerns that TJF was developed. The Minister of HRDC announced TJF in December 1995 as part of the major reform to employment insurance, unveiling the program in skeletal form. It was to be a three-year, $300-million program to encourage small and medium businesses to create sustainable jobs in areas of high unemployment. The areas of the country where projects would be funded were primarily in Atlantic Canada and Quebec, in those areas hardest hit by Employment Insurance reform. The type of projects to be funded would be those proposed by small enterprises and include the creation of new start-up businesses or the expansion and diversification of existing ones. These projects ranged across the broad spectrum of industrial sectors, including aquaculture, tourism infrastructure, silviculture, manufacturing and light industry, food processing, and retail.

There had been a long and sordid history with direct job-creation programs by the federal government. Because there had been such limited success with many of these programs, the department was particularly attentive to how any new program could best be designed, and drew upon its experience with job-creation programs of the past. An immediate reading of the seemingly unending stream of program evaluations and reviews of previous programs provided the general answer to the often asked question of 'what works and why.' In short, the answer was 'not much and there are lots of problems.'

To the experienced program designer this suggested three things. One, any new program had to recognize the inherent scepticism concerning the effectiveness of direct job-creation programs undertaken by a remote federal government in the absence of locally developed initiatives and without the benefit of a broader regional economic-development scheme.[3] Second, any new program, if it was to be successful, had to be limited in scope, restricted to small projects, focus on results, engage partners, lever private sector funding, ensure clarity and transparency in the approval process, and minimize administrative processes and maximize flexibility to deal effectively with the private and voluntary sector partners. Third, job-creation programs were often perceived as prone to excessive political influence by ministers and Members of Parliament.

The program was therefore developed to accomplish only a few objectives. Experience indicated that the greater the number of objectives, the greater the likelihood of conflicts among them and the greater the implementation problems. TJF was designed to be simple, with one objective: 'To create long-term sustainable jobs for individuals in high-unemployment regions affected by EI reform.'[4] It is a tall order to create sustainable jobs in areas of high unemployment, but by limiting the program to one objective and by maximizing flexibility in its implementation, there was a better chance of some success. The program explicitly emphasized collaboration through 'partnership initiatives with the private sector, provincial and municipal governments, other federal departments, community groups and other organizations.'[5] Four specific program criteria were set out publicly:

1 Proposals must clearly demonstrate that they will lead to the creation of sustainable jobs.
2 Other partners must contribute at least 50 per cent of the total project costs.
3 Proposals should be consistent with the strategic plan for local/ regional economic development.
4 Proposals must have the support of the province/territory in which the activity will take place.

In addition, two other guidelines were established as part of the Treasury Board approved terms and conditions, namely, 'flexibility to allow activities to reflect and respond to local and/or regional needs' and 'implementation of TJF activities within a framework for evaluating their success in creating sustainable jobs and leveraging funds from other partners.'[6]

TJF was designed not only to minimize constraints but also to maximize flexibility in delivery. To ensure maximum flexibility and to increase the likelihood of creating sustainable jobs, officials with the support of the Minister and Members of Parliament emphasized decision-making at the local level. The department did not establish a criterion or strict rule for defining high-unemployment regions. Instead, it allowed considerable flexibility for interpretation by HRDC regional managers in determining high-unemployment regions and hence eligible projects. This meant that regional managers could respond to local needs, partners, and circumstances, and that the program could be tailored to the different labour market conditions in different regions.

There were four definitions for high-unemployment regions. The first was straightforward and open to little interpretation. It involved EI economic regions where the unemployment rate in 1995 was above 12 per cent. This amounted to twenty of the fifty-four EI economic regions in the country, all of which had comparable unemployment data. Two-thirds of the over 1,000 projects were approved on this basis. The second definition allowed projects within EI regions with unemployment rates less than 12 per cent but only in a specific subregion, or 'pocket of high unemployment' with a rate above 12 per cent, as derived from labour market information calculated by the department and statistical data from Statistics Canada surveys. These projects were open to more local interpretation and involved about one-third of the total projects. Less than a handful of projects took place under the third and fourth definitions. These projects involved considerably more discretion and were approved on the basis of 'community needs,' such as high-unemployment rates in communities of Aboriginals or persons with disabilities, or 'spin-off benefits' where projects could be eligible in low-unemployment areas (less than 12 per cent) if they produced jobs in immediately surrounding areas of high unemployment (greater than 12 per cent).

Because the program emphasized local partnerships and collaboration, HRDC employees worked at the local level with private sector sponsors, community and business groups, provincial and municipal governments, other federal departments, and the local Members of Parliament. This was based on the view that local needs were best defined locally and that flexibility was required in order to ensure that projects would have a positive impact on the community and create sustainable jobs.

To ensure that timely decisions could be taken on individual projects, HRDC put into place a streamlined and decentralized project approval process. Projects were reviewed and negotiated by HRDC officials at the local and regional level with recommendations flowing directly from the departmental regional executive to the Minister for approval. HRDC headquarters provided an overview and monitoring function, intervening only on a limited number of contentious cases – for example, when the expected jobs might not materialize or the cost per job was considered too high. The limited role of national headquarters in the review of individual projects meant that there was no comprehensive central source of reliable project-specific information. National headquarters did, of course, have information on the program and projects, especially those projects that came under scrutiny by the media. This information, however, was neither completely accurate nor totally reliable for effective and quick response in publicly explaining and defending a project in the national media or in question period in the midst of a crisis.

A cardinal rule of public administration and an implicit assumption of the new public management is that the more decision-making is decentralized, the more information should be centralized. While this assumption is true in theory, experience suggests that it is very difficult and costly to attain in practice. Accurate, timely, and reliable project information is very costly to acquire and assemble centrally when the project assessment, analysis, negotiations, and approval are decentralized. While in theory the dichotomy of decentralized decision-making and centralized information may be addressed by achieving the right balance, in the real world of strict limits on budgets, human resources, and information systems, it is more likely to be a hard trade-off involving considerable risk. In short, more decentralized decision-making in TJF meant less centralized information.

TJF was developed and implemented within the constraints and opportunities faced by the department. This meant that TJF was designed to minimize its draw on internal HRDC resources, to maximize (or lever) the resources of other partners outside government, and to secure results through flexible partnerships in delivery. At the same time that HRDC was launching its new TJF program, it was also dramatically cutting its operating expenditures. Faced with the immediate need to reduce departmental staff by 20 per cent and achieve $200 million in annual savings, the department launched a series of mutually reinforcing initiatives to restructure and improve service delivery, increase productivity, improve and measure performance, streamline administration and reduce overhead, eliminate 'red tape,' and empower employees. The principles underlying these initiatives were incorporated into the design of TJF.

Because of overall fiscal restraint across government and the operating reductions in HRDC, Treasury Board provided no new resources to the department for the administration and delivery of TJF. This meant that only limited implementation resources could be squeezed from other programs and that staff responsible for other programs had to be multi-tasked in order to support the delivery of TJF. It also meant that external partners were expected to assist in delivering the program and in measuring its results.

The Role of Members of Parliament

All the features outlined above were important in the design and implementation of TJF; however, in many ways, the most significant and unique feature of the program was the role and involvement of Members of Parliament in individual TJF projects. This particular feature of the program had important ramifications for the way in which the internal audit came to be viewed by the media, Members of Parliament, and the general public. The involvement of Members of Parliament was also related to the way in which public management reforms were being conceived and implemented in the federal government, and had important and far-reaching implications for accountability within government – government Members of Parliament needed to support the government while meeting the needs of their constituents; opposition Members of Parliament needed to hold government to account while serving their ridings; and public servants had to be seen as politically neutral while responding to the different needs of citizens.

Public servants knew that this would not be the first program in which Members of Parliament were involved in the delivery of employment programs – MPs had been explicitly involved in providing advice to the HRDC Minister on project approvals within their ridings under the Student Summer Employment Program. Before the Chrétien government, Members of Parliament and their offices had been consulted in less formal ways on other employment-related initiatives. No other programs included in the grants and contributions administrative audit, however, contained explicit provision for a formal role for Members of Parliament in the advisory process.

The idea of involving Members of Parliament in individual TJF projects originated with the members of the Liberal caucus. They strongly pressured the Minister and the Prime Minister for a direct employment program to offset the loss in benefits to those affected by employment insurance reform. They also believed that decisions should be made at the local level and that the local Member of Parliament had an important role to play in the process. They argued that it was the Member of Parliament who best knew the needs of the local community, and that individual members could work cooperatively with community organizations and businesses to ensure effective employment projects were developed and implemented. The Minister agreed with the view that all Members of Parliament should be involved and HRDC officials were asked to incorporate this feature into the design and delivery of the program.

The first fundamental question that had to be addressed was the nature of MPs' involvement in the TJF approval process. Would they have a decision-making role or would their input be advisory? There was an important consideration related to this question. It was already recognized that one of the problems with previous employment programs had been the inability to engage provincial governments in a meaningful way so that individual projects would be an integral part of provincial regional development plans rather than simply a one-time federal initiative that may be inconsistent with provincial growth and investment strategies. In the past, the federal government's commitment to consultation had often resulted in only paying lip-service to provinces. It did not necessarily result in a more coordinated approach nor translate into public support by provinces for individual projects, some of which were contentious. Giving the provincial governments co-decision-making authority on TJF projects, in effect veto power, signalled the federal government's willingness not only to work closely with provinces but also to listen to them. It also provided the opportunity for broader and hence more credible political support for job-creation projects, which in the past were sometimes viewed as motivated by narrow political interests. One other important consideration was weighed in the balance. Giving the provinces a veto over individual project approvals strengthened the hand of the federal government to insist that provinces bring some of their funding to the table for the projects.

Even with a provincial veto over the projects there were other important reasons the Minister and officials preferred that the role of the

Member of Parliament be advisory and not decisional. First, the Minister wished to retain the authority to decide what projects would go where, given the inevitable competition for projects across ridings, regions, and members. Second, some Members of Parliament (government as well as opposition) could stymie the wishes of the Minister and the provinces if they had a veto. Third, the accountability for public servants would be significantly confused and divided with their accountability fragmented between their constitutionally appointed minister and the democratically elected local Member of Parliament. It was therefore concluded that the MPs' role would be advisory in nature.

The question then centred on how the advisory role would be best performed within the decision-making process. Essentially, there were two ways. One was through informal arrangements along the lines that had existed for a number of years. This took many forms, but in general it involved the Minister, and more often the Minister's office, 'sounding out' the views of Members of Parliament on their support for specific projects in their ridings. Sometimes correspondence might be exchanged and other times there would be simply discussions and conversations. More often it involved both. This approach tended to be private, undertaken behind close doors, and was therefore not seen by other partners to the project as being open and transparent. Because it was informal there was less requirement to involve public servants in the process.

The other option was a more formalized set of procedures, similar to those that existed for the Student Summer Employment Program. This involved the obligation to ensure that the local MP was consulted and had the opportunity to express his or her views and support, or lack thereof, in writing to the Minister or the Minister's office. It was also coupled with a more formalized process of securing the views and advice of those involved in the project – the local community, business, and voluntary sector, and the municipal and provincial government partners. Because it was a formal process requiring procedures and documentation, there was a requirement for greater involvement of public servants.

The minister of the day, on the advice of the department, decided that the role of Members of Parliament should be advisory in nature. As a result, formal program guidelines were established requiring that, as part of the project assessment process, the local HRDC manager would receive input from community partners, provincial/territorial governments, regional development agencies, the local Member of Parliament, and the regional minister. This information was provided to the Minister as input for making decisions on individual projects. At the time, HRDC noted that by involving MPs, there was a greater assurance that the project proposals would take into account regional and local needs.

Although Members of Parliament had an advisory role, it became evident in the aftermath of the release of the grants and contributions audit that this advisory role was not fully understood by the media, the opposition, and the public. There was a broadly held perception that MPs were actually approving the projects or, at the very least, determining whether or, not projects would proceed. Adding to the confusion was a criminal investigation in 1997 of a Liberal Party fund-raiser who approached at least five proponents of TJF projects seeking political contributions in exchange for the promise of project approval. A 1998 evaluation report of the program, which referred to 'the presence of political factors' without elaborating on the advisory role of MPs in the approval process, added more confusion. The involvement of MPs in an advisory capacity to the government in the development and implementation of programs was not new. Members of Parliament were there to serve the interest of their constituents. In direct job-creation programs like TJF, where the benefits were geographically concentrated, MPs had traditionally taken a great interest in projects in their own constituencies and generally found ways to express their views. What was new was the formality of the advisory process.

Program Assessment and Evaluation

Throughout the course of implementing TJF, officials placed considerable emphasis on program assessment and evaluation. An early external review of the program noted:

> The partnering model of federal, provincial, and non-profit and private sector organizations should continue to be encouraged. The model enables the efficient use of resources, expertise and knowledge, provides for one-window approach to clients, and ensures that proper skills are applied to the analyses of proposals.[7]

A separate independent evaluation[8] was undertaken that gathered information through interviews with 300 of the nearly 1,000 project sponsors. This formative evaluation noted that the 'vast majority of key informants' indicated that partnerships were 'an important component of effective delivery.' They approvingly cited the 'extensive use of formal and informal partnerships at the local and regional levels, particularly in the review process,' and noted that 'the partnership approach brings increased scrutiny to the proposal review process, and tends to lead to the approval of projects which are most likely to succeed.' They emphasized that 'a good mix of partners helps sponsors identify and leverage funds from other sources.'

The evaluation suggested that the program was doing reasonably well by standards associated with previous direct job-creation projects in areas of the country with chronically high unemployment. During the period (1996–98), the program helped to create some 30,000 jobs with 22,000 considered to be incremental.[9] Comparing jobs expected with jobs created, 79 per cent of the jobs expected were actually created. The evaluation concluded that, without the program, one half of the projects would not have been pursued, and that the program had accelerated the creation of jobs in one-quarter of the projects. Of the private sector sponsors over nine out of ten were 'satisfied' with the program and emphasized its flexibility and partnership. The average cost per job of just over $8,000 was less than past experience.

A subsequent analysis undertaken by HRDC in May 2000 supported the overall positive results of the program and the evaluation. A regression analysis of TJF data found that several variables were important in influencing the number of jobs created. For example, smaller projects (less than $500,000) did better than larger projects; the larger the TJF contribution, the greater the number of jobs created; projects in Montreal in designated 'pockets' of unemployment did better than those in the rest of the country; and projects created more jobs as time went on.

Not surprisingly, the research organizations and the senior analysts responsible for both the external review and the independent evaluation were the subject of vigorous questioning by members of the Parliamentary Committee during the course of its hearings. In testimony before the committee, the analysts defended their findings, emphasizing that the number of jobs should be considered as 'short term' since there was insufficient history with the program to know if they were sustainable. The Auditor General, in his audit in October 2000, noted the limitations of the formative evaluation and concluded that the incremental job creation effect of 22,000 was 'overstated,' but he did not question the total number of 30,000.

On the basis of the apparent success of the three-year TJF program and its broad support from Members of Parliament and provincial governments (especially in Atlantic Canada and Quebec), the federal government put into place a permanent program: the $110-million Canada Jobs Fund (CJF) in April 1999. This new program was similar to TJF, with heavy emphasis on collaborative community partnerships and advice from Members of Parliament. There were, however, three key differences between the programs, two of which were:

1 the eligibility requirement for CJF was an EI economic region with over 10 per cent unemployment, as compared with 12 per cent under TJF – this was related to the decline in the overall rate of unemployment in the country, and
2 to ensure CJF funding was 'last resort' and avoid competition with repayable loans from the federal regional development agencies, there would be closer coordination between HRDC and the agencies in the delivery of the program.

Unlike TJF, which had minimal program guidelines, CJF had a two-inch-thick set of national guidelines covering areas of program administration such as eligibility, performance and accountability, partnership, planning and consultation, assessment and recommendation, project contracting, and monitoring. By 1999 it was apparent to HRDC that regional and local officials required a common set of detailed national guidelines for the consistent implementation of the program. One of the most significant guidelines was greater clarity and hence less discretion concerning the eligibility of projects in subregions (the 'pockets' of unemployment) within economic regions. In reaction to concerns about the flexible administration of TJF, the department significantly 'tightened up' the administration of its new program, CJF. Two very significant features remained, however – the advisory role of Members of Parliament in the approval process and the flexibility to use subregions for eligibility.

Despite the positive program evaluations, the achievement of job results, the support of effective partnerships, the replacement of TJF by CJF, and the reduced flexibility through national guidelines, the TJF program came under increasingly sharp criticism from the media and the opposition. The *National Post* and the opposition Reform Party focused their attack almost exclusively on the seventeen projects in the Prime Minister's riding. They flooded HRDC with access to information requests about these and other projects. Responding to these requests in a timely manner posed an increasingly difficult challenge for the department, diverting staff from program delivery. It also touched on the fundamental issue surrounding the qualified right of public access to government information and the information requirements of the department in managing its programs and activities.[10]

As the *National Post* and the Reform opposition mounted a sustained public campaign, they began to put into question a number of the TJF projects in the Prime Minister's riding. The concerns ranged across a wide spectrum of issues, including allegations of jobs not being created, financial mismanagement, the inappropriate use of trust funds, and political interference in the approval of projects. It was in this environment that HRDC released its internal grants and contributions audit, at which time the media put the spotlight on TJF and the $100-million program immediately became 'the billion dollar job fund' and 'the billion dollar boondoggle.'

Learning the Right Lessons

There are a number of lessons that can be learned about partnerships in employment programs that flow from the experience of TJF/CJF and the administrative audit of grants and contributions. One of the difficulties, however, with 'lessons learned' is that they are often so general as to merely sound like statements about the virtues of motherhood. The other difficulty is that they usually appear rather conventional, often a restatement of what should be done in an unconstrained idealized world, but rarely if ever totally achievable in a constrained real world. The lessons learned usually focus on what was not done and then prescribe what should have been done. This is usually cast under the general dictum of greater clarity for almost everything: clear program objectives; clear and focused accountability; clear roles and responsibilities of partners; clear and reliable information about program results. The reality is that the objectives in employment partnerships, as they are in most government programs, are usually multiple, conflicting, and vague. Accountabilities among partners are always multiple, inevitably complex, and often fuzzy. The roles and responsibilities are often both contradictory and complementary at the same time, and the information about program results is rarely totally accurate and often incomplete. TJF/CJF was no exception.

The reality is that achieving greater clarity in one area – be it objectives, accountability, or results – will invariably come at a cost. That cost might be rigidity, paper burden, slow responsiveness, missed opportunity, or increased resources. The lessons learned, therefore, for employment partnerships become not just what should be done but also what should be sacrificed. Invariably there will be a need to balance seemingly conflicting values. Getting the balance right means learning the right lessons.

Employment programs – whether delivered directly through conventional government machinery or through innovative collaborative partnerships with private and voluntary sponsors – are of intense interest to Members of Parliament. The benefits as well as the costs of such programs are geographically specific. Therefore, those who benefit are often different from those who pay. Some Members of Parliament strongly support these programs while others strongly oppose them. Even among the supporters, there is invariably competition for projects. This means that even if the explicit objectives of the program are singular, non-conflicting, and clear (e.g., to create sustainable jobs) and at the same time shared by most partners, there will be other implicit objectives that will be important to other partners. For example, an MP, particularly one representing an area of high unemployment, all too quickly comes to see that attracting employment projects to his or her riding is a part of doing the job as well as keeping the job. All this leads to an opposition and a media that are highly attentive and critical of the way these programs are delivered. Partners in employment programs need to be prepared for this.

Partnership arrangements can be helpful in providing public support for employment projects. They can help develop a broader based consensus for the program and increase the likelihood that better projects will be selected. For example, TJF/CJF project proposals involved a great deal of collaboration among all the partners – the private or voluntary sector sponsor, the local community, the province, HRDC, other federal departments, and the local Member of Parliament. The approval of both the province and the federal minister was required. Explicit provincial approval was important not only because it helped to ensure that the project was consistent with the regional development plan but also because it provided broader political support for the enterprise. However, as we have seen, partnership support for a project will not materialize into public support for the program when it is under strong attack.

There are sharp limits on the extent to which flexibility for partners can be built into the delivery of employment programs. For example, when it comes to defining those geographic regions of eligibility, the

TJF experience suggests there is little room for flexibility, and any flexibility that is provided should be spelled out publicly in advance through explicit rules and guidelines. Further, the flexibility should also be thoroughly communicated and explained at the outset of the program to all potential partners, including Members of Parliament. It would also be important that there be public documentation supporting this process. The Standing Committee report, prepared after hearing from an extensive list of witnesses, was particularly explicit on this point. It noted that 'HRDC officials assured the Committee that regional offices informed MPs of these selection sub-criteria (the so-called "pockets of unemployment"). We cannot support this claim because the Committee found no evidence that HRDC was able to apply the eligibility criteria for the Transitional Jobs Fund equitably across the country.'[11] The TJF/CJF case suggests that in the absence of communicating explicit rules and guidelines at the outset of an employment program, subsequent explanations about program eligibility provided at a time of intensive probing and questioning, no matter how logical, are likely to lack credibility.

On the important matter of accountability for the results of employment programs, this case suggests that partners are under considerable pressure to provide both independent and detailed documentation of the results achieved. For example, while the Auditor General approvingly concluded that the project results of TJF were 'defined in measurable terms,' he was sharply critical of what he considered to be 'a lack of follow-through in their measurement and reporting.'[12] A Member of Parliament during the lengthy Parliamentary Committee hearings expressed scepticism with the findings of the independent evaluation, despite extensive and thorough testimony from the professional evaluators. He argued that the evaluators' survey of project sponsors was inadequate, since it included only 58 per cent of the total, and concluded that the 42 per cent who did not respond 'were embarrassed at the negligible or zero jobs (they) created.' The media adopted an even higher standard for determining the number of jobs created, concluding that the evaluators could not rely upon the information provided by sponsors but had to speak individually to those actually employed. While no one would deny that the determination of the number of incremental jobs actually created is tricky business, it would appear that these outside critics were proposing standards of accountability that even the most trusting of partners in a collaborative arrangement would not, given reasonable capacity, be able to meet.

It can be argued that the media spotlight made TJF/CJF into an extreme case and that, in more normal circumstances, the requirements for accountability and results reporting would be considerably less onerous. Even if we assume that the accountability critics are 'half right,' then it is still the case that in collaborative employment partnership arrangements the public's expectations for accountability of results will be significant. The challenge is made considerably more difficult because the benefits for decision-making of flexibility and decentralization that come from partnerships demand that information on results be standardized and centralized. This requires a large investment by all partners in providing information about program results, in the systems that can generate the information, in the independent professional external evaluators that can assess and assemble the information, and the independent cross-checking that will be required. Perhaps what is even more important is that governments, as the principal partners in these collaborative arrangements, must be prepared to make the investments with their private and voluntary sector partners to increase the overall capacity to secure reliable, timely, and credible information about program results. The size of these investments and the time required to undertake them should not be underestimated.

The one question that dominated much of the controversy surrounding the TJF/CJF partnership centred on the extensive debate around the appropriate role of Members of Parliament in the review and approval process. At one level, there were those who argued that Members of Parliament should have no formal role in the decision-making process. The Auditor General in his testimony before the Parliamentary Committee and in his report concluded that 'written recommendations from the Member of Parliament for the area as one of the inputs for the project approval process ... confuses traditional accountability relationships.'[13] At another level, the Liberal Members of Parliament in their majority committee report, while cautioning that 'direct political involvement in HRDC's project selection can potentially create a conflict for parliamentarians, whose role is to hold the government accountable,' concluded that 'MPs' involvement in the project selection process should remain advisory.'[14]

If no formal role is provided to Members of Parliament in the approval process of employment programs, our analysis suggests that they are likely to find and create an informal and unstructured role for themselves primarily because they care deeply about the employability of their constituents. Indeed, evidence suggests that even when there is a formal and visible advisory role, less formal and more invisible parallel ways for

Members of Parliament to provide additional representation are likely to emerge.[15] One of the realities of involving Members of Parliament in an advisory capacity in TJF projects was the inability to consistently and credibly explain and defend that role in the face of a suspicious media, a tenacious opposition, and a sceptical public. Indeed, partners themselves, who were uncertain and confused about the role of Members of Parliament, expressed concern about the 'presence of political factors' in the approval process. In short, accountability *was* confused and accountability *looked* confused.

If we were to assume that Members of Parliament should be involved in a formal advisory capacity in the project approval process, then what would be the essential conditions that would have to be met? There are at least four. First, the role of MPs must be clearly defined both in terms of what is expected from them and how they relate to others in the advisory process. Second, the process must be open, transparent, and understandable to all parties, both those in the partnerships arrangement and those outside it. Third, the political neutrality of public servants must not be, nor seen to be, compromised. Fourth, the accountabilities of partners must be sufficiently clear.

Let's start with accountability. The formal involvement of Members of Parliament in an advisory capacity requires that it be clearly understood who makes the final decisions on the projects and who is accountable. In theory, it is always the minister who takes the project decision in the sense that the minister can always overrule a decision that has been delegated to officials. In practice, however, in a number of programs the responsibility for project approval is often delegated to officials because of the sheer volume of project proposals and the need for timely responses. Under TJF/CJF, the minister approved the projects except for those in the minister's riding, which in all cases were delegated to the deputy minister. With an average of over 300 projects requiring approval each year, there was considerable criticism from partners, provinces, proponents, and MPs concerning the delays in the approval process. The involvement of MPs in the advisory process would require that the minister and not an official have and be seen to have final approval, otherwise it could put undue political pressure on public servants. This also means the minister is to be held accountable for the project decision, and suggests that if Members of Parliament are to be involved as advisors in the process, then no one should expect the timely approval of projects.

How Members of Parliament might be involved in a formal advisory capacity speaks to the important need for transparency, openness, and understandability of the decision-making process. It also speaks to the fundamental need for political neutrality of public servants. All Members of Parliament, whether government or opposition must be, and be seen to be, treated the same. Some Members of Parliament will not want to be involved; others will be personally involved in the details of every project; and still others will leave it to staff in their offices. All these and other possibilities will need to be handled and explained to all partners in an open and transparent manner. Throughout the entire process, public servants must be, and be seen to be, politically neutral. There is considerable evidence from the experience with TJF/CJF to suggest that the involvement of Members of Parliament in providing separate advice directly to the local HRDC director is flawed. First, it is not open and transparent since the advice of the Member of Parliament is available only to the HRDC director and the minister and not to the community partners. Nor is this advice generally known to those outside the partnership arrangement. Second, providing the advice directly from a Member of Parliament to the local HRDC director can create a perception of compromising the political neutrality of the public servant.

One way of trying to address these important requirements, as suggested by the Parliamentary Committee, might be to create project selection advisory groups that include community partners and Members of Parliament. These groups would be responsible for advising the minister on whether or not the project should be funded. The Parliamentary Committee noted that this arrangement had the advantage of broadening the decision-making process, thereby permitting broad representation from within the community. But how would this work in practice? In many local communities it would prove very difficult to separate the project selection advisory group from the project development and advocacy group, which would invariably be put into place to develop and promote the project to governments and other funding sponsors. The question of who would chair the advisory group would be problematic. If chaired by the local MP, it could give the appearance of political pressure at the project assessment stage. If chaired by the local HRDC director, it could well raise issues of the perception of political neutrality for public officials. Not all Members of Parliament want be involved in advising on direct job-creation projects; and many in the opposition explicitly choose to provide no formal input to projects. This results in a pattern of activity where public officials are involved with government members but not those in the opposition, once again possibly creating a perception of differential treatment. Effective accountability depends upon clarity in the roles of ministers, public officials, and parliamentarians, and that would become further confused and made more complicated under the scheme proposed by the Parliamentary Committee.

From the above it would seem that Members of Parliament cannot have it both ways. They cannot advocate for projects in their ridings, formally advise the minister on the approval of these same projects, and at the same time fulfil their role as parliamentarians in holding the same minister to account. This is not so much a matter of finding the right balance, as suggested by the majority report of the House of Commons, as involving a tough trade-off. If accountability is important, and is not to be further confused and further complicated, then we should expect Members of Parliament not to be formally involved in advising on projects within their own ridings.

I have suggested that when it comes to partnerships in the development and delivery of employment programs there are likely to be some significant limitations – both real and perceived. Unless accountability is to be further complicated and eroded, Members of Parliament should not be formally involved in the project advisory process. Within the limited resources for program delivery that are normally expended on such programs, it will not always be possible to achieve both flexibility and accountability, particularly during periods of intense media and opposition scrutiny. This will require that trade-offs be made and that they be made among the partners in an open and transparent manner so that those outside the partnership – the media, the opposition, the auditors, the public – have a greater appreciation for the potential as well as the limits of partnerships.

I began by asking what the practical limitations to partnerships are between the public sector and the private and voluntary sectors in the development and implementation of employment programs. By focusing on a situation and a program where things went wrong – the administrative audit and the TJF/CJF programs – we have seen that there are likely to be significant limitations to such partnerships. This case does not foreshadow 'a public sector without boundaries,'[16] as some might advocate, but rather a public sector under pressure. It suggests that if the boundaries are not skilfully determined by governments and their partners, they will be clumsily drawn by opposition parties, the media, and internal and external auditors.

Determining new boundaries is hardly an easy task. Like any matter that involves limits, it will require not only the balancing of competing objectives and interests but also some hard trade-offs. It is not surprising that there will continue to be confusion over where the new boundaries should be. As this case indicates, determining the new boundaries for 'new governance' arrangements touches on some basic tensions across important values – accountability and quality service, political responsiveness and political neutrality, resource efficiency and building capacity, engaging citizens and political representativeness.

If some of the promises of partnerships are to be realized while avoiding the worst pitfalls, then the capacities of governments and their partners will need to be increased. Doing partnerships without capacity is risky business. Having capacity means that both governments and their private and voluntary sector partners be 'partnership ready.'[17] This will require clearer articulation of the requirements for accountability; underwriting the costs for improved information and evaluation strategies; investing in public servants who can deal publicly with outside partners and outside critics; recognizing the limits to flexibility for public sector organizations; calibrating and sharing risks across the sectors; and strengthening the human resource capacity of the voluntary sector.

It will also require that those outside the partnership – the media, the opposition, the auditors, and the public – be 'partnership tolerant.' If the outcomes of partnerships continue to be judged by the traditional standards that have been applied to public administration – that is, determining whether the processes and procedures been followed, mistakes avoided, benefits equitably distributed, and public servants remaining anonymous – then we are unlikely to move the boundaries of the public sector.

This chapter has taken a closer look at the 'billion dollar job fund' that came to be viewed as the central and only program contained in the grants and contributions audit, and has described how a number of the principles underlying new public management where used in the design and implementation of TJF/CJF. In the next chapter, I look outward, taking a broader focus to assess the implications of the grants and contributions audit on the way in which new public management has been conceived and implemented by the federal government.

CHAPTER SIX

Looking Around

Implications for New Public Management

The case of the HRDC grants and contributions audit provides an important window through which to view and better understand how public administration is conceived and actually practised within government. Up to this point, we have seen how the context of public sector reform shaped the way in which the department went about its work, how the media interpreted the internal audit and shaped the ensuing events, how the department dealt with the crisis it faced, and how direct employment programs – which came to be seen as the focus of the audit – were designed, implemented, and dismantled. Because this case provides such a broad window on both the theory and practice of public administration, it also affords a rare opportunity to examine new public management. This chapter, therefore, explores the implications of the internal audit for new public management, that is, how new public management was conceived and implemented by the federal Canadian government.

At one extreme, there are those who will say that one case study, no matter how significant and far-reaching, provides scant evidence from which to draw meaningful conclusions about either the essential features of new public management or the manner in which it was implemented. How could the conclusions drawn about a single case have meaning for a much broader process of public sector management reform that has been formulated and implemented in various ways in the Canadian federal government, in provincial governments, and in many other countries? At the other extreme, there are those who will say that the adoption of new public management principles, with their emphasis on service delivery, increased autonomy of public managers from central controls, rewarding individuals for performance, and cutting public programs and public servants, significantly contributed to the grants and contributions crisis. I reject both of these extreme views. Instead, I argue that because the case touches so fundamentally on such a broad array of the central issues of public administration, and because it took place at the very time that the public service was in the midst of implementing variations of new public management, it can provide important insights into new public management.

Based on the HRDC experience, I argue that some of the essential concepts of new public management place requirements on public sector managers that cannot be achieved in the practice of public administration without making trade-offs. It is not just a matter of improving the implementation of new public management. Rather, if new public management is to be successful, adjustments need to be made to some of its underlying concepts in a manner more consistent with the political context within which public administration is carried out. As Christopher Pollitt and Geert Bouckaert emphasize, 'Public management cannot be adequately comprehended without reference to the crucial relationships which exist between administration and politics and between administrators and politicians.'[1]

As the case of the HRDC grants and contributions audit has illustrated, paradoxes and contradictions are an inherent aspect of public administration and by definition the new public management. Addressing these conundrums through balance, where it can be done, and through direct trade-offs, where it is necessary, is becoming increasingly complicated, complex, and delicate. The literature on new public management provides some general guidance on how this might best be done, but it also makes a set of rather optimistic assumptions about what public servants can actually produce by way of information, feedback, and accountability.[2] It also makes a number of implicit assumptions about how ministers and parliamentarians actually use information to hold public servants to account.[3] The glare of the media and the intensity of the opposition, both of which reflect in part public concerns about the integrity and legitimacy of government and its institutions, mean that securing balance in administrative reform has become and will continue to be ever more delicate and difficult. This is not a call for reducing our efforts at reform. Rather, it is a call to recognize the need for a broad assessment of the risks inherent in any effort to fundamentally change approaches to public administration and some thoughts on how best to mitigate those inevitable risks.

This chapter begins with an articulation of the federal government's approach to new public management – how it was conceived and how it was implemented. This approach has been called the 'Canadian model.'[4] Because public administration and politics are so closely related, as illustrated in the case of the HRDC grants and contributions audit, I examine those distinct aspects of Canadian politics that underpin the 'Canadian model' of public management. New public management requires an effective system of accountability, a challenge that is particularly difficult for public management when practised within the context of Canadian politics. I therefore analyse three different and competing perspectives on accountability – control, assurance, and learning – each of which, to varying degrees, is found in the HRDC grants and contributions case. A major challenge for strengthening public sector management in the Canadian federal government is reconciling and integrating these competing perspectives on accountability.

New Public Management and the 'Canadian Model'

What is new public management (NPM) and how has it been conceived and implemented in the Canadian federal government? Two students of public administration, Christopher Hood and Michael Jackson, provide an important insight: 'Whether there is in fact a single "new public management" or whether NPM is a better seen as something like a flu virus, continuously mutating and having several different strains at once, is debatable.'[5] There is little debate, however, about how Canadian practitioners and public servants see new public management. Practitioners rarely use the term and they do not envisage a single approach. Instead, based on what they experience, they speak in terms of mutations: 'public service reform,' 'public service management reform,' or 'public sector reform.' Indeed, the Canadian approach has, for a number of reasons, been less clearly articulated and less discernable than the new public management models of the United Kingdom, New Zealand, and Australia.

In reflecting on the 1990s, former Clerk of the Privy Council Jocelyne Bourgon articulated a definition of the 'Canadian model' in her annual report to the Prime Minister.[6] Like other things Canadian, she saw that this reform was carried out 'calmly, competently, without much fanfare.' Its distinguishing features were pragmatic and non-ideological. Its approach was practical and not doctrinaire, reflecting the evolutionary history in the practise of public administration within a Westminster system of cabinet government in a decentralized federation. It also reflected a broadly shared set of values about the role of government in a country of large geography, close proximity to the United States, and a society with diverse ethnic origins and different regional experiences. The central features of the 'Canadian model' described by Bourgon were:

- Less government is not better government, but government must be affordable.
- The role of government can vary from leader, to catalyst, to partner.
- Both strong policy and modern service delivery are required; policy and service delivery functions should not be separated as a universal principle.
- A well-performing, professional, and non-partisan public service is important.
- Leadership is required from both politicians and public servants.

In this sense the 'Canadian model,' as Peter Aucoin explains, is most closely associated with a view of new public management that has as its most central feature the concept of a professional public service.[7] This view of new public management is in sharp contrast to, and in some ways competes with, three other paradigms of public service reform – politicization, privatization, and performance measurement – which are more characteristic of the UK, the US, Australia, and New Zealand. The politicization paradigm begins from the premise that strong political conviction is what drives public service reform, and the privatization paradigm emphasizes subjecting public service functions to the competitive forces of the market. Performance measurement, however, focuses on clearly established contractual arrangements specifying the results that public servants and their organizations are expected to achieve.

Appreciating the importance of a professional public service concept is key to understanding the 'Canadian model,' how it has been conceived, how is it being implemented, and the challenges it faces. Underlying the 'Canadian model' is an important set of assumptions about the current and future role of the public service. Canadian governments have not seen the public service as an obstacle to achieving their political and policy objectives, but rather as an essential partner in the enterprise. As a consequence, political and ministerial attention has not been directed at how to reform or change the public service, but at how to achieve particular policy and political objectives – for example, maintaining national unity in the face of intense pressures that would pull the country apart, securing freer trade in a global world, restoring fiscal sovereignty in the face of escalating government deficits and ballooning government debt, or restructuring government programs and operations in the face of outmoded and ineffective programs and demands from the public for greater efficiency in government and improvements in service delivery.

During the 1995 Program Review, public servants helped the government of the day to reduce expenditures and restructure programs in a manner in which the divisive regional interests could be considered and taken into account.[8] Affordable government, not necessarily less government, was a mixed blessing for the public service. On the one hand, it was a welcome sign since, for much of the 1970s and 1980s, the public service had been trying to manage programs which were increasingly overcommitted and underresourced. On the other hand, Program Review did more than cut programs. By reducing support, administration, and personnel, it diminished the capacity of the public service.

A model that sees varying roles for government in the economy and society, suggests a government that will be increasingly dependent on a skilled and professional public service. In this model, the traditional instruments of governance – expenditure, taxation, regulation, and exhortation – are not only refined but also expanded and extended.[9] This model foresees a government that can move from 'provider' to 'enabler or facilitator,' a government that can spend less and regulate smarter through partnership, leadership, and strategic alliance. It suggests a government that can deal with important new challenges by encouraging and providing reliable and accurate information (as opposed to self-serving exhortation) to citizens concerned with choices about their health, education, safety, and lifestyles. All of this change in government requires that its public servants are not just spending money, collecting taxes, and enforcing regulations but also undertaking new roles as partners, brokers, mediators, information disseminators, and facilitators.

This model does not accept that policy and service delivery should be institutionally separated as a matter of principle. Instead, it emphasizes government-wide efforts to strengthen policy capacity, including policy research and policy analysis across departments and central agencies[10] and integrated citizen-centred service delivery. Enhanced performance of the public service both in terms of the quality of the policy advice tendered to ministers and the quality of public services delivered to citizens, can be achieved without institutionally separating policy and operations. Depending upon the nature of the policy to be developed or the service to be delivered, this model offers a wide variation of how the tasks are best organized and structured.

For example, the model permits a mixture of cooperative and competitive policy analysis and advice. This is perhaps best represented in the competing and complementary policy interests between and among the key central agencies of the Privy Council Office and the Department of Finance, and the major line departments of HRDC and Industry Canada. The model also permits 'portfolio management,' ranging from its earliest forms of 'light coordination' by the Solicitor General of the Royal Canadian Mounted Police (RCMP), the Canadian Security and Intelligence Service (CSIS), and Corrections Canada, to the more recently formulated 'Industry Portfolio' which, in addition to the industry department, includes the regional agencies, the scientific research institutes like the NRC, industry-related research granting councils, and Crown corporations like the Business Development Bank of Canada. This model also permits relatively low-profile modest experimentation with institutional forms, such as Special Operating Agencies functioning within departmental mandates, as well as legislatively based Operating Agencies such as the Canadian Food Inspection Agency, the Canada Customs and Revenue Agency, and Parks Canada.

In the 'Canadian model,' each of these institutional organizations, whether at the policy centre of government in the Privy Council Office or the service periphery of government in Parks Canada, requires a well-performing, professional, and non-partisan public service. Where public servants in the Privy Council Office operate at the heart of government, those in Parks Canada are only an 'elbow length' away. With the exception of Crown corporations, independent agencies and commissions, and the newly formed independent foundations in the areas of scholarships and innovation, no one in Ottawa works at arm's length. Despite all the discussion over the past decade about new forms of organizational structure for both policy and service delivery, when it comes to the essential features of government – performance and accountability – the Privy Council Office and Parks Canada – have more in common than they do in difference. The status of separate employer, probably the most significant distinguishing feature that led Parks Canada to become a separate operating agency, offers some prospect for escaping the rigidities of central staffing through the Public Service Commission and centralized labour negotiations through the Treasury Board. But even here these new-found flexibilities are sharply limited in part by the ever-restricted operating budgets that the Treasury Board is prepared to provide to Parks Canada. If salaries are to be increased beyond the government-wide notional rate in order to attract and retain more skilled personnel, then there will be fewer superintendents and wardens to protect the national parks.

If the 'Canadian model' requires a public service that is 'well-performing, professional, and non-partisan,' then it also requires one that is politically sensitive, that is, public servants must be able to deal with conflicting values. Indeed, it is probably not an exaggeration to see political sensitivity as one of the most important characteristics of a professional, non-partisan public service with the capacity to serve the government of the day whatever its political stripe. It has been widely understood and accepted for many years that officers in the Privy Council Office must be 'politically sensitive.'[11] What has not been so widely appreciated is the extent to which public service professionals in agencies and departments like Parks Canada, HRDC, or Health Canada are expected to share this same attribute.

Lest anyone be in doubt about the importance of political sensitivity for park wardens, superintendents, and regional directors generals of Parks Canada, he or she only needs to read the diary accounts of Henry Mintzberg's 'a day in the life' of eight federal public servants observing the 'what' and the 'how' of their jobs. In reference to the Western Region of Parks Canada he writes, '... one begins to get an idea of just how delicate managing on the edge can be (for public servants), between the developers and environmentalists, the politicians and the public servants, the department and the Parks Service, the Parks Service headquarters in Ottawa and its regions, and this particular region and its parks, leaving aside the truckers and the tourists in the front-country and the bears from the back.'[12]

The 'Canadian model' depends upon leadership by both politicians and public servants. If political leadership is required to articulate directions and sustain political and public support, public service leadership is required to put forward bold ideas, marshal support, and ensure smooth implementation. 'Speaking truth to power' requires that public servants be fearless in their policy advice and loyal in their implementation. This requires public service employees who are 'knowledge workers' and can find innovative resolutions to complex public issues, share information with others, and keep their skills and knowledge current. It also requires public service managers who are 'leaders and champions' and can create a climate of trust for their employees, encourage collaboration, and share power in exchange for everyone gaining a greater sense of collective responsibility.

Examining the public service features in the 'Canadian model' is one way of understanding it. But it is not the only way. Another way is to compare and contrast the model with the characteristics that have generally been associated with new public management. Sandford Borins[13] has put forward a list of five important characteristics of new public management (which are set out in chapter 2). When assessed against these we see that the Canadian federal government has emphasized 'high-quality services that citizens value' as reflected in the government-wide initiatives on citizen- (not customer-) centred service, service standards, and service quality. This, however, has not been at the cost of institutionally separating service and policy. Nor has it detracted from the modest efforts to strengthen policy and research capacity within government.

With respect to 'increasing the autonomy of public managers, particularly from central controls,' the focus in the 1990s embodied in Public Service 2000 was clearly directed at loosening both financial and administrative controls, with considerably less emphasis and success in reforming and streamlining central constraints in the area of human resource management. 'Measuring and rewarding organizations and individuals on the basis of whether they meet demanding performance targets' has not been a defining characteristic of the Canadian approach. Overall, compared with the UK, New Zealand, and Australia, there has been considerably less emphasis in the Canadian federal government in defining expectations, monitoring results, and reporting on performance. Unlike other countries, Canada has focused considerably less on such activities as performance contracting, market-testing, and contracting out.

'Making available the human and technological resources that managers need to perform well' was not a hallmark of the mid- to late 1990s, when expenditure budgets were severely reduced through Program Review and attention was focused on the need to address the widely anticipated Y2K computer problems. Despite the efforts of La Relève and the more recent commitment of a Clerk of the Privy Council that the public service provide an 'exceptional workplace of choice,' the Canadian model has not distinguished itself in the area of human resource management. Indeed, there has been considerable criticism of the federal government's inability to reform its human resources[14] despite specific proposals for change.[15] In terms of 'maintaining an open-minded attitude about which public services should be performed in the private sector,' Canada has been considerably less vigorous on the privatization front than the UK, New Zealand, and Australia. It has however, privatized a number of commercial operations (e.g., Petro Canada, Canadair) and taken an opportunistic approach in dealing with such areas as airports and the air navigation system. It has been quite successful in implementing an overall management regime for its forty-one Crown corporations through Part X of the Financial Administration Act, with an emphasis on corporate plans and public reporting.[16]

Canadian Politics and the 'Canadian Model'

If there is a distinctively 'Canadian model' of new public management, then there must also be a distinctively Canadian politic that is relevant to that model. Knowing that the public service is important to the 'Canadian model' of new public management is not enough. Public management does not exist in isolation from politics. Indeed, public choice and public action require that politics and management be joined. Understanding the politics should help us to better understand the management. What, then, are the central characteristics of Canadian politics that underpin the 'Canadian model' of new public management? While the annual *Report to the Prime Minister on the Public Service* from the Clerk of the Privy Council and Secretary to the Cabinet helps us to understand the 'Canadian model,' we have no public report from the Prime Minister to help us understand the politics.

Most college students know that the Canadian federal government operates as a responsible parliamentary government in the Westminster tradition. Executive authority is exercised by the Prime Minister and cabinet, which constitute the government. The political dynamic that underpins responsible government is partisan politics as organized by parliamentary political parties. Political parties provide the means by which governments are formed and are held responsible to the House of Commons and, in turn, to the public. The government of the day is supported by a public service staffed on the basis of merit. Canada is a decentralized and evolving federation with the two levels of government – federal and provincial – having the constitutional authority to act within their respective areas of jurisdictions. Sometimes they operate in cooperation and sometimes in conflict. For most citizens, the window on Canadian federal politics is through question period in the House of Commons.

If most college students know that the federal government operates as responsible government, then every citizen knows that question period operates as political theatre played out in the glare of the media. What most citizens know about politics and Parliament is learned through the images and sound bites they get from question period on their televisions. There are three players in question period – the opposition, the government, and the media – and two observers, the public service and the public. The opposition uses question period to embarrass the government, highlight issues, and influence public opinion. Their task is to 'unmake the government.' The government does not use question period in the same way, but rather tries to escape unharmed and occasionally score a counter-punch. Its task is to never admit to error. The media uses question period to get short, snappy rhetorical sound bites, good for print but even better for television. The public service monitors question period so it can prepare the ministers for the next day. The public listens to the question period sound bites for 'infotainment.'

Question period is undoubtedly a time of great strain for ministers who are under ongoing attack either because of the admission of error or the hint of scandal. Occasionally, the opposition can get the government into a sustained defensive posture. Yet for all the bravado, there are few instances were sustained opposition attacks have severely damaged a government or caused it to change its policy. Despite the nearly year-long attack by the opposition on both the Minister and the Prime Minister surrounding the HRDC grants and contributions audit and the linked issues surrounding the 'Shawinigate,' the Liberal government escaped largely unharmed. These matters did not become an election issue nor did they appear to affect the results of the November 2000 election. There was, however, significant unintended collateral damage that fell on the public service in the form of an unhealthy and excessively high level of aversion to risk.

When it comes to Canadian politics, there would appear to be four distinguishing features that bear upon the way in which new public management has been conceived and implemented in the Canadian federal government. First, brokering competing regional interests to maintain regional support is essential for sustaining the government of the day. In the United States, 'all politics is local,'[17] whereas in Canada, politics is regional. Regional interests are represented outside the federal government by provincial governments, opposition parties, and regional interest groups, and inside by regional ministers and government caucus members. Second, for much of the twentieth century there have been relatively strong majority governments and most notably a single governing party, the Liberal Party, which has been able to secure varying configurations of sufficient regional and popular support for its political platform. Third, in the face of a significant number of majority governments, opposition parties have become relatively weak, increasingly fragmented, and unable to reunite. Fourth, the media has always been an important independent critic of government, on occasion almost casting itself as the opposition. With public pressure for more openness and transparency and increased competition within the media, the media are increasingly putting government under more intense and critical scrutiny as illustrated in the case of the HRDC audit. While not all of these characteristics are unique to Canadian federal politics, when taken together they are highly interrelated and mutually reinforcing.

If politics is about who gets what, then Canadian federal politics is about who gets what and where. In Canadian politics, place matters deeply. To secure and maintain political support, every Canadian federal government needs to attend in varying degrees to the specific needs of specific regions. This invariably means that politicians and public servants spend a great deal of their time grappling with and attending to regionally targeted initiatives and the regional dimensions of national initiatives. Initiatives targeted to one region are commonly seen to be at the expense of another, invariably leading to sharp criticism and resentment from other regions.[18] Because national policies and programs play out differently in different regions, handling the impacts and designing and negotiating regionally flexible programs, such as the Transitional Jobs Fund, is a major preoccupation for politicians and public servants.

When it comes to politics (and administration), the language of regional considerations is apparent everywhere. It is found in the political demands for 'fair share' from the provinces. It is found in the occasional 'provincially friendly' language of the federal government, and incorporated into major federal–provincial agreements such as the Social Union Framework Agreement that gives the flexibility to 'a provincial/territorial government ... (to) reinvest any funds not required for (Canada-wide) objectives in the same or related priority area.'[19] It is enshrined in the Constitution in the form of 'making equalization payments to ensure that provincial governments have sufficient revenues to provide reasonably comparable levels of public services at reasonably comparable levels of taxation,' and also in the form of 'furthering economic development to reduce disparity in opportunities.'[20] And it is found in countless individual pieces of legislation, for example, the provisions for 'extended regional benefits' in the Employment Insurance Act.

The language takes the form of 'regional flexibility' and 'regional configuration' in national programs. It was called 'cushioning the impact' when the Transitional Jobs Fund was created, in part to reduce the regionally skewed negative impact of the reforms to the Unemployment Insurance Act. It goes by the name of 'regional set-offs' in government contracting. It takes on a form that is less direct but no less important for each region under the guise of special industrial assistance programs – R&D in Ontario; defence contracts in Quebec; 'final cash payments' for fishers in Atlantic Canada; programs for grain farmers in Western Canada, and forestry initiatives for British Columbia. It comes to life in the political actions of current 'regional ministers' and has found expression within the public service in the former Federal Economic Development Coordinators.

The fundamental nature of Canadian politics is the need to understand the entire country and not just particular regions. Brokering the competing regional interests is essential to framing policies and crafting messages that can be appreciated by the whole country. Viewed from this perspective, the 'Canadian model' is not one of less government but of active and affordable government. The reason there is a reluctance to separate policy and service delivery as a universal principle is partly because federal politicians want to touch citizens in regions in a direct and immediate way. A multiplicity of roles for government – leader, catalyst and partner – are especially important in dealing with regional demands and in maintaining sufficient regional political support.

A parliamentary system, coupled with an electoral system based on a simple majority vote, has tended to produce majority governments formed by a single party. Strong majority governments over the last twenty-five years, coupled with the single governing party of the Liberals, have afforded the opportunity for a close working relationship between the government and the federal public service. This is not to suggest that a close functional relationship did not develop over time between the Conservative Mulroney government and the public service. Although the adjustment period in the early stages of its first mandate was rough, by the end of the second mandate in 1993, Conservative ministers were satisfied with 81 per cent of the minister/deputy minister teams.[21]

The strength of majority governments and the absence of minority governments has meant that elected governments have had a relatively free hand in determining and implementing their policies and programs. Managing the opposition within the government caucus has quite often been as challenging as dealing with the opposition parties across the floor in the House of Commons. In both the Mulroney and the Chrétien governments, numerous efforts have been made to provide modest opportunities for government Members of Parliament to participate in policy making and implementation, but not through restructuring of the government's decision-making process nor at the expense of reducing the authority of cabinet ministers. The role of Members of Parliament in advising on TJF/CJF projects, with its attendant difficulties, was one such initiative.

Strong majority governments, led by a single governing party, go hand in hand with weak opposition parties. This, coupled with the more recent and dramatic fragmentation of opposition parties, means that there is not a 'government in waiting' capable of replacing the governing party. If the role of the opposition is to 'unmake the government,' then any fragmented political party based more on ideology than ideas will find it very difficult to put forward a platform that embraces the whole of the country. As Jeffrey Simpson has astutely observed: 'Successful parties ... learn a quite simple lesson: Procrustean politics do not work in Canada. Parties that try to shape the country to their message rather than shaping their message to the country – the whole country, not just elements of it – are going to lose.'[22]

Under these conditions, 'unmaking the government' then becomes not a contestation over ideas and policies but a strategy to unearth government mistakes and errors, possibly leading to scandal and even corruption. Focusing on the management (and more directly, the mismanagement) of government then becomes a more productive area for opposition attack than do the policies of government. As the HRDC case illustrated, it is easier to get people worked up about the prospect of administrative mismanagement than about the consequences of major policy failure. The targets for the opposition attacks are what they have always been – any hint of mismanagement of public funds and any suggestion of corruption. The major difference now is the vigour and intensity with which the opposition parties pursue these targets illuminated by the glare of a competitive and probing media.

As we saw in chapter 3, the media shape both the content and the way in which the government and the opposition deliver messages to citizens. They also shape the way in which citizens come to view their governments. The constraints and deadlines of the media mean that question period, the scrums, and press conferences deliver sound bites of information to citizens and not the fulsome details and nuances that governments and officials might want to be delivered. The dramatization and personalization of the news mean that citizens receive the dramatic visual effects with the stories played out in terms of the clash of political personalities and not the content of the issues. The rise of critical journalism has meant that the media are now participants rather than mere observers and reporters of the political process. Journalists, through their national exposure in the electronic and print media and through their investigations and editorials, have emerged as celebrities, often more trusted than politicians and public servants. Because journalists can and are expected to simplify and contextualize the news, they can appear to be more principled and bolder than politicians and public servants who must invariably balance conflicting and diverse interests, and publicly defend uneasy and often temporary compromises.

What happens when we combine Canadian politics and the 'Canadian model' of new public management? The key elements of Canadian politics – the need for the governing party to broker regional differences, the existence of a single governing party, the fragmented opposition, and the intensity of the media spotlight – reinforce the important need for sound management in government. The ability of the governments to demonstrate that they are managing the public enterprise with prudence and probity and to perform well takes on added importance especially with a strong, independent Auditor General reporting directly to the legislature. Ironically, the 'Canadian model' of new public management, operating under the paradigm of the professional public service, has not made accountability and performance a primary element. Indeed, for new public management itself, it is not an exaggeration to say that securing accountability is almost universally viewed as the 'the missing link' and 'the most elusive dimension.'[23]

If the 'Canadian model' has retained its traditional Westminster concept of accountability, the new public management, as it has been implemented in Canada and elsewhere, has made accountability increasingly more complex and more confusing. The complex accountability associated with the CJF/TJF program is a case in point. This, of course, is hardly surprising. As Peter Aucoin[24] has observed, there is a tension at the centre of the public service reform process between the need for greater managerial discretion and the degree of political direction, control, and accountability over public bureaucracies. Paul Thomas has noted that 'the extent to which this dichotomy becomes a problem in practice ... depend(s) upon the willingness and capacity of political officials to set directions, to develop indicators of progress, and to compel the production of the relevant information needed to hold public servants accountable for the exercise of discretion and the achievement of results.'[25]

Accountability: Control, Assurance, and Learning

New public management has placed new and increased demands on governments for improved accountability and performance. As the responsibility for the delivery of government services have been pushed down and out to the front line, governments have found it increasingly difficult to get accountability and performance information up and into the centre. This was illustrated by the inability of the Minister Stewart and senior HRDC officials at headquarters to secure timely and accurate information about the numerous grants and contributions projects where management and decision-making authority was delegated to lower levels in the department. As governments have decentralized, devolved, and de-bureaucratized the management of public affairs, and as they have moved to shared governance and collective management, accountability has become more complicated and elusive for politicians, public servants, and citizens. The 'Canadian model' has not made the accountability problem go away; Canadian politics has not made accountability less important but rather more important.

What is meant by accountability and how, under the new public management, is it increasingly being related to performance? Peter Aucoin and Ralph Heintzman[26] provide a useful framework for thinking about accountability and the requirements for performance in the new public management that is particularly relevant to the 'Canadian model' and to Canadian politics. In essence, accountability can be viewed from three perspectives: accountability for control, accountability for assurance, and accountability for learning.[27] Not only are these perspectives different but, more important, there are also inherent tensions and contradictions both within and among them. Indeed, Robert Behn has written about similar concepts of accountability, emphasizing 'the accountability dilemma – the trade-off between accountability for finances and fairness and accountability for performance.'[28] By separately analysing these three perspectives – control, assurance, and learning – and by pushing them a bit to their extremes, we can get a better idea of the pressures that new public management is placing on traditional accountability.

Accountability for Control

When public organizations think about accountability for control, they are focused on control for the abuse and misuse of public authority. From this perspective, the ideal organization would be self-controlling through an effective accountability process. It would have in place a comprehensive set of accountability processes and mechanisms to control the exercise of power and discretion. These processes and mechanisms would be arranged in a hierarchical framework, ranging from laws to regulations, to rules and guidelines, to policies and procedures that would help public servants and politicians be self-controlling. Some mechanisms would be of the 'command and control' nature that would prescribe what was to be controlled, who would do it, and according to what standard. Other mechanisms would be less prescriptive and directive, requiring that public servants exercise judgment within the confines of prescribed laws, guidelines, procedures, and public service values.

Ideal members of the self-controlling organization seek to minimize their own discretion and that of their fellow workers. They believe in clarifying rules and instituting documented procedures that they and their fellow workers can follow to ensure that control is maintained. They believe in the 'chain of command' and see accountability as 'an obligation to explain and justify how one discharges responsibilities, the origins of which may be political, constitutional, statutory, hierarchical or contractual.'[29] Experience has told them, however, that accountability as control is closely related to blame, because 'conventional media interpretation and ordinary discourse often interpret accountability simply as a process of assigning blame and punishing wrong-doing.'[30] It is not surprising, therefore, that the goal is 'error-free' government. Errors are to be avoided and eliminated by narrowing the discretion of public servants and prescribing detailed rules to govern the situations about what must be done, who should do it, and how it should be done.

To self-controlling officials, the public organization matters to the extent that it can maintain its legitimacy and integrity by minimizing any perception of abuse or misuse of public authority. Officials are not concerned with the purpose or the performance of the programs of the organization but with ensuring the proper exercise of powers entrusted to employees. By exercising powers according to prescribed procedures, control can be maintained and the potential for abuse and misuse minimized. Actions and inactions down the line are judged not by how they contribute to the programs but by how they are consistent with the prescribed rules and defined guidelines. Officials are concerned not with whether public money has been effectively spent, but with whether public money has been lost, spent illegally, or used for purposes not authorized by Parliament.

The self-controlling organization is interested in the use of scientific tools to detect and then reduce or eliminate abuse and misuse of authority. The compliance audit is the principle vehicle because it can produce regular and reliable reports about whether or not public servants have followed the prescribed laws, regulations, rules, and guidelines. The compliance audit methodology, with its emphasis on whether or not officials have complied with the written procedures (and there is evidence of that effect in files), provides the organization with a measure of the extent to which it is in control. Just how compliance with administrative procedures provides the assurance of control is rarely fully explained. In the case of the HRDC internal grants and contributions audit, the auditors equated control with the completeness of forms, and officials questioned neither this underlying premise nor the conclusions about control that auditors drew from their findings. The ritual of the audit, however, coupled with external pressure is sometimes sufficient to galvanize support for improvements in internal control. The general practice of having the organization prepare a 'management response' to the audit provides an assurance that the organization intends to take action to ensure that public servants are following the prescribed procedures.

The self-controlling organization and its employees soon learn, however, that there cannot be a rule and regulation for every eventuality. The new public management, with its emphasis on greater degrees of devolution and delegation of authority and more emphasis on partnering and collaboration, raises important new challenges for the self-controlling organization. Self-controlling officials sometimes have to exercise political or professional judgment. At other times the heavy weight and burden of a multiplicity of central rules and guidelines can result in conflicts and dilemmas making it difficult to effectively circumscribe discretionary decision-making. It is at such times, which are increasingly more frequent, that public servants must focus on risk assessment and risk management. In short, risk-averse, self-controlling officials must take risks, but only after careful and thorough calculation and calibration.

Self-controlling officials soon learn that they must live with some contradictions if they are to control the abuse and misuse of public authority. While they need central rules, they must also reduce their commitment to some of the old rules they have developed. They must decide which are the rules that are not to be broken and which are the guidelines that can be bent. They must reduce their commitment to the strict chain of command and understand when to issue an order to be obeyed, a functional direction to be followed, or an advisory to be considered. They must decide what the audit results really mean. Does compliance with the rules mean that there is little risk of abuse or can it be that the rules themselves do not provide an adequate standard against which to determine abuse and misuse? Where there is not or cannot be a rule or guideline, they must calibrate the risks for abuse and then ensure that an adequate system of public service values is in place so that their subordinates can deal ethically and properly with the dilemmas that they face. The more that self-controlling officials grapple with the contradictions, the more they begin to look like self-assuring officials. This takes us to accountability for assurance.

Accountability for Assurance

When public organizations think about accountability for assurance, they are concerned about providing 'assurance to citizens, legislatures and governments that public authority and state resources have been used in ways that adhere to the law, public policy and public service values in the administration of public affairs.'[31] The ideal organization would be self-assured with an effectively functioning accountability system to provide that assurance. It would have in place a complete set of tools and techniques for establishing its performance targets, measuring progress in reaching these targets, and reporting publicly on its progress. The ideal self-assuring member of the public organization knows that he or she is 'an agent' of his 'principal,'[32] the minister. A good performance measurement system is needed to provide the assurance to principals that agents are meeting the intended objectives. By being self-assured and providing assurance to principals and citizens, public confidence in the organization is maintained.

Ideal members of the self-assuring organization want to clarify objectives and assess the performance of the programs against these objectives. In short, they want both assurance that systems are in place to measure and report publicly on program results and the assurance that intended results are being achieved. Unlike, self-controlling officials, they are not interested in whether their fellow public servants have followed the rules in implementing the programs, but rather in how effectively the programs are designed, the extent to which the public expenditures are wisely made, and the degree to which programs have achieved intended results. For them, accountability is the 'the obligation to answer for the fulfillment of assigned and accepted duties within a framework of authority and resources provided.'[33] Or even more to the point, accountability is 'a relationship based on the obligation to demonstrate and take responsibility for performance in light of agreed expectations.'[34] But they draw an important distinction between accountability and answerability: 'answerability does not include the personal consequences that are part of accountability.'[35] Like other public servants, self-assuring officials are answerable and not accountable to Parliamentary Committees. It is their ministers who are accountable to the committees. While self-assuring officials would accept being accountable for the adequacy of the systems to measure the achievement of program results, they would be answerable, but not fully accountable, for the results achieved.

Self-assuring officials know that if their organization cannot provide assurance about the efficiency and effectiveness of the program, others will, and they are likely to use political rather than performance criteria. Self-assuring organizations, therefore, invest heavily in program monitoring, assessment, and evaluation. They focus on the results achieved as well as the inputs used. To ensure objectivity and assurance, these organizations contract out their evaluations to independent professional evaluators and report the results publicly.

Self-assuring officials want more than the assurance that their programs are effective. Increasingly under new public management, they want a broader sense of assurance about the organization's performance. As they and their colleagues interact more directly with citizens in the delivery of public services, they want the assurance that the highest quality of service has been provided. Through the use of service standards, client surveys and other quality assurance techniques, they are able to secure citizen feedback firsthand and information that has not been filtered through the political system. More recently, they have come to understand that they need assurance with respect to the management performance of their staff. Not only do they need to know who is doing a good job so they can be rewarded, but who is doing a bad job so that 'poor performers' can be weeded out. They need the assurance that employees understand the values and ethics that underlie the organization, and the assurance that they are being put to use as they exercise increasing discretion in dealing with complicated issues of devolution, partnership, horizontal collaboration, and alternative service delivery arrangements.

As the activities and decision-making of the organization are decentralized and devolved, the self-assuring organization comes to learn that assurance can only be provided to its principals if more and more reviews are undertaken. The self-assuring organization soon learns that it is increasingly difficult and costly to provide assurance to everyone on everything at every time. If self-assuring officials could have their way, they would continuously evaluate, review, assess, and audit every program, system, and individual in the organization. But there are only so many value-for-money audits, inspections, summative evaluations, and systems-under-development reviews that can be done at any one time. Not only is it a matter of the limits of time and resources but it is also a question of the capacity to the organization to deal with the findings of the reviews. It is, however, one thing to be assured about what is working and what is not, and quite another thing to internalize the learning and do something about it. This takes us to accountability for learning.

Accountability for Learning

When members of public organizations think about accountability for learning, they are concerned with continuous learning for continuous improvement. The ideal organization would be self-learning and seek continuous improvement in its operations and management. To members of the continuously improving organization, accountability is celebrated as the means for learning and self-improvement. Organizational actions and programs are viewed as the opportunities around which learning can take place, and accountability the means through which it is done. Accountability is the means by which the assessment of performance becomes the stimulus for promoting improvement.

Ideal members of the learning and continuously improving organization instinctively know that learning is not automatic. They therefore seek to maximize, not minimize, learning opportunities. Continuous improvement officials believe in consciously structuring programs as experiments for learning and not just entitlements to be delivered. They believe in taking action first and then learning from that action to improve subsequent actions. They believe that they can learn from their successes, but experience tells them that they can learn as much from their mistakes. If anything, they believe that governments must design error-detection systems to learn from mistakes and not be paralysed by them,[36] and they know that the process by which organizations learn from their errors is too slow. They are concerned not just with learning from errors of commission, when the organization undertakes programs or actions that are not successful, but also from errors of omission when the organization fails to act when it should have. More than anything, they are risk-takers when it comes to learning opportunities.

The continuously learning organization believes that hierarchy often stands in the way of learning. Team-based approaches are better suited to harness knowledge and the unique talents of public servants. Managers act as coaches and leaders, and employees as learners and innovators. These organizations avoid learning traps, believing that mistakes are opportunities to learn, the workplace is a complex web of learning opportunities, and people have an inherent curiosity for ideas and a motivation to learn.

Continuously improving officials are interested in reliable and accurate knowledge that is publicly verifiable. They seek out information and knowledge that has withstood the test of public scrutiny, open academic debate, and professional peer review. Ensuring that their organization has world-class knowledge means that they must interact with policy researchers and policy advocates across different 'schools of thought' around policy issues of varying degrees of urgency and visibility to their political masters. Engaging in public policy networks requires a greater openness and exposure on their part and greater risk of being seen as taking sides in public on important policy issues.

When it comes to accountability, continuously improving officials are both smart and naïve at the same time. They are smart because they know that improvement lies at the heart of organizational survival. As an agent of their principals, they instinctively know that having a track record of demonstrated improvement is important to provide a credible promise of future improvement when things go wrong. They know that to recruit and retain knowledge-workers to the public service, they need the competitive edge of an organization committed to lifelong learning and knowledge development for their employees. They are smart because they know that knowledge and research strategically positioned in hands outside government can bring about positive change and policy improvement inside government. Even in the face of errors, they believe that published admissions can sometimes bring about the external pressure needed for improvement.

But these officials are also naïve because they believe that accountability can be primarily about the positive aspects of learning without the negative aspects of 'assigning blame and punishing wrong-doing.' They view experiments and innovations, whether successful or not, as organizational opportunities for learning and not as public episodes pointing to failure and blame. Over time, these officials come to learn that it is better to be smart than to be naïve. In short, they must curtail their appetite for learning. Rather than maximizing every opportunity for learning, they come to minimize most, but not all, opportunities for mistakes.

Balancing the Tensions

I have painted each of these perspectives on accountability in their extremes. Public officials, as far as I can tell, do not operate this way all the time; some many never operate this way. But as the HRDC grants and contributions case has indicated, at various times and in various circumstances, men and women in public organizations do behave this way. Sometimes the vigorous pursuit of one perspective is at the expense of others. There are tensions and contradictions across these three perspectives on accountability – control, assurance, and learning – as well as tensions within each of them. The new public management has placed greater emphasis on accountability as assurance because central information is required for the assurance that decentralized organizations are performing. The 'Canadian model,' which embraces new trends in collaborative and horizontal governance, is beginning to give greater importance to accountability as learning. Accountability as control, which is perhaps most closely associated with traditional public administration, has waxed and waned, often coming to the fore during periods of crisis or scandal as was the case in the aftermath of the release of the HRDC audit. What is important is that accountability in new public management and the 'Canadian model' cannot just contain one perspective.

Accountability and the Limits of New Public Management and the 'Canadian Model'

The new public management, with its emphasis on alternative service delivery, devolution of administration, de-bureaucratization, partnership arrangements, and performance results depends heavily on accountability as assurance. The more that services and programs are developed and implemented with partners outside government through innovative service delivery arrangements or flexible grants and contributions programs, the more the government needs a steady stream of high quality and reliable reviews, evaluations, and audits about its performance. That governments should 'manage for results' is hardly new. Efforts to measure the performance of government have spanned forty years since the Glassco Commission's report in 1962. Since the early 1970s, the Treasury Board has promoted performance measurement through a series of government-wide initiatives, including Planning, Programming, and Budgeting Systems (PPBS); Operational Performance Management Systems; Management by Objectives; Program Evaluation; and various reforms of the Estimates. More recently the government launched the Modern Comptrollership initiative and, every year since 1995, the President of the Treasury Board has reported to Parliament on the government's progress towards managing for results. In 2000, the President of the Treasury Board underlined the commitment of the government with the publication of *Results for Canadians: A Management Framework for the Government of Canada.*

Despite these initiatives, the Auditor General has been rightfully critical of the government's overall effort, noting that

> the main barrier is less a technical than a cultural problem: there is little pressure at any level to make performance information available. Public servants detect this, and moreover, are not inclined to produce information that could embarrass their ministers. The accountability battery thus never gets charged up.[37]

Information on performance is supposed to serve not only public servants who manage the programs and ministers who are accountable, but also parliamentarians who have an oversight role. Initiatives to improve reporting to Parliament began in 1981 with the implementation of Part III of the Estimates, in an effort to provide information on departmental spending plans and on the results achieved. More recently in 1995, Parliamentary Committees received departmental Plans and Priorities documents to permit parliamentarians to input to future spending plans. They also received departmental Performance Reports for assessing results achieved. Once again, the Auditor General has rightfully been disappointed with the results, describing the process as 'painfully slow' and 'flat,' with Parliament 'still not informed enough about the results of government programs.'[38]

It seems that when it comes to program performance information for the purposes of accountability, public servants don't publish it for fear of embarrassing their ministers, and Parliamentary Committees don't use what is published because it cannot embarrass ministers. Little wonder progress has been slow and reliable information limited. All this suggests some important limits to new public management. If public servants, ministers, and parliamentarians lack the incentives to respectively produce, demand, and use reliable performance information, then there are greater limitations than we might have initially thought on the extent to which operations can be devolved, services decentralized, programs made flexible, and public servants empowered. Performance has been a component of the 'Canadian model,' but it has not been nor does it appear likely that it will become a central and critical feature.

While new public management has focused primarily on accountability for assurance, the 'Canadian model' is beginning to give greater emphasis to accountability for learning. Individual and organizational learning are increasingly seen as an important means of increasing performance and promoting change and innovation.[39] According to Peter Aucoin, a learning organization requires a commitment to three things: the necessary resources, the appropriate systems, and learning networks.[40] Resources require a high level of ongoing investment in professional staff. Appropriate systems require that there be effective incentives within organizations for continuous learning in the workplace; collaborative working arrangements within organization that can link policy and operations; and the appropriate capacity of central agencies to challenge the entire governmental system to enhance performance. Learning networks across organizational boundaries are critical because they provide the formal and informal means by which public servants learn through connections with others in their own organization, throughout their government, with other governments, and experts outside government.

The federal government, in its 1999 Speech from the Throne, recognized the importance of a 'public service equipped with the skills for a knowledge economy and society' and committed itself to the concept of a learning organization. Through the leadership of the Canadian Centre for Management Development, an effort has begun along the 'learning journey' to help public servants transform their culture and workplace into a continuously learning organization. The groundwork is beginning to be put in place for the policies, programs, and tools to integrate learning into the missions, practices, and operations of the public service.[41]

Becoming a learning organization, however, will not be an easy transformation for a public service that is under intense strain. Even with the right level and combination of resources, systems, and networks, there are significant forces that at best might throw the initiative off track and at worst contribute to its demise. Foremost are the external threats to a safe, yet challenging, public service environment within which individual, organizational, and corporate learning can take place. One of the most common traps to learning is how errors and mistakes get treated once detected. In the world of practise, where public policy and public management interact with politics, we can sometimes find that inside government, mistakes are not discussible, team members avoid blame for mistakes, mistakes get buried, and if mistakes are discussed no one seeks out the root causes.[42] We can also find, as was the case with the HRDC grants and contributions audit, that mistakes in government can be so amplified and distorted through the interaction of politics and the media that overreaction and excessively risk-adverse behaviour on the part of the public service can result.

Therefore, the major challenge for a public service that wants to become a learning organization is how best to cope with the inevitable uncertainty that lies behind nearly every public policy and public management decision. Invariably the objectives are fuzzy, the information incomplete, the means messy, the outcomes uncertain, and the risk of political embarrassment great. As Charles Lindblom and Edward Woodhouse explain, most public policy analysis, and for that matter public management decision-making, usually proceeds through trial-and-error learning based on experience.[43] The major pitfalls inherent in most trial-and-error learning is that the policy or management 'trial' might produce unbearably costly outcomes, the policy or management change contains too little flexibility to permit ongoing adjustment and correction, and learning about errors is too slow. The challenge, then, is to make errors less costly, build in greater flexibility, and speed up the learning process.

The focus of much of traditional public administration has been on accountability for control. At a time when organizations were viewed as machinelike, with a clearly defined hierarchical structure and a well-established command and control regime of decision-making, it was easy to see accountability as the basis for control. This, of course, was the much-celebrated bureaucratic organization.[44] New public management and the way it has been implemented, often viewed in juxtaposition to traditional public administration, has tended to downplay and even obscure the concept of accountability for control.

Kenneth Kernaghan, Brian Marson, and Sandford Borins provide a comprehensive comparison of the characteristics of the 'bureaucratic organization' and the 'post-bureaucratic organization.' Accountability in the bureaucratic organization is 'process-oriented,' and in the post-bureaucratic organization, 'results-oriented.' While it is noted that not every organization should or can adopt all the characteristics of the post-bureaucratic organization, the authors do recommend that when it is in the public interest, organizations should move away from the characteristics identified on the left to those identified on the right:

- organization-centred   citizen-centred
- position power   participative leadership
- rule-centred   people-centred
- independent action   collective action
- status-quo-oriented   change-oriented
- process-oriented   results-oriented
- centralized   decentralized
- departmental form   non–departmental form
- budget driven   revenue-driven
- monopolistic   competitive[45]

The HRDC audit raises the question of whether and when public organizations should retain some of the characteristics in the left column associated with the bureaucratic organization? Some will argue that there are important reasons some public organizations and parts of organizations need to be rule-centred, process-oriented, and budget driven. There is also the question of whether it is always possible and desirable for public organizations to achieve the characteristics in the right column associated with the post-bureaucratic organization. How difficult is it for organizations to become results-oriented, people-centred, and revenue-driven? What is the cost of achieving these characteristics? In theory, there seems to be little reason to believe that in moving to accountability for assurance and accountability for learning it is necessary to give up accountability for control. Yet, in practice, the HRDC grants and contributions case suggests that some of this may have happened.

One of the dilemmas with public sector reform that the HRDC case illustrates is the difficulty of getting it right. Like the swinging pendulum, reform seems to take too much time to get going, only to find that once it gets going, it is too difficult to adjust. Like Goldilocks's porridge, it can take more that two tries to get it just right. In the eyes of most public servants, public service reforms quickly come down to simple one-liners and slogans – 'let the managers manage,' 'serve the public,' 'empower employees,' and so on. This is understandable because to change organizations, cultures, and behaviour, a broad-based and sustained commitment is required. Leaders, therefore, need to communicate repeated messages that are clear, simple, and consistent. Change also comes at a cost, because behind each prescriptive slogan lies a submerged and often hidden dichotomy of competing values that at some point will need to be reconciled through rebalancing or, in some cases, trade-offs.

The HRDC case suggests that the natural adjustments of balance and rebalance throughout the implementation of public service reforms do not always work as well as they should. At one level, the department took the initiative on its own to recognize that there could well be problems with the administration of its grants and contributions after having seen the results of its internal audit of the TAGS program. The department requested its Internal Audit Bureau to undertake an audit of the administration of all of its grants and contributions programs. Upon seeing what the auditors described as deficiencies in the documentation contained in the files of the grants and contributions projects, HRDC immediately launched a comprehensive action plan, with the support of its employees, to address the problems. No doubt this would have led to some improvement and rebalancing. But would it have been sufficient? One might legitimately ask, what would have happened had the audit not been made public in the high-profile manner it was? In the absence of a crisis, would the dramatic and widespread reaction have taken place within HRDC and within the federal government? While no one can say for sure, it seems likely that the deep and comprehensive nature of the accountability and administrative controls that are now in place in HRDC to ensure that sufficient documentation is in the files would not have occurred. Nor would the accompanying re-bureaucratization.

There are important and significant limitations to new public management and to the 'Canadian model.' These limitations revolve around the critical requirements for accountability in public governance and public sector management. There can be little doubt that new public management is straining the accountability systems of public sector organizations. The additional pressures placed upon traditional accountability have not been met with any comprehensive reformulation of accountability to deal with the new challenges. But breaking accountability down into its essential features of control, assurance, and learning is a useful start. By describing how different sets of real and imagined instruments are used (or not) by different participants, (public servants, ministers, parliamentarians, and auditors), we can better appreciate the accountability limits of new public management. It also helps us to recognize that, when it comes to public governance and public management, accountability can never be just one thing. Any single accountability perspective is partial, incomplete, and in competition with the others. It is by skillfully combining and balancing all three that we are likely to see the most progress. We have also seen that there are dichotomies and differences within each of the perspectives and contradictions, and dilemmas across all of them.

This chapter has illustrated the pressures on accountability from the new public management, particularly how it has been conceived under the 'Canadian model' and how it has been implemented in the context of Canadian politics. The purpose has not been to call for a totally new reformulation of public sector accountability or to abandon Canadian efforts at public management reform. Rather, as governments continue to implement pieces of new public management there will be an increasing need to come to grips with the various and competing requirements for accountability and the means for its improvement. Both the experience with the HRDC grants and contributions audit and the strains that new public management is placing on the traditions of accountability suggest that there must be a better   way – a topic to which we now turn.

CHAPTER SEVEN

Looking Forward

Speaking Up for a Better Way

The HRDC grants and contributions audit provides an important springboard for exploring broader questions about how public management is done in government and how it might be improved. The examination of this case has emphasized the fundamental dichotomies and contradictions that underlie public management and the ongoing efforts of reform. The case itself has illustrated the significant and increasing difficulties in achieving balance and effecting sustainable trade-offs in the practice of public management. It has detailed the high costs that can result from imbalances and inappropriate trade-offs in the world of pressure politics, competitive media scrutiny, and a sceptical and often untrusting public. If we are to avoid, or even minimize, future problems like those found in the HRDC grants and contributions case, then there must be a better way to achieve balance and to effect trade-offs in public management. This chapter looks at ways to improve public management.

But where do we start? As the HRDC case has indicated, when it comes to public management, politics and administration are intertwined. Do we rescue administration from politics or do we rescue politics from administration? Is it that politicians have become too engaged in public administration and that public administrators have become too close to politicians? Or is it that administration has become too divorced from politics and there is a danger of making government less politically responsive and more managerial and bureaucratic? Instead of preventing administration from being contaminated by politics, maybe we need to insulate politics from the rigidifying effects of bureaucracy? Is it that we have focused too much on good public management and not enough on good governance? What do we actually need? Is it TQM (total quality management) as many would advocate, or TQP (total quality politics) as others have suggested?

Some critics, like the American public administration scholar H. George Frederickson, have argued that most countries would benefit more from 'total quality politics' than from 'total quality management.'[1] A key part of this approach would be significant reform to the central institutions and processes of governance beginning, for example, with parliamentary reform.[2] It would also include ongoing measures to increase public trust in government. Others, however, put their emphasis on improvements in public sector management.[3]

One of the clues in knowing where to start is the understanding that a dichotomy cannot exist between politics and administration. History has shown that it has been difficult to have 'politics' and 'administration' as two exclusive or nearly exclusive categories.[4] Calling for reforms to public administration that are not grounded in political reality are not likely to get us very far. Simply improving management does not necessarily guarantee better public administration, nor does improving politics guarantee improved public administration. By viewing the politics-administration dichotomy as a continuum along which politicians and public servants must operate, we can see that modest, but complementary, improvements in both management and politics are likely to be more realistic in improving public administration than dramatic and wholesale changes in either one or in both.

Experience at every level and size of government in Canada has indicated that politicians (ministers) do not want to be told by their officials that the public servants will do the rowing and leave the steering to them.[5] Ministers want to be engaged in the administration and management of programs in part because it is something that can actually be done that directly touches citizens. Steering, which not only includes determining the directions for society but also ensuring that effective and legitimate political institutions are in place, is considerably more difficult. No wonder so little steering gets done and that there is limited appetite to try. Success in steering is hard to come by. Rowing is a better bet. It can involve some steering (perhaps counter-steering) and at least both hands are firmly attached to the oars. Besides, it looks like the rower is actually going somewhere and accomplishing something.

But emphasizing rowing without steering will not take us very far in the right direction. Steering may be difficult and risky, but it needs to be done. A steady hand at the tiller is necessary. But in the increasingly open and democratic society of the twenty-first century, characterized by a continuing decline in deference to political authority, there is not just one hand on the tiller.[6] There are several, and all are struggling to pursue their own interests while hoping that the ship of state remains afloat. If we want better public administration, there must be greater understanding and cooperation between those whose hands are on the tiller. No one, however, has an interest in removing his or her hand for fear of being crowded out by someone else. We do not have the luxury of an automatic pilot to keep the boat on course while permitting time for everyone to simultaneously readjust their grip. Nor is there an agreed upon master chart that tells everyone how to reposition their hands to improve direction and stability. Movement must therefore be incremental. All must be prepared to adjust a bit if anyone is prepared to adjust at all. The risk associated with adjustment and change must be shared by each participant in order that all benefit.

Looked at from a different perspective, the participants in public management face 'the prisoner's dilemma'[7] and 'the tragedy of the commons.'[8] Individual action taken by each participant for his or her own benefit leads to inferior results for all. If there is to be a better way, it must therefore involve cooperation and mutual agreement. This suggests that improvements in public management will be found in mutual adjustments on the part of each participant and not in unilateral changes on the part of only a few.

If we compile all the players who shape public administration within democratic society, it will be, a long list. All players will need to adjust, some more than others, if sustained improvement is to be made. The list includes ministers of the government, backbench government Members of Parliament, opposition Members of Parliament, the public service, the Auditor General, the media, citizens (as clients and taxpayers), and organizations within the private and voluntary sectors. Within any one of these are a host of institutions and participants, and within and across all of them are a broad range of processes, structures, and individual incentives. For example, within the public service there are the most senior public servants dealing with politicians on a regular basis, and managers with responsibilities for administering programs and front-line staff delivering benefits and information to citizens. There are central agencies of all sorts and a multiplicity of line departments, each with specially mandated responsibilities and particular interests. Within central agencies there are specific yet overlapping responsibilities across the Privy Council Office, Department of Finance, Treasury Board Secretariat, and the Public Service Commission.

If there is to be a better way, then it must come from the participants themselves. As far as I know, there is not a blueprint of public management reform to which all will agree. Change will require that participants not only speak up for their interests but also look out for the interests of others. It is against this backdrop of fundamental issues in public management raised in the HRDC case that I examine the central participants and make some suggestions for change, beginning with the public service and ending with the media.

The Public Service

Public servants have a strong interest in public service reform. Unlike the United Kingdom, public service reform in Canada has usually been led by the public service and not by the politicians.[9] At the federal level, there has been little political interest in public service reform because governments and ministers see limited political advantage in it. The public service has been the leader of public service reform, be it the 'Glassco' reforms of the 1960s, the Lambert and D'Avignon reforms of the 1970s and 1980s, or the Public Service 2000 and other reforms of the 1990s. The absence of political leadership has a disadvantage and an important advantage.

On the one hand, there is little doubt that a lack of political interest makes it difficult to get public service reform on the government's political agenda and to give it the sustained push that it may require. Experience also indicates that it is even more difficult to get public service reform integrated with the central priorities of government, such as restructuring of policies and programs, restraint in government expenditures, and reorganization and development of new delivery mechanisms. Once on the agenda, or more likely on its edges, experience indicates that public service reform will not be there for long. It will invariably be overtaken by the government's more pressing priorities of day, be it the pending crisis in the unity file, the deteriorating fiscal situation, the emergence of unforeseen international events, or the global risks to human security. On the other hand, the advantage is that most ministers have not come to view the public service as an obstacle to achieving their policy agendas. As a consequence, the Canadian federal public service has had greater latitude in designing and undertaking reforms, rather than having politicians doing it for them.

Public servants in Canada have greater scope to shape the precise nature of the management reforms than do their counterparts in other countries. This provides them with the opportunity and the obligation to make the most of their expertise and advice. One of the keys to improvement is for public servants to 'speak administrative truth to political power,' to 'speak the contradictions of administrative reform to politicians and administrators,' and to 'speak public service values and ethics to everyone.'[10]

Speaking Administrative Truth to Political Power

A great part of public administration deals with the need to balance conflicting and competing values. Public servants are constantly faced with the need to tender balanced advice to ministers in the face of competing priorities and limited resources. Sometimes, however, as the HRDC case has illustrated, there are such fundamental and inherent contradictions in public administration that hard trade-offs are required and one value must be explicitly sacrificed in order to achieve others. It is at times like this that speaking administrative truth to political power becomes critical.[11] The analysis of the HRDC case indicates that this task is ever more important and is increasingly difficult to do. When public servants challenge ministers who want to significantly cut operations and still maintain service quality, public servants are speaking administrative truth to political power. When public servants explain to ministers that programs cannot be as flexible and responsive as they might wish, public servants are speaking administrative truth to political power.

It is one thing for ministers to be told that they cannot have both program X and program Y because resources are limited. Not only are the ministers likely to hear this from their own officials but also from the Minister of Finance, the President of the Treasury Board, and their spending ministerial colleagues with whom they are in competition for limited public resources. Ministers do not want to be told that they cannot do something because it is not administratively feasible. Where there is a political will there must be an administrative way. This, however, is not always the case, as the grants and contributions episode has revealed.

The grants and contributions case indicates the critical importance of speaking administrative truth to political power. If the administrative functions that support program delivery are severely cut through expenditure restraint, it is extremely difficult, and in many cases impossible, to maintain service standards for citizens. If there is to be significant flexi-

bility in determining the geographic regions eligible for direct employment programs like TJF and thereby tailor particular solutions to
address specific problems, then there will be charges of political interference. If Members of Parliament are to be involved in an advisory
capacity in the approval of employment projects, then the decision-making process will be considerably longer, more time consuming, complicated, and politically contentious. If decision-making approval for
projects in a complex program is to be decentralized to regional authorities, then do not expect to have timely, detailed, and accurate centralized information at the project level that can withstand an onslaught of
questions in the House of Commons. Since these 'hard truths' of public
administration will come to ministers from only one source – their
departmental officials – the ability of deputy ministers to authoritatively
speak administrative truth to political power is and will continue to be
especially important. This will require reliable data and information;
firsthand experience of lessons learned; skilled and forceful staff; and
perseverance and determination.

In dealing with ministers, most deputy ministers have traditionally
focused their attention on matters of policy and not on matters of public
administration. Indeed, there has been sharp criticism that too many
deputy ministers were appointed for their skills in 'managing up' and
providing policy advice to their ministers rather than for their skills in
'managing down' and effectively running their departmental operations.
Over the past decade, the situation has been changing somewhat and
deputy ministers are increasingly expected to be skilled enough to handle both the policy and the operational dimensions of their departments.
While the Deputy Minister of Finance must be first and foremost a policy
adviser, and the Deputy Minister of Public Works and Government Services an operational manager, each must take an interest in and have
skills in the other area. Dealing successfully with administration is not just
about internal management, it is also about managing the external communications of administrative decisions. Skillfully handling the administrative function is hardly a matter of just 'managing down' to the staff, it
is increasingly a matter of 'speaking up' to the ministers on matters of
complexity and contradiction in public administration.

Speaking Administrative Contradictions to Politicians and Administrators

Just as many administrative reforms continue well beyond their useful
life, many others start up only to flounder and peter out before they

have taken hold. The 'flavour of the month' is not uncommon in Ottawa. The job for leaders of public service reform is not an easy one. The standard rule for leaders of any such reform is to provide clear, simple, and consistent communications. This rule invariably has several consequences. First, the new reform is presented in sharp contrast to the existing practice. It is only if the new reform measures can be recognized and distinguished from the background of everyday administrative clutter that they can be quickly recognized and understood by others in the organization. As a result the background gets painted as old and black – 'command and control' – and the foreground as new and white – 'service and flexibility.' If anything, as indicated in chapter 2 the problems associated with the old practices are overstated and so, too, are the benefits promised from the new ones.

Second, the reform gets cast in simple language and communicated as a slogan – 'let the managers manage,' 'empower employees,' and 'break the barriers.' This undoubtedly helps to ensure that a simple, understandable message is clearly communicated to employees who must in turn explain it to others with sufficient precision, determination, and conviction that implementation will actually occur. The rhetoric focuses on selling the sizzle and not the steak. Third, the communications message of reform must be internally reinforcing and consistent to avoid confusion and scepticism. Leaders therefore emphasize the reform's features that complement other initiatives and minimize it's contradictions.

Making the message clear, simple, and consistent at the outset is often necessary in order to create sufficient organizational momentum that gets the new policy 'up and running' and into practice. Although administrative reforms are usually designed by a few people, invariably they are implemented by many. It is through the implementation, and not the design, that the issues, contradictions, and dilemmas rise to the surface and become grounded in the reality of administration and politics. And it is often the implementers, not the designers, who are called upon to reconcile them. Breaking a barrier for some often means eliminating protection for others. Flexibly serving the needs of citizens through a third-party service delivery agency can mean confusing the accountability of public servants to their ministers. Receiving input from Members of Parliament to help public servants deliver services that better reflect community and constituency needs confuses accountability and rubs up against political neutrality and citizens' perceptions that services are impartially and fairly administered.

Administrative reforms must be more than just balanced. An essential task for the leaders (and the implementers) of any administrative reform is to unearth and expose their inherent contradictions. Public service leaders should view their jobs not as decorators who wallpaper over the cracks but as workers who expose and highlight the cracks so that they can be properly filled in. Leaders should see their mission as exposing conflicts so they can be resolved rather that absorbing conflicts so that underlying issues and conflicting values remain hidden. But how best to do this? Uncover too much contradiction at the outset and nothing gets off the ground; too little later on and a crash landing could result. One way to encourage the exposure of contradictions and dilemmas is to establish a dialogue that can help public servants deal with them. This brings us to the importance of public service values and ethics.

Speaking to Public Service Values and Ethics

There is little doubt that the significant work of the Tait Taskforce Report in 1996 marked a significant renewal within the public service about the importance of values and ethics in government. The report triggered a fundamental discussion of public service values and ethics, and recommended that two far-reaching actions be undertaken within one year. The first recommendation called for a 'wide-ranging and honest dialogue' within the public service, about public service values and ethics. The taskforce proposed that the dialogue start at the top with public service leaders, embrace the entire public service and extend to and include ministers and members of Parliament. The second recommendation called for the adoption by the government and Parliament of 'a statement of principles for the public service, or a public service code.' The taskforce noted approvingly that the UK Civil Service Code focused on the principles of responsible government and set out not only the duties of public servants to ministers but also the duties of ministers to officials.

It is both surprising and yet not surprising that four years later the Auditor General in his 2000 Report would conclude that 'most initiatives promoting values and ethics are in their early stages.'[12] Despite the considerable desire of public servants to discuss values and ethics, concrete action takes time. The Secretary to the Treasury Board in his response to the report captured it best by describing 'the dialogue as a journey [that] will touch many public servants, and in many ways, the journey is as important as the destination.'[13] The experience with the HRDC audit indicates that the continuation of that journey is more important than ever.

As illustrated in the HRDC grants and contributions audit, public servants in their day-to-day work are being confronted with increasingly more complicated and difficult value and ethical dilemmas. Consider, for example, some fundamental value dilemmas that emerged from the grants and contributions case. They raised new and significant challenges not only for HRDC officials but also for all public servants:

- Accountability and service: To what extent are program delivery staff accountable for outcomes outside their control or for the results of taking risks that they are encouraged to take?
- Political neutrality and political sensitivity: How does the increasing contact between the public service and politicians and their offices reconcile with the value of political neutrality?
- Public duties and private interests: How should public servants deal with the real and apparent conflicts of interest that can emerge when their public duties and private roles intersect through partnership arrangements?
- Confidentiality and openness: How much information should public servants share with partners, clients, and others, and how proactive should they be in providing that information?
- Privacy in an information society: How to best balance the protection of privacy with its safety and security against the efficiency and effectiveness benefits that modern data collection, integration and information sharing can provide?[14]

These dilemmas do not emerge for public servants as abstract concepts to consider but as specific cases requiring choice. Consider, for example, a case concerning accountability for public servants as it relates to service delivery by a government funded non-profit organization. The following conversation represents a probable exchange between two HRDC employees with responsibilities for grants and contributions in the area of youth employment:

Joan: You look pretty upset. What's up?
Bill: Do you remember Young Adventurers? It's one of the new non-profit delivery agencies we're working with. There's evidence that some coun-

sellors from Young Adventurers have been engaging in sexual activity with teenage clients in their job skills workshops.

Joan: That's a problem; but it's not *your* problem. After all, Young Adventurers is an independent agency. It's not as if you supervise these people.

Bill: I'm bound to be blamed for it, though. I encouraged Young Adventurers to apply. As part of the contribution agreement I certified that the agency was credible and reputable. They provided criminal record checks for their counsellors, but I didn't ask them to dig any deeper than that.

Joan: Well, our bosses up the line and the minister still can't hold you accountable for the inappropriate behaviour of some employees in a third-party, arm's-length delivery agency. Where does our responsibility end and somebody else's start?

Bill: Look, Joan, my boss is really upset. The press and parents are calling and they want to know 'who is responsible?' and 'who is accountable?' The media already seem to be blaming the department. They say our procedures for managing delivery organizations that deal with vulnerable youth are inadequate. Apparently, there were similar problems a couple of years ago with another youth training group we funded.

Joan: I still don't get it. Everybody agrees these arrangements with specialized agencies are more effective and efficient than having public servants directly provide these services. The department funds hundreds of them. Between you and me, we probably oversee twenty-five to thirty similar arrangements and we don't have the resources to monitor their every move. When a few idiots in one of these organizations screw up, how does that become your responsibility?

Bill: I don't know, Joan. I feel at least partly responsible for what happened and I'd like to be able to explain my role to the parents and kids. I feel caught in the middle here.

To what extent and to whom should Bill be held accountable for the actions of counsellors employed by Young Adventurers?

Public servants face issues like this on a daily basis. Having the opportunity for 'honest dialogue' and for taking the time to discuss these issues in the workplace are essential prerequisites for exposing the dilemmas and subsequently finding the means for their reconciliation. The development and application of meaningful public service values helps public servants to clarify directions and deepen trust, thereby minimizing rigid, counter-productive rules.

The Auditor General and Internal Audit Bureaus

Like the public service, the Auditor General has a strong interest in improving management within government. At times the Auditor General has been in significant conflict with the public service and the government of the day over issues of management and administration. This was the case in 1976 when the Auditor General claimed that 'Parliament – and indeed the Government – has lost control or is close to losing effective control of the public purse.'[15] It was also the case in 1982 when he recommended an accountability regime to bring public servants 'out of the closet'[16] through a new system of accountability of public servants to the public rather that through their ministers. At other times, there has been a greater degree of cooperation between the Auditor General and the public service. For example, there have been efforts by the Auditor General and the Treasury Board Secretariat to work together in such areas as assessing the merits of Special Operating Agencies, reforming the Estimates process, the reporting of results to Parliament, and modernizing accountability.[17]

Internal Audit Bureaus within departments also have an interest in improving management within government. Throughout the mid- to late 1990s, the Internal Audit Bureau in HRDC and those in most other departments were treated like all other administrative support services. They were downsized, restructured, combined with evaluation functions, and had their lines of reporting downgraded. They were left with little staff and significantly diminished capacity.[18] Once reporting directly to deputy ministers, many internal audit executives have spent more time with assistant deputy ministers and other officials than with their actual bosses over the past decade. More recently, in the aftermath of the HRDC internal audit, efforts have been made to provide these audit units with functional guidance from the Treasury Board Secretariat, more support from departmental officials, and more attention from deputy ministers.

The new public management, with its emphasis on reducing and eliminating administrative constraints and focusing on results and accountability, is asking a great deal from Auditors General and Internal Audit Bureaus. The delegation of increased responsibilities from the central agencies and departmental headquarters to departments and regional delivery units, along with increased flexibility in exchange for improved performance has generated increased demands for timely and accurate flows of financial and non-financial information. In this world, the role of Auditors General will become increasingly more important, as will the role of their colleagues in Internal Audit Bureaus and those working in program evaluation and management review functions throughout the government. We will be hard pressed to escape 'the audit society.'[19] Responding to these challenges will require a shift in the traditional way in which auditors have conceived and undertaken their tasks. One such shift will be for auditors to 'speak to audit humility and not to audit rhetoric' and to 'speak administrative reality to political power.'

Speaking to Audit Humility and Not to Audit Rhetoric

The practice of the audit is steeped in great tradition, and one of the most important is what Michael Power has described as the 'expectations gap.'[20] This is the gap between what the public expects from an audit – the detection of fraud – and what auditors claim to be delivering – an opinion on the financial statements that appeals to notions that the statements are 'true and fair.' Power points out that a main preoccupation of audit methodologies since the mid-1900s has been to narrow the expectations gap between what the public expects to receive from an audit and what it actually does. As he concludes:

> ... the knowledge base of the financial audit process is fundamentally obscure. It is this obscurity which sustains the expectations gap, an obscurity which practitioners overcome by appealing in the end to the authority of their own judgment in determining what is reasonable practice ... Auditing remains at the level of a folk craft or art.[21]

Traditionally, auditors have systematically attempted to narrow the 'expectations gap' between what the public expects of an audit – a detailed financial account indicating prudence and probity in public expenditure – and what many audits actually do – simply verifying that management practices have been followed.

The expanded mandates of both the Auditor General and Internal Audit Bureaus beyond traditional financial audits have significantly reinforced the narrowing of the expectations gap. While Auditors General continue to undertake traditional financial audits, this responsibility is now a small part of their overall work and is increasingly being offloaded to Internal Audit Bureaus in departments. The Auditor General is increasingly focused on performance, or 'value for money,' audits of the management of government programs as well as studies of management practices within government. Internal Audit Bureaus are also devoting more of their limited resources to performance audits and management studies. While auditors make a distinction between audits and studies, this is not something that parliamentarians, the media, and the public understand. Nor is there a complete understanding and agreement within government over what constitutes an audit and what is really a study. This is important because while many people might question the validity of a study, few question the validity of an audit.

Within the audit community, the definition of an audit has expanded dramatically to include a host of activities that were traditionally more akin to studies than to audits. To auditors, the audit activity now includes such activities as performance audits, management audits, systems under development audits, and environmental audits. None of these so-called audits directly deal with public money. Yet those outside the audit community, like parliamentarians, the media, and the public view all audits as dealing with money. In fact only a very limited number of audits – financial audits and forensic audits – focus on money.

It is probably not an exaggeration to conclude that the events associated with the audit of the HRDC grants and contributions programs have forever changed the way in which internal audits will be undertaken and reported within the federal government. In one sense, an internal audit has become more closely fused with an external audit. There can be little doubt that, in the future, departments will give much more attention to their own internal audits simply because to the outsider they will be viewed as external audits. If there was one overriding sentiment that HRDC officials received from their fearful colleagues in other departments in Ottawa it was 'Oh, but for the grace of God.' In short, public servants recognized that they were all vulnerable to any paper audit that simply reviewed the extent of documentation contained in individual project files. The Information Commissioner had for sometime lamented what he called 'the collapse of the culture' of internal record-keeping in the public service in the aftermath of downsizing and in the midst of dramatic innovations in e-mail technology. It is, however, one thing to have inadequate documentation in project files and quite another to misspend, illegally spend, or lose public money.

The government and departments will need to clarify the 'expectations gap' between what the public thinks an internal audit can do and what it can actually deliver. The Auditor General and departmental auditors will also need to contain their audit rhetoric. To the public, parliamentarians, and the media, any audit in government is about the use (occasionally the misuse) of public money. In short, the public has come to view audits in terms of what they have been historically – financial audits. A 'performance or a management audit' of government operations is a term that the public and the media do not understand.

The Assistant Auditor General engaged in audit rhetoric when she commented in the media immediately following the public release of the HRDC administrative audit that, 'once that kind of paperwork isn't there, anything can happen. There could be abuse, or there could be no abuse. You have no way of knowing.' When the internal HRDC auditors set as one of their review objectives 'protect(ion) from errors, misappropriation, misuse and abuse ... and [to] provide an estimate of the magnitude of the loss,'[22] and then did not examine any financial information, they engaged in audit rhetoric. While the audit talked of and detected missing paper, it did not audit or document any missing money. As a management audit as opposed to a financial audit, the grants and contributions audit did not examine any financial transactions. The use of rhetoric by auditors and exaggeration by the media are not new. A quarter of a century earlier, when J.J. Macdonell stated that 'parliament has lost, or is close to losing, effective control of the public purse,'[23] the media understood him to mean that the government had actually lost control of the public purse. Mr Macdonell was speaking of 'management controls,' that is, the application by public sector managers of the 'three E's' – economy, efficiency, and effectiveness.

To most people, an audit is an audit is an audit. It is thought to deal directly with money. In the world of the audit, there is a large array of different types of 'audits,' most of which do not deal directly with money. While financial audits and forensic audits in government examine financial transactions, most other 'audits' address financial matters only indirectly. There are a host of terms for these so-called audits, including management audits, performance audits, systems under development audits, environmental audits, studies, reviews, management reviews, assessments, risk assessments, check-ups – the list goes on. Each of these different audits is distinct and each has a specific and important purpose. Given the complexity of these audits, it does not seem possible to distinguish between them in a manner that is understandable, even for those inside government let alone those on the outside. Therefore, departments with the support of the Treasury Board Secretariat should restrict the use of the term 'audit' only to those internal audits that directly address financial matters. Use of the term 'management audit' should cease and such activities should be called what they actually are – management studies or reviews.

Changing terminology is hardly a complete answer. It never is. It would, however, signal an important start within government to ensure that the important function of an internal audit and all other internal reviews are more clearly understood for what they really are, rather than for what some would wish them to be. By restricting internal audits to direct financial matters, program managers are more likely to request and support such audits as well as the other non-financial and management reviews that they need in order to effectively manage their operations. Some will argue that the word 'audit' is so widely entrenched in the language of our 'audit society' that it is not possible or desirable to reduce the scope of its meaning. Auditors General around the world have long promoted the concept of management audits and value for money audits that are now well established in their legislative mandates and in their practices and procedures. But this misses the point. The dramatic and rapid expansion of the audit culture has been both a blessing and a curse. Should government decide that it wants to reserve the term 'audit' to include only financial audits, this will not prevent the Auditor General from continuing, or even modifying, his current practices.

Auditors need to describe their performance audits in terms of what they really are, rather than what the media and the public might like them to be. Performance audits are based upon social and management science, not on the universal accounting standards associated with financial audits. Unlike financial accounting, social and management science are hardly an exact science. They are based on separate and partial social, economic, political, and organizational theories about human behaviour. At best, performance audits are an heroic attempt to explain and predict human and organizational performance in the face of considerable uncertainty, partial theories, limited tools, inadequate experimental design, and incomplete evidence. This is not a call to weaken the audit but rather to strengthen it by being more explicit and realistic about what it is and how it is limited.

Speaking Public Administrative Reality to Parliamentary Power

Auditors General lament the complexity of managing in the federal government. In reflecting on a decade of serving Parliament, a former Auditor General described his first impressions on coming to Ottawa:

I was also struck by the complexity of managing in the federal government. Many activities involved more than one department as well as provincial and municipal governments. Duplication in services and problems in co-ordination marked the management of agriculture, the environment, and fisheries. Devolution of responsibilities to First Nations added to the complexity of their relationship with government.[24]

Complexity in public sector management stems not from a natural desire of public servants to be complicated, but rather from the complexity of the public management challenge itself. Consider the seemingly simple matter of service delivery. Publicly serving citizens is considerably more complicated than privately satisfying customers. Take customs officers who must serve entrants at the border. These public officials need to be efficient and respectful to the person at the front of the queue but also need to protect the security of the other citizens already in the country. The customs officers have only a few seconds to size up the visitor and make an initial determination. Do they wave the visitor through and go on to the next person, or do they give the visitor a special card and send him or her off for further review?

Take meat inspectors who must also serve several different citizens. They are expected to serve the meat industry through cost-efficient inspection without a heavy burden of intrusive rules and regulations. They are also expected to protect the consumer who depends on the public assurance and confidence that comes from knowing that properly inspected meat products are safe to eat. Take employment insurance agents who not only need to serve the EI claimant by meeting service standards and maintaining 'an ethics of care' with respect to proper entitlements, but they also need to protect the employer and employee contributors who have paid their premiums into the EI account. In each of these cases, public officials make difficult individualized public judgments and exercise discretion in the context of complicated, and sometimes conflicting, laws, regulations, and policies.

Public servants operate in a constraint-filled world. Yet the performance audits that review their management rarely consider the constraints in public management under which they must work. As Peter Aucoin has noted, 'If (performance) audits are to be credible, they must explicitly consider and assess the constraints in public management.'[25] There are several types of constraints.

Consider the objectives of programs. The development of objectives is not a natural act where heavenly principles are divined into worldly directions. It is invariably earthy, messy, and artificial. Some have appropriately considered the development of objectives to be a 'hostile act' involving 'violence to reality'[26] because some activities must be emphasized over others. Little wonder that program objectives turn out to be multiple, conflicting, and vague. For politicians, this ambiguity not only makes political life tolerable but it also ensures that a policy or program will gain sufficient political support to actually see the light of day. Ambiguities in policies and programs must be left in place in order to manage the politics of governance. For public servants, however, this ambiguity is a major constraint to effective management. It means that public servants are significantly constrained in 'managing for results.'

The Auditor General has reported on 'the painfully slow progress of departments toward managing for results,' noting that 'the trend in reporting accomplishments to Parliament is equally flat.'[27] Why is this so? According to the report, there are three basic reasons for this lack of progress:

1 Public servants still have not completely accepted management based on measuring results and reporting on their achievement to Parliament.
2 Reporting performance to Parliament has political consequences and there is fear that performance reports could become a political tool of ministers and the Opposition.
3 Few incentives for reporting have been offered to individual managers or to departments as a whole. Nothing really happens to an organization that does not improve its reporting. In fact, because of our political culture, poor reporting is safer.[28]

In short, the problems and the proposed solutions are largely addressed to public servants who, according to the Auditor General's report, must increase their acceptance of reporting, reduce their fear, and be offered incentives. Politicians, however, must change their political culture. While few would disagree with the conclusions of the Auditor General, it is questionable whether the report sufficiently recognizes the real constraints faced by public servants and their inability to remove a number of them. This report seems to conclude that managers can and should be doing much better even within a political culture where poor reporting is safer. Auditors appear to be asking a lot, perhaps too much, of public servants, and they may be asking too much of politicians as well.

There are a significant number of constraints to public sector management that find their origins in the administrative laws, regulations, rules, and guidelines under which public servants operate. When looked at individually, each of these constraints has a particular purpose in its own area of public administration. The dilemma of course is that when taken together, it is hard to image an area of public administrative activity that is not governed by a large volume of legislation, regulation, and policies. Nearly every aspect of public administrative activity is covered. The Treasury Board Secretariat Web site of on-line publications and policies contains twenty-four major categories – including financial management, human resources, compensation, contracting, access to information and privacy, materiel management, real property management, Crown assets, common services, official languages, employment equity, federal identity program, performance reporting, information management, public key infrastructure, evaluation, audit, risk management, and security, – to name a few.[29] Much has been done to eliminate and streamline unnecessary constraints. But in reality, constraints are an important and essential feature of good public management. While it is currently fashionable to focus on 'constraints *to* productive management' too little emphasis is being given to 'constraints *for* productive management.' A former Secretary to the Treasury Board Secretary reminds us that 'centralization and control are not dirty words.'[30] While these constraints are intended to prevent abuse, they are also intended to encourage better management.

Audit reports that ignore these constraints on the public service provide a distorted and incomplete picture of reality. The underlying assumption is that administration can and should be separated from politics and that public sector management is best improved by focusing on the managers. This has led to an increasing and disturbing tendency to address external audit recommendations to public servants rather than to politicians. While public servants are important players in improving management within government, it must be remembered that only ministers have the authority to make policy, set direction, and instruct public servants to take corrective action. External audits can improve public management, but their findings and recommendations must be directed not to public servants who operate as the agents of ministers, but to the ministers themselves, who have the authority and the responsibility to take action.

The increasing tendency in external audit reports to focus findings and recommendations on 'managers' as opposed to ministers has led the media and opposition Members of Parliament to direct their attention to public servants. This is particularly the case when things go wrong, or appear to go wrong, as we have seen from the HRDC case. This has reinforced and encouraged opposition Members of Parliament to attempt to use legislative committees and other means to hold public servants directly accountable to Parliament in the place of, or in addition to, their responsible ministers.

Ministers

Relative to other countries and jurisdictions, Canadian federal ministers involve themselves more directly in the delivery and administration of government programs and services. The constant search for federal visibility and regional presence has been a long-standing quest of all federal governments. It is also one reason ministers in both the Conservative and Liberal governments have been reluctant to embrace wholeheartedly those public sector reforms that more clearly delineate either functionally or organizationally the boundaries between policy development and service delivery. Ministers have never found it compelling to be told by public servants that establishing separate service delivery organizations would free up precious ministerial time to focus on the bigger issues of setting policy, thereby leaving the more mundane operational issues to public servants. To Canadian federal governments and ministers, matters of service delivery, operations, and public administration are not mundane matters to be left exclusively to bureaucratic experts. They are important matters of governance that have significant political ramifications, carrying citizen support for programs and, by extension, public support for governments and ministers.

There are several reasons federal governments and ministers involve themselves so deeply in matters of public administration. First, in a significantly decentralized federation, characterized by large governmental transfers in important areas like health, education, and social assistance, federal ministers are anxious to ensure that they can directly touch Canadians who have come to view provincial and municipal governments as more relevant to their day-to-day lives. Second, the intensity and competition of the diverse and different regional interests means that ministers pay careful attention to regional ministers, Members of Parliament, and others who advocate on behalf of their regions. Third, federal governments, in the face of threats to national unity through Quebec separation or Western alienation, have continuously searched for new ways to increase federal visibility and regional presence.

Listening to Administrative Advice

Just as Auditors General need to recognize the constraints in public management, ministers need to recognize the constraints on public servants. If deputy ministers need to speak administrative truth to political power, then ministers need to listen. Listening to administrative advice from deputy ministers about what cannot be done is never easy for ministers. Better to listen to them, though, than to seek such advice from one's own political office. A former secretary of the Treasury Board makes a telling point: '... it is sobering to contemplate a future Prime Minister's response to the proposition that a major public service reform initiative could be launched to improve services with only one downside: that it would somewhat increase the possibility of an "HRDC affair" in some department during his mandate.'[31]

When it comes to deputy ministers and ministers, it is generally understood that administration is the domain of the deputy. Most experienced ministers who are new to the department express it in different ways when first meeting with their deputies: 'You run the department and I'll look after the politics,' or 'you manage and I'll govern.' But it all comes down to the same thing. While it is the rare minister who will propose an administrative change to a deputy minister, it is the rare minister who will accept administrative advice from the deputy that might significantly undermine or thwart a favoured policy proposal or project. Demands by ministers for a more flexible and responsive program that might better address the unique needs of the local community, comes at a price. As the HRDC case has illustrated, that price might be less central information; more risk of perceived unfairness; a lack of consistency; increased risk of perceived political interference in projects; more ambiguous and complex accountability; and reduced service and program monitoring. Administrative advice is almost never an opportunity; it is invariably a constraint. Assessing the administrative advice, adjusting the program in light of that advice, and publicly defending the eventual design of the program is an important job for the minister.

It is the rare occasion in which an administrative issue takes on such importance that it is elevated to the level of exclusive consideration by the cabinet. During the run-up to Y2K, officials regularly briefed their ministers on the risks and the state of preparedness. On more than one occasion, officials briefed the full cabinet under the watchful eye of the Prime Minister, sharply cautioning them to curtail any proposals that required new information systems in order to ensure that all existing information systems could be made Y2K compliant. The result – New Year's Day 2000 came and went without an administrative glitch. The delivery of difficult administrative advice by deputy ministers and the acceptance of that advice by their respective ministers needs to be visibly supported by the Treasury Board, as a collectivity of ministers, and by the Prime Minister.

Speaking Publicly in Defence of Public Management Reforms

Canadian politicians' general disinterest in public management reform provides no guarantee that at some point the reforms themselves will not become embroiled in political controversy. What it can mean, however, is that politicians who have been less politically and ideologically wedded to particular management reforms may find it more difficult to come to a vigorous public defence when things go wrong. That certain features of any public management reform can and will go wrong can almost be taken as a given. It is not a matter of subsequently dealing with the much-celebrated 'unintended consequences' that accompany any contemporary public policy, but rather accepting that some undesirable consequences will often occur in the normal course of events. The public service authors of Public Service 2000 must have had this in mind when they astutely wrote:

> [Ministers] know that any reform, particularly to deregulate the administrative processes of an organization as large as the Public Service, cannot proceed without mistakes. Ministers know that they will have to steel themselves not to react to political and media outcry against some particular error by reimposing central controls. They believe that better service to Canada and Canadians outweighs the embarrassment that such mistakes cause.[32]

The HRDC case suggests that it is extremely hard not to reimpose controls in the face of an intense political and media outcry about mistakes and errors.

The political task of ministers to publicly defend public management reforms is, however, more difficult when the reforms are not conceived by politicians and are not integral to their political platform or governing priorities. It was one thing for Prime Minister Thatcher to vigorously defend the virtues of her 'next step agencies' in the face of inevitable problems and growing pains, and quite another for Prime Minister

Chrétien to defend 'the Canadian model' of public management when an internal audit in a department indicated there could be problems. Ms Thatcher was ideologically committed to her reforms and would vigorously defend them in the face of problems. Mr Chrétien, who did not see the model as his own creation, defended his minister rather than the reform and downplayed the problems.

If ministers want to leave public management reform largely to public servants and if they also want government programs to be flexible, responsive, and adaptable to the unique characteristics of regions and citizens throughout the country, then they will have to make special efforts to publicly defend these reforms when things invariably go wrong. This is not to suggest that ministers and the Prime Minister have not and do not come to the support of the public service when things go wrong. The desire to maintain a political reputation as a prudent government manager is an important incentive. However, in the face of continued administrative reform to make government more flexible and responsive to citizens, a competitive media with a keen eye for any hint of scandal, a fragmented opposition hungry to embarrass the government, and a distrusting public, it may not be enough for politicians to simply downplay the problems and support the programs. It may be necessary for politicians to give vigorous political support in public to the management reforms themselves. In short, they will need to defend not only what is being done but also how it is being done. This will require that ministers become more engaged with the public service in determining and supporting the directions for public management reform and in ensuring that the major reform initiatives become an integral part of the government's overall agenda.

Members of Parliament

The role of any Member of Parliament is to represent the views of constituents. This means securing benefits, services, and projects for the constituents in one's riding. As a government member, the job is to support the government. This means partisan political support for the government to maintain the confidence of the House of Commons. As an opposition member, the job is to hold the government and its ministers to account. This means embarrassing and criticizing the government to ensure its defeat.

As we know and have seen from this case, Members of Parliament are fundamentally concerned with politics and not with public administration. What Members of Parliament know about public administration and how it is practised in government has been largely garnered from the steady stream of Auditor General's reports that are critical of management in government. Their understanding of public administration has also been shaped through their personal experience and that of their constituents with what is often seen as an insensitive and rule-bound bureaucracy on matters of service delivery, benefits programs, and projects. Not surprisingly, when it comes to public administration, what Members or Parliament see are fundamental dichotomies. On the one hand, programs and services to the public are often seen as inflexible and unresponsive. On the other, when programs become flexible and responsive, as was the case with TJF and other HRDC grants and contributions, they are seen as inconsistent and unfair. Ministers are responsible for the policy, yet public servants seem to be making many of the important decisions in terms of the delivery of programs, services and projects on the ground. For Members of Parliament, management in government is an oxymoron. The ministers are too political and the public servants are too bureaucratic. To Members of Parliament, no one person seems accountable, responsible, and answerable.

Holding Ministers Accountable and Public Servants Answerable

The HRDC case confirms what has worried many academics and practitioners of public administration for some time – there is much confusion about how the concepts of accountability, responsibility, answerability, and blame are applied in the real world of politics and public management.[33] Chapter 3 illustrates how this confusion emerges in the media and how politicians often use these terms loosely and interchangeably. If there is particular confusion on the part of Members of Parliament, it is easy to understand why. The increasing participation of public servants as witnesses at Parliamentary Committees in the absence of their ministers, as was sometimes the case with the HRDC audit, can leave the impression with Members of Parliament that public servants have a direct responsibility to Parliament rather than to their ministers. This, of course, is not the case. Under responsible government, it is ministers and not public servants who are accountable to the House of Commons for what is done by the government. Public servants appear before Parliamentary Committees on behalf of their ministers to answer questions and provide information and explanations on details that ministers could not be expected to provide personally.

Members of Parliament who attempt to make public servants rather than ministers accountable to Parliament may score momentary political points. In doing so, however, they undermine their own capacity and their responsibility to hold ministers accountable to Parliament. It means that ministers can push off poor decisions and errors unto their officials and thereby escape responsibility and accountability for their actions. Politicians, the media, and the public sometimes assume that ministerial accountability supports and protects public servants from their actions. In reality, it supports Members of Parliament by providing them with a single ministerial target to be held to account and it protects ministers by not having their authority undercut by public servants.

If in Canada, ministers continue to increasingly involve themselves in the details of public administration through the design and delivery of programs and services, then it is natural to expect that parliamentarians should hold ministers accountable for the consequences of these decisions. This will require that parliamentarians be provided with more systematic and useful information about the actual performance and results of programs and services. It also suggests that parliamentarians will need to increase their substantive expertise in matters of public administration, which, to date, has been more difficult given the greater turnover of Members of Parliament compared with other democratic legislatures.[34]

Members of Parliament can and must ensure that public servants provide information to Parliamentary Committees about the government's policies and programs and give explanations about their actions. Public servants, appearing before committees on behalf of their ministers, have a duty to inform and explain. For Members of Parliament to do their jobs, they will need more regular and relevant information on the government's programs and on their performance. For public servants to respond, they will need to adjust their long-held tradition of anonymity. This will mean that anonymity not be viewed as an absolute to be maintained but as a concept that evolves. As Members of Parliament put public servants more and more into the public eye, under the accompanying glare of the media, the question will not be whether public servants should remain anonymous but rather how they behave. Having the information and the explanations to be answerable to parliamentarians with the full knowledge and acceptance by all that it is ministers who are accountable, will become an increasingly more important part of their jobs.

Speaking More to Policy and Less to Administration

Members of Parliament are political and partisan. But the question is where to focus their political attention along the policy-administration continuum. The incentive for MPs is to focus on where the pay-off is the greatest. In an environment where the opposition effort is directed at assigning blame and the government effort at avoiding blame, the focus with the best pay-off is often on administration and management in government rather than on policy. There are two reasons for this. First, in any area of management and administration there are bound to be problems which can be readily communicated to the public through the media in convincing newsworthy terms with an emphasis on simplicity, drama, and personality. Try as it will, no government can be 'error free' in its management and administration. Second, Members of Parliament, both government and opposition, have limited opportunity to influence policy. From time to time government members might have some impact on government policy by exerting pressure in caucus. Less often and with less influence, MPs might deal with policy through their partic-ipation in Parliamentary Committees, in the review of legislation, or in preparing reports on emerging issues of public concern. In short, when it comes to Members of Parliament, the politics of administration signif-icantly overshadows the politics of policy.

Consider, for example, the impact of reports of Parliamentary Com-mittees. As noted in chapter 4, the majority report of the Standing Com-mittee, aptly called *Seeking a Balance*, provided broad but useful advice on the major elements around which an administrative balance might be constructed, and it warned against the re-bureaucratization of grants and contributions. Yet this report of the Liberal majority, along with the four other minority reports from each opposition party, had limited impact on policy. The media dismissed them as a partisan effort. Indeed, as Peter Dobell has indicated, 'the net effect of the current emphasis on submitting minority views is to limit the influence of com-mittee reports and diminish the contribution of Parliament to policy development.'[35] A less partisan Parliamentary Committee might have produced a single report, thereby having greater influence on policy.

How can Members of Parliament be encouraged to focus more on policy and less on administration? The answer does not lie in asking Members of Parliament to be something they are not. It is not a ques-tion of curtailing their efforts to focus on errors in management and administration but rather giving them considerably more scope and opportunity to meaningfully engage in and influence public policy. Significantly strengthening the analytical support to Parliamentary Committees would be one step in the right direction. But more is needed than this. Members of Parliament will not demand information that they cannot use and if committees and MPs have little or no sway over policy, why demand policy analysis and advice? Considering every piece of government legislation to be a matter of confidence on which the government must stand or fall significantly limits the policy role of Members of Parliament and Parliamentary Committees. Yet not every government initiative is central to its party's platform or the core of its agenda. Selectively loosening the whip of party discipline for both government and opposition Members of Parliament would allow them greater opportunity to shape and influence policy.

The Media

As we saw in chapter 3, the media is not objective nor do most people expect it to be. Indeed, the so-called golden age of journalism in the middle of the twentieth century, when fact and opinion were supposed to be separated, is probably largely mythical, not unlike the wishful separation of politics and administration. Today, analysing and commenting on the events that reporters cover as news is an essential part of the journalist's job. Television, with an average time of less than sixty seconds for each story, makes it impossible to be objective and comprehensive. In the print media, analysis, commentary, interpretation, and opinion are found on every page. Indeed, 'the subjectivity of contemporary news media redefines their role.'[36]

Objectivity as a standard of journalism has fallen out of favour and has been replaced by more realistic objectives – 'accuracy' and 'fairness.' As Nick Russell has noted in his book on ethics in journalism, 'objectivity *is* impossible, but ... every reporter should make every effort to be objective – to be fair, full and accurate – nonetheless.'[37] While the public may not expect the media to be objective, they do expect it to be accurate and fair.

Speaking to Accuracy and Fairness

What does it mean for the media to be accurate and fair? While there is no universal agreement within society or for that matter within the media itself, codes of conduct for the profession do provide some general guidance. For example, the Statement of Principles adopted by the Canadian Daily Newspaper Publishers Association in 1977, and significantly shortened and revised in 1995, devotes one of its six paragraphs to 'accuracy and fairness.' It states: 'The newspaper keeps faith with readers by presenting information that is accurate, fair, comprehensive, interesting and timely. It should acknowledge its mistakes promptly and conspicuously. Sound practice clearly distinguishes among news reports, expressions of opinion.'[38] Interestingly, the more subjective electronic media attempt to go further in their search for accuracy and fairness. The recently adopted Code of Ethics and Professional Conduct of the Radio and Television News Directors Association, under one of six headings entitled 'Truth,' states that 'professional electronic journalists should pursue truth aggressively and present news accurately, in context, and as completely as possible,' and that they 'should not report anything known to be false.' Under 'Fairness,' professional electronic journalists 'should present the news fairly and impartially placing a primary value on significance and relevance ... [and they] should present a diversity of expressions, opinions, and ideas in context.' Under 'Accountability,' professional electronic journalists 'should correct errors promptly and with as much prominence as the original report.'[39]

In light of these standards, several questions come to mind about the accuracy of the reporting by the media of the HRDC grants and contributions audit. Did the print and electronic media fulfil their commitments to accuracy and fairness when they continuously reported that 'a billion dollars had been lost,' that there was 'a billion dollar job fund,' and that the audit revealed 'a billion dollar boondoggle'? Why did some reporters even complain privately that their stories would say one thing, while the headlines – 'bungling bureaucrats to receive bonuses' – would say something else? How could the media inaccurately conclude that the wage subsidy program had been manipulated for election purposes?

It is probably unrealistic to believe that media can and will ever live up to these standards of conduct. The media do not act as innocent bystanders to the political process but rather as active participants through critical journalism and 'infotainment.' The simple fact is that the newsmedia have become a considerable power and influence in Canadian politics. In that regard, like others in the public arena, they do have a responsibility for a level of fairness and accuracy. The media, however, are more likely to be accurate and fair if those on whom they are reporting can provide detailed information to their requests. The media will need to ensure that, in their daily practice, they speak to the language of accuracy and fairness as promised in their published codes of ethics and conduct.

Speaking Together

In this book I have not offered a single and simple solution to the dichotomies and contradictions that underlie much of public administration. In such an enterprise, there can be no single and simple answer. I have, however, indicated that there is an urgent need for all participants to speak up for a better way and to find a safe way for honest dialogue. I have sketched out some of the key elements for improvement. However, little of this will happen without greater cooperation among the key participants. As a modest first step, an ongoing forum on public management in a neutral environment, where the key participants could come together, could provide an opportunity for some honest dialogue. Such an ongoing forum, involving both current and former inside participants and others on the outside who have observed and reflected upon these matters, could allow for active listening and the beginnings of positive change. Alternatively, or in parallel with such a forum, greater efforts could be made to broaden the normal single participant-led dialogues, such as discussion among public servants and academics, to include other participants, such as current and former ministers, Members of Parliament, auditors, and representatives of the media.

This analysis indicates that without any change or adjustment by anyone, governments and citizens will be increasingly vulnerable to a continuation of high-profile problems in public administration, which will result in the pendulum swinging towards re-bureaucratization. The 'Canadian model' of new public management, deeply embedded in the Canadian politics of public management and magnified by an influential media, makes it so. Modest changes and adjustments by everyone can lead to important improvements for all. In the end, however, it will be citizens who will benefit most from these improvements through efficient service and effective programs, a government that is trusted and performs, an opposition that vigorously holds government to account, a public service that is professional, auditors that work within the units of their craft, and a probing media that are accurate and fair.

Postscript

'Well, Mr Good, you were the Assistant Deputy Minister for the Human Resources Investment Branch of HRDC with responsibilities for grants and contributions at the time of this audit scandal. What did you personally learn from the experience, what would you have done differently?'

No one can replay the wheel of history, but we can all learn from the past in order to perform better in the future. From my own experience, I learned a number of lessons, some the hard way. They are perhaps best expressed in terms of what I would have done differently.

Speak to the contradictions that underlie public management. In the mid-1990s when I was leading a number of efforts to get public servants to focus on the results achieved by programs and to 'break the barriers' of excessive administration, I should have continuously reinforced the need to ensure that minimal but adequate documentation and information be contained in the project files of discretionary grants and contributions programs. No matter how positive the program outcomes, the media, Parliament, and the public will invariably be interested in the program inputs, especially when there is considerable discretion in decision-making.

When balance is not possible, speak out strongly about the trade-offs required. When the government decided in 1995 to significantly reduce the number of staff in HRDC as part of Program Review while attempting to maintain levels of service for citizens, I should have recognized that these two objectives were inconsistent and that balance was not immediately possible. It takes considerable time to put into place cost savings and efficiency measures and, as a consequence, service must be reduced. Expressing these as sharp trade-offs and pressing for quantifiable measures (e.g., a 10 per cent reduction in staff reduces service standards by 5 per cent) is an important part of 'speaking administrative truth to political power.'

When taking on a new job, immediately ask to see all the audits and the evaluations of programs for which you are responsible. When I took on the responsibility of assistant deputy minister, Human Resources Investment Branch in May 1997, I examined the program evaluations that had been undertaken. I recall, for example, the positive but preliminary formative evaluation of the Transitional Jobs Fund. Unlike some previous programs, it indicated that jobs were being created in areas of chronic high unemployment through flexible partnership arrangements among the public, private, and voluntary sectors. I did not ask for, nor did I review, any audits that had been undertaken of grants and contributions programs. If I had done so, I would have been aware of the two administrative audits undertaken in 1991 and 1994 that highlighted missing documentation in the project files. I might well have given greater priority within my branch to the risks inherent in grants and contributions programs and mobilized my staff to strengthen administrative procedures.

Carefully read the external environment, especially when it sends out negative signals. In the early stages of implementing the Transitional Jobs Fund, a political party fund-raiser was charged and subsequently found guilty of 'influence peddling' as he attempted to secure political campaign contributions in exchange for commitments for job-creation projects. When the department was informed of these serious allegations, it immediately referred the matter to the police for investigation. After questions in the House of Commons and the normal media attention, the Transitional Jobs Fund emerged unblemished, or so I thought. I implicitly felt that since the integrity of the program had been sharply tested and it came through largely unscathed, it was therefore not a source of major vulnerability. This was an incorrect interpretation. Flipping the issue around one hundred and eighty degrees, it would have been more prudent and accurate to have viewed this episode as pointing to a potential risk for the program.

Know when an audit is the wrong instrument. When the Auditor General asked HRDC's Internal Audit Bureau to undertake an audit on its behalf of the management of projects under The Atlantic Groundfish Strategy (TAGS), I should have advised against the use of an audit. When the stated purpose was to review the management of projects, I should have insisted upon a management study and not an audit.

Probe the terms of reference to get them right. When the Internal Audit Bureau came to see me with the draft terms of reference for the proposed grants and contributions audit, I should have sharply questioned how a review of the documentation contained in project files would be used to draw conclusions about the management and control of expenditures in these programs. Asking tough questions is a good way to understand difficult problems.

Know what underlies internal audits and challenge both their findings and their conclusions. In the summer of 1999, when the Internal Audit Bureau came to brief me on the preliminary results of the grants and contributions audit, I should have asked for a list of the 461 project files that were sampled by the auditors. I then should have randomly selected ten files from the list and asked to see the actual project files and the audit findings for these ten files. This would have helped me to appreciate, in a very real way, the nature of the 'audit' that had been done, why documentation could be missing in a project file but exist in another file, why some projects did not require application forms, the importance of the missing documentation, and the conclusions that could and would be reasonably (and unreasonably) drawn from these findings. At the very least, I would have had a greater appreciation for how long it takes to retrieve project files from regional offices and assemble them in Ottawa. This would have prompted me to more critically assess the findings and the conclusions of the audit, rather than spending almost all of my efforts on preparing an action plan to address the problems.

Be prepared for the unexpected. I thought I was prepared for a low-profile release of the grants and contributions audit. The release was to follow the normal procedures for the handling of internal audits by posting the results on the department's intranet Web site. I was not prepared, however, for the higher-profile public release of the audit that included a technical briefing by officials and a media scrum by the Minister. Public servants, like every boy scout, must be prepared for any option, even 'last-minute' options that might have been previously rejected.

Be overly prepared for the expected. I was not overly prepared for the low-profile release of the audit. My colleagues and I devoted a great deal of effort preparing our regional and headquarters staff so they would understand the nature of the problems contained in the audit and begin to address them. This required some rebalancing between the requirements for service on the one hand, and control on the other. By focusing on the internal environment, I spent less time in understanding the nature of the external environment, particularly in appreciating the intensity of the competition within the media and the determination of the opposition.

If there is a change in strategy, push back forcefully if you have strong convictions and compelling evidence. Once I became aware that it was decided to proceed with the higher-profile public release of the audit and a technical media briefing, I should have pushed back more forcefully. Officials have the responsibility to speak up when they foresee that major problems might be overlooked, even within a chosen course of action. To do this, one needs to express more than deep concerns and severe warnings. One needs strong convictions and compelling evidence that there is a significantly better course to take and that it can work. While I was uneasy, I lacked both strong conviction and compelling evidence. I did not push back forcefully.

Quickly recognize when a crisis emerges. When I returned from the technical briefing of the media just before noon on Wednesday, 19 January, I did not know that a crisis was in the making. Despite the extensive media coverage Thursday and Friday, and a foreshadowing of the issues that could play out over the course of the next ten months, when I left the office late Friday evening, I believed that the matter would 'blow over.' In retrospect, I should have read the media reports in a more pessimistic manner to prepare myself, and my staff, for what lay ahead.

Establish a central crisis unit when you first think of it, not when you think it may be needed. A central crisis unit is essential to ensure quick response and coordinated communications in the beginning stages of a crisis. 'Daily panics' can quickly turn into full-blown crises, and without strong central coordination there is great risk of error. Although I did not appreciate it at the time, the benefits that could have been realized from immediately establishing a coordinated quick response team far outweighed the small risk that such a unit might be construed as an overreaction pushing the department and government into crisis. Weeks later, when we did establish the unit, we responded faster and more accurately, corrected inaccurate stories in the media, and made many fewer mistakes, and the crisis gradually began to dissipate.

In a crisis you must be able to respond immediately to media questions with accurate and detailed answers. In a number of the media briefings and inquiries I was not able to respond quickly and with precision to their many detailed questions. In the rush of the crisis I was unable to quickly assemble sufficiently accurate and detailed information in order to deal with the media's storyline. Providing the media and the public with detailed and timely information on request contributes to accuracy in media reporting.

Notes

Introduction

1 Donald J. Savoie, *Ottawa Citizen*, 15 February 2000.
2 HRDC expenditures for 1998–99 have been referenced, since the 2000 HRDC Internal Audit of Grants and Contributions was based upon that year.
3 Contributions are conditional payments requiring an arrangement between the recipient and the donor that identifies the terms and conditions governing the payment. Grants are not conditional payments and do not require arrangements and terms and conditions.
4 The annual expenditure for the Transitional Jobs Fund was $100 million. The amount in 1998–99 was slightly higher because of the reprofiling of $25 million in unspent funds from 1997–98 to 1998–99.
5 These programs were excluded from the 2000 Internal Audit for several reasons: they involved transfers to the provincial and territorial governments; the program was not yet implemented (the case of the fisheries adjustment and restructuring program); or a previous administrative audit had recently been undertaken (the case of TAGS).
6 Human Resources Development Canada, *News Release*, 19 January 2000.
7 Christopher Hood, *The Art of the State: Culture, Rhetoric and Public Management* (New York: Clarendon Press, 1998), v.
8 B. Guy Peters and Donald J. Savoie, eds., *Taking Stock: Assessing Public Sector Reforms* (Montreal: McGill-Queen's Press, 1998), 11.
9 Herbert Kaufman, 'Reflections on Administrative Reorganization,' in J.A. Pechman, ed., *Setting National Priorities: The 1978 Budget* (Washington, DC: The Brookings Institution, 1978).

Chapter 1: Looking Underneath

1 Peter Hennessy, *Whitehall* (London: Martin Secker and Warburg Ltd., 1989), 19.
2 B. Guy Peters and Donald J. Savoie, eds., *Taking Stock: Assessing Public Sector Reforms* (Montreal: McGill-Queen's Press, 1998), 3.
3 Christopher Hood, *The Art of the State: Culture, Rhetoric and Public Management* (New York: Clarendon Press, 1998).
4 Peter Aucoin, *The New Public Management: Canada in Comparative Perspective* (Montreal: Institute for Research on Public Policy, 1995), 23–5.
5 Charles Perrow, *Complex Organizations* (Glenview: Scott Foreman, 1972).
6 Christopher Hood and Michael Jackson, *Administrative Argument* (Aldershot: Dartmouth Publishing Company Limited, 1991), xi.
7 B. Guy Peters, 'What Works? The Antiphons of Administrative Reform,' in Peters and Savoie, eds., *Taking Stock*, 80, 100.
8 Peter Aucoin, 'Administrative Reform in Public Management: Paradigms, Principles, Paradoxes, and Pendulums,' *Governance* 3, no. 2 (April 1990), 115–37.
9 Gareth Morgan, *Images of Organization*, 2nd ed. (Thousand Oaks, CA: Sage Publications Inc., 1997), 293.
10 Kenneth P. Ruscio, 'Trust, Democracy, and Public Management: A Theoretical Argument,' *Journal of Public Administration Research and Theory* 6, no. 3 (1996), 474.
11 Kenneth Kernaghan, Brian Marson, and Sandford Borins, *The New Public Organization* (Toronto: Institute of Public Administration in Canada, 2000), 284.
12 Christopher Pollitt and Geert Bouckaert, *Public Management Reform: A Comparative Analysis* (Oxford: Oxford University Press, 2000), 7. See especially chap. 7, 'Trade-offs, Balances, Limits, Dilemmas, and Paradoxes.'
13 Ibid., 153.
14 Ibid., 154. The list of contradictions by Pollitt and Bouckaert is similar to the list of 'paradoxical tensions' set out by Morgan, *Images of Organization*, 292–3:
   • Innovate but avoid mistakes
   • Think long term but deliver results now
   • Cut costs but increase morale
   • Reduce staff but improve teamwork
   • Be flexible but respect the rules
   • Collaborate but compete
   • Decentralize but regain control

- Specialize but be opportunistic
- Lower costs but improve quality.

15 Christopher Pollitt, Testimony before the UK Government House of Commons Select Committee on Public Administration, 14 June 2000.

16 Report of the Standing Committee on Human Resources Development and the Status of Persons with Disabilities, *Seeking a Balance: Final Report on Human Resources Development Grants and Contributions* (Ottawa, June 2000).

17 Auditor General of Canada, *Report of the Auditor General of Canada* (Ottawa: Minister of Public Works and Government Services Canada, 2000), chap. 11, 'Human Resources Development Canada,' 60.

18 Peters, 'What Works?' 80.

19 It was widely reported in the media and by the opposition that these programs were a 'billion dollar job fund.' In fact only 10 per cent of the total expenditures of the programs were direct employment programs. The eight grants and contribution program areas included in the internal audit are discussed more fully in the Introduction.

20 The direct quotations in this and the following paragraph are from Human Resources Development Canada, *News Release*, 19 January 2000.

21 The author was one of the officials.

22 Transcript, 'Briefing Regarding the Release of an Internal Audit Report on HRDC Grants and Contributions Programs' (Ottawa, 19 January 2000).

23 This quote and those in this paragraph are from Transcript, 'Release of an Internal Audit Report on HRDC Grants and Contributions Programs' (Ottawa, House of Commons Foyer, 19 January 2000).

24 CBC Radio, *As It Happens*, 19 January 2000.

25 *Global News*, 19 January 2000.

26 Arthur Kroeger, 'The HRDC Affair: Reflections on Accountability in Government' (speech to the Canadian Club of Ottawa, 12 December 2000).

Chapter 2: Looking Back

1 Ian D. Clark, *Distant Reflections on Federal Public Service Reform in the 1990s.* Report prepared for the Office of the Auditor General (Ottawa, September 2000), 2.

2 The Auditor General produced a major report on constraints to productive management in government. See Auditor General of Canada, *Report of the Auditor General of Canada to the House of Commons for the Fiscal Year Ended 31 March 1983* (Ottawa: Minister of Supply and Services Canada, 1983), chap. 2, 'Constraints to Productive Management in the Public Sector,' 53–87.

3 John Edwards, *Looking Back from 2000 at Public Service 2000*. Report prepared for the Office of the Auditor General (Ottawa, September 2000), 8.

4 Auditor General of Canada, *Public Service Management Reform: Progress, Setbacks and Challenges* (Ottawa: Minister of Public Works and Government Services, 2001), 3.

5 Peter Aucoin, *Comparative Perspectives on Canadian Public Service Reform in the 1990s*. Report prepared for the Office of the Auditor General (Ottawa, September 2000), 6.

6 Herman Bakvis, 'On Silos and Stovepipes: The Case of the Department of Human Resources Development' (paper prepared for the Canadian Centre for Management Development, Ottawa, 1995), 1.

7 The reduction in expenditures from $69 billion in 1993–94 to $58 billion in 1998–99 is the result of the folding in of the Canada Assistance Plan and the fiscal transfers payments for health and post-secondary education under Established Programs Financing to the Canada Health and Social Transfer (CHST) in 1995. CHST expenditures are reported in the Estimates of the Department of Finance.

8 See, for example, Jane Pulkingham and Gordon Ternowetsky, eds., *Remaking Canadian Social Policy: Social Security in the Late 1990s* (Halifax: Fernwood Publishing, 1996), and Keith Banting and Ken Battle, eds., *A New Social Vision for Canada? Perspectives on the Federal Discussion Paper on Social Security Reform* (Kingston: Queen's University School of Policy Studies, and Caledon Institute of Social Policy, 1994).

9 Herman Bakvis, 'Shrinking the House of "HRIF": Program Review and the Department of Human Resources Development,' in Gene Swimmer, ed., *How Ottawa Spends: Life Under the Knife, 1997–98* (Ottawa: Carleton University Press, 1996).

10 Peter Aucoin, *Comparative Perspectives on Canadian Public Service Reform in the 1990s*. Report prepared for the Office of the Auditor General (Ottawa, September 2000), 2.

11 See for example, Peter Aucoin, *The New Public Management: Canada in Comparative Perspective* (Montreal: Institute for Research in Public Policy, 1995); Donald Savoie, *Thatcher, Reagan, Mulroney: In Search of a New Bureaucracy* (Pittsburgh: University of Pittsburgh Press, 1994); Christopher Pollitt, *Managerialism and the Public Services: The Anglo-American Experience* (Oxford: Basil Blackwell, 1990); and M. Brazelay and B. J. Armajani, *Breaking through Bureaucracy: A New Vision for Managing Government* (Berkeley: University of California Press, 1992). For a debate on new public management, see Donald Savoie, 'What Is Wrong with the New Public Management?' *Cana-*

dian Public Administration (Spring 1995), 112–21, and Sandford Borins, 'The New Public Management Is Here to Stay,' *Canadian Public Administration* (Spring 1995), 122–32.

12 Borins, 'The New Public Administration Is Here to Stay,' 122.

13 Ibid.

14 For a critique that public administration literature has focused too much on senior public servants and too little on 'state workers,' as well as a case study of the impact of public management reforms on 'state workers,' in the former Employment and Immigration Canada (EIC), see Greg McElligott, *Beyond Service: State Workers, Public Policy, and the Prospects for Democratic Administration* (Toronto: University of Toronto Press, 2001).

15 Canada, *A Public Service Learning Organization: Progress Report* (Ottawa: Canadian Centre for Management Development, 2001).

16 Ian Lee and Clem Hobbs, 'Pink Slips and Running Shoes: The Liberal Government's Downsizing of the Public Service,' in Gene Swimmer, ed., *How Ottawa Spends: Life under the Knife* (Ottawa: Carleton University Press, 1996), 337–78.

17 F. Leslie Seidle, *Rethinking the Delivery of Public Services to Citizens* (Montreal: Institute for Research on Public Policy, 1995), 129–31.

18 Testimony, House of Commons Standing Committee on Human Resources Development and Persons with Disabilities, 21 March 2000.

19 Instilling a greater emphasis on service to the public was one of the important legacies of Public Service 2000. As John Edwards has noted, 'There can be little doubt that the work of the Task Force on Service to the Public was a major factor in bringing about a strong shift in the public service culture toward meeting the needs of the public' (*Looking Back from 2000 at Public Service 2000*, 9).

20 Human Resources Development Canada, *A Quality Services Journey* (Ottawa, 1996).

21 Report of the Auditor General of Canada, *Human Resources Development Canada: Service Quality at the Local Level* (Ottawa, April 2000), 2–5.

22 Martin Landau, 'Redundancy, Rationality, and the Problem of Duplication and Overlap,' *Public Administration Review* 29, no. 4 (1969), 346–58.

23 Hal G. Rainey, 'Assessing Past and Current Personnel Reforms,' in Guy Peters and Donald J. Savoie, eds., *Taking Stock: Assessing Public Sector Reforms* (Montreal: McGill-Queen's University Press, 1998), 187–220. Rainey notes that successful public sector pay-performance systems require three conditions: (1) trust within the organization between leaders and subordinates, (2) a performance rating system that employees consider fair, and (3) ade-

quate funding to provide appreciable pay increases. None of these conditions existed in HRDC during a period of severe restraint, wage freezes, and
dramatic organizational and program change.

24 See for example, Kimball Fisher, *Leading Self-Directed Work Teams* (New York:
McGraw-Hill, 1993).

25 Human Resources Development Canada, *The HRDC Leadership Profile*
(Ottawa, 1995).

26 Evert Lindquist, 'Getting Results Right: Reforming Ottawa's Estimates,' in
L. Pal, ed., *How Ottawa Spends, 1998–99* (Ottawa: University of Carleton
Press, 1998), 155. For an examination of performance reporting from the
perspective of departments and agencies, see Evert Lindquist, 'On the Cut-
ting Edge: Program Review, Government Restructuring, and the Treasury
Board of Canada,' in Gene Swimmer, ed., *How Ottawa Spends, 1996–97: Life
under the Knife* (Ottawa: Carleton University Press, 1996), 205–52, and Evert
Lindquist, 'Business Planning Comes to Ottawa: Critical Issues and Future
Directions,' in Peter Aucoin and Donald Savoie, eds., *Managing Strategic
Change in the Public Sector: Lessons Learned from Program Review* (Ottawa: Cana-
dian Centre for Management Development, 1998).

27 Human Resource Development Canada, *Results-Based Accountability Framework* (Ottawa, 1996).

28 David A. Good, 'Breaking the Barriers: Improving Accountability for Results
Government-Wide' (notes for Armchair Discussion Group, Canadian Centre
for Management Development, Ottawa, 18 March 1997).

29 Canada, *Breaking the Barriers: Innovation in the Public Interest, Summary
Report* (Ottawa: Minister of Public Works and Government Services Canada,
1997), 1.

30 Rodney Haddow, 'How Ottawa Shrivels: Ottawa's Declining Role in Active
Labour Market Policy,' in Pal, ed., *How Ottawa Spends, 1998–99*, 99–126.

31 Human Resources Development Canada, *Making a Difference in Human Development: A Vision for HRDC* (Ottawa, April 1998), 2.

32 'La Relève: Our Greatest Challenge' (notes for an address by the Clerk of the
Privy Council and Secretary to the Cabinet, Ottawa, November 1996).

33 Canada, *A Strong Foundation: Report of the Task Force on Public Sector Values and
Ethics* (Ottawa: Canadian Centre for Management Development, 1996). See
also Kenneth Kernaghan and John W. Langford, *The Responsible Public Servant* (Toronto: The Institute for Research on Public Policy and the Institute
of Public Administration of Canada, 1990).

34 Auditor General of Canada, *Report of the Auditor General: Values and Ethics in
the Public Service* (Ottawa: Minister of Public Works and Government Services
Canada, October 2000), chap. 12.

35 Human Resources Development Canada, *Handbook on Values and Ethics in HRDC* (Ottawa, 2000).

36 Human Resources Development Canada, Internal Audit Bureau, *Final Report: Audit of TAGS Grants and Contributions* (Ottawa, April 1999).

37 Human Resources Development Canada, Internal Audit Bureau, *Final Report: Program Integrity/Grants and Contributions*, Project No.: 429/98 (Ottawa, January 2000), 3.

38 Ibid., 4.

39 Michael Power, *The Audit Society: Rituals of Verification* (Oxford: Oxford University Press, 1997).

40 Ibid. See especially chap. 1, 'The Audit Explosion.'

41 Ibid., 85.

42 Christopher Pollitt and Geert Bouckaert, *Public Management Reform: A Comparative Analysis* (Oxford: Oxford University Press, 2000), 138.

43 For a thorough examination of the audit of HRDC grants and contributions, see Sharon Sutherland, '"Biggest Scandal in Canadian History": HRDC Audit Starts Probity War,' *Critical Perspectives on Accounting* 14, nos. 1–2 (January 2003), 187–224.

44 Employment and Immigration Canada, Internal Audit Bureau, *Audit of Significant Contributions: National Report* (Project X-200) (Ottawa: Human Resource Development Canada, December 1991); Internal Audit Bureau, 'Employment Follow-up Audit,' Draft Report: Project No.: 413/93 (Ottawa, December 1994); and Human Resources Development Canada, Internal Audit Bureau, *Final Report: Program Integrity/Grants and Contributions*.

45 HRDC, *Final Report*, 7.

46 The author was one of those officials.

47 The communications plan was subsequently released under the Access to Information Act in late February 2000 and immediately reported in the media.

48 Ian Clark, 'Restraint, Renewal and the Treasury Board Secretariat,' *Canadian Public Administration*, 37, no. 2 (Summer 1994); Paul M. Tellier, 'No Time for Half-Measures: The Urgency of Re-engineering the Public Service of Canada' (remarks to the Canadian Institute, Ottawa, 21 February 1994). An abridged version of Tellier's remarks is printed in *Canadian Speeches: Issues of the Day* 8, Issue 1 (April 1994), 45–8.

49 Jocelyne Bourgon, *Fifth Annual Report to the Prime Minister on the Public Service of Canada* (Ottawa: Privy Council Office, 1998).

50 Auditor General of Canada, *Report of the Auditor General of Canada to the House of Commons* (Ottawa: Minister of Supply and Services, 1993), 159–85; Auditor General of Canada, *Public Service Management Reform*, 25.

51 Pollitt and Bouckaert, *Public Management Reform*, 211; Aucoin, *Comparative Perspectives on Canadian Public Service Reform in the 1990s*, 6.

52 Kenneth Kernaghan, Brian Marson, and Sanford Borins, *The New Public Organization* (Toronto: Institute of Public Administration, 2000), 29–30.

Chapter 3: Outside Looking In

1 Sharon Sutherland, '"Biggest Scandal in Canadian History": HRDC Audit Starts Probity War,' *Critical Perspectives on Accounting* 14, nos. 1–2 (January 2003), 187–224.

2 These theories and models are drawn from David Taras, *The Newsmakers* (Scarborough, ON: Nelson, 1990).

3 Peter Desbarats, *Guide to Canadian News Media* (Toronto: Harcourt Brace, 1996), 136.

4 Quoted in Daniel Hallin, *The Uncensored War: The Media and Vietnam* (Berkeley: University of California Press, 1986), 5.

5 Desbarats, *Guide to Canadian News Media*, 136.

6 The recent 'Mills Affair,' in which the publisher of the *Ottawa Citizen* left his job after a meeting with a senior executive of CanWest Global, does suggest that owners can and do determine editorial content. See the interviews by Anthony Germain with Peter Desbarats, and Peter Mansbridge with Leonard Asper, and separate commentary by James Ferrabee and Tom Kent in *Policy Options* 23, no. 7 (October 2002), 17–18.

7 Taras, *The Newsmakers*, 14.

8 Ibid., 17.

9 Ibid., 19.

10 Ibid.

11 The study was published in two separate volumes. See Richard V. Ericson, Patricia M. Baranek, and Janet B. Chan, *Visualizing Deviance: A Study of News Organizations* (Toronto: University of Toronto Press, 1987), and *Negotiating Control: A Study of News Sources* (Toronto: University of Toronto Press, 1989).

12 The author was one of the officials.

13 Arthur Kroeger, 'The HRDC Affair: Reflections on Accountability in Government' (speech to the Canadian Club of Ottawa, 12 December 2000).

14 Ekos Research Associates, 'Rethinking Government' (Toronto, May 2000).

15 Angus Reid Group, 'Public Views on HRDC Programs' (Toronto, May 2000).

Chapter 4: Inside Looking Out

1 For example, the Institute for Crisis Management has a large and extensive

biography of books and articles on crisis management in the private
sector. See 'Publications Research' on its Web site at <htpp://
www.crisisexperts.com>.

2 Christine M. Pearson and Judith A. Clair, 'Reframing Crisis Management,'
   Academy of Management Review (January 1998), 66.

3 Peter Meyboom, 'Crisis Management in Government: Lessons Learned from
   Twelve Case Histories in the Department of Fisheries and Oceans' (Ottawa,
   1988).

4 This was the author.

5 For example, a memorandum was sent from the Deputy Minister to executives on 23 September 1999, stressing the need to strengthen administrative
   practices regarding grants and contributions. It noted:

   > Increasingly in recent years, we have emphasized the need for flexibility,
   > making things happen, and focusing on results. At the same time, as we
   > have lost staff and their expertise, we have put less emphasis on docu-
   > menting and monitoring our agreements. Now it is necessary to renew
   > our attention to these aspects of public administration, while maintain-
   > ing the client focus for which staff are rightly proud.

   The memorandum went further and emphasized the importance of balance:

   > ... we must also keep our focus on serving clients and achieving results
   > for Canadians. In many cases our partners have modest administrative
   > capacity, so our expectations need to be adapted accordingly, while still
   > respecting good administrative practices. Our challenge is to balance
   > results with probity in practical ways that suit the circumstances. As
   > managers we are accountable for both.

   A week later a follow-up memorandum from two assistant deputy ministers
   (ADMs) provided details on the steps to strengthen the administration of
   grants and contributions, the establishment of a National Performance
   Tracking Directorate to regularly monitor grants and contributions files,
   plus several other initiatives. On 17 January, another memorandum from the
   two ADMs, as a follow-up to the BTV session convened by the deputy ministers on 11 January, reinforced the importance of adhering to Treasury Board
   guidelines, especially with respect to 'advance payments at year-end.'

6 For a complete critique of the audit, see Sharon Sutherland, '"Biggest Scandal in Canadian History": HRDC Audit Starts Probity War,' *Critical Perspective
   on Accounting* 14, nos. 1–2 (January 2003), 187–224.

7 In fact, there were 461 project files in the audit sample.

8 Michael Power describes in great detail the importance of having a random

sample in an audit for the purposes of drawing meaningful conclusions, and yet how difficult and costly this is to achieve in practice. See *The Audit Society: Rituals of Verification* (Oxford: Oxford University Press, 1997).

9 See Sutherland, '"Biggest Scandal in Canadian History."'

10 Arthur Kroeger, 'The HRDC Affair: Reflections on Accountability in Government' (speech to the Canadian Club of Ottawa, 12 December 2000).

11 Donald Savoie, *Governing from the Centre: The Concentration of Power in Canadian Politics* (Toronto: University of Toronto Press, 1999), 131.

12 Testimony, The House of Commons Standing Committee on Human Resources Development and the Status of Persons with Disabilities, 10 February 2000.

13 Donald Savoie is quoted in the *Ottawa Citizen* (15 February 2000) expressing concerns that the role of Members of Parliament in the decision-making process of TJF projects 'opens the door to political pressure on bureaucrats.'

14 Testimony, The House of Commons Standing Committee on Human Resources Development and the Status of Persons with Disabilities, 16 May 2000.

15 Ibid., 9 May 2000.

16 Ibid.

17 Ibid., 16 May 2000.

18 Ibid.

19 Privacy Commissioner of Canada, *Annual Report: 1999–2000* (Ottawa: The Minister of Public Works and Government Services Canada, 2000).

20 The House of Commons Standing Committee on Human Resources Development and the Status of Persons with Disabilities, *Seeking a Balance: Final Report on Human Resources Development Grants and Contributions* (Ottawa, June 2000).

21 Ibid.

22 Canadian Centre for Management Development, *A Foundation for Developing Risk Management: Learning Strategies in the Public Service* (Ottawa: Canadian Centre for Management Development, 2001), 20.

23 Human Resources Development Canada, *Third Progress Report on the Six-Point Action Plan for Strengthening Administration of Grants and Contributions* (Ottawa, December 2000).

24 House of Commons Standing Committee, *Seeking a Balance: Final Report on Human Resources Development Grants and Contributions.*

Chapter 5: Looking Closer

1 This chapter draws upon David A. Good, 'Public, Private and Voluntary Sec-

tor Partnerships in Employment Programs: What Are the Practical Boundaries?' in Meredith Edwards and John Langford, eds., *New Players, Partners
and Process: A Public Service Without Boundaries?* (Canberra and Victoria: ING
and CPSS, 2002), 37–55.

2 See for example, Keith G. Banting, ed., *The Nonprofit Sector in Canada: Roles
and Relationships* (Montreal: McGill-Queen's University Press, 2000), and
Kathy L. Brock and Keith G. Banting, ed., *The Nonprofit Sector and Government
in a New Century* (Montreal: McGill-Queen's University Press, 2001).

3 For one perspective on the evolution of regional economic-development
approaches and programs and the illusive search for solutions, see Donald
Savoie, *Regional Economic Development: Canada's Search for Solutions*, 2nd ed.,
(Toronto: University of Toronto Press, 1992), and Donald Savoie, *Rethink-
ing Canada's Regional Development Policy* (Moncton: Canadian Institute for
Research on Regional Development, 1997).

4 Human Resources Development Canada, *Terms and Conditions: Transitional
Jobs Fund* (Ottawa, 1996).

5 Ibid.

6 Ibid.

7 Consulting and Audit Canada, *Review of the Transitional Jobs Fund* (Ottawa,
August 1997), v.

8 Human Resource Development Canada, *Evaluation of the Transitional Jobs
Fund, Phase 1* (Ottawa, 1998). An evaluation study conducted by Ekos Research Associates under the direction of the Evaluation and Data Development Branch of HRDC.

9 'Incremental jobs' refers to the number of new jobs that have been created
as a direct result of the employment project, 'Total jobs' refers to the number of jobs that are associated with an employment project. It is difficult to
attribute the creation of new jobs directly to an individual project. There are
various methodologies used for calculating incremental jobs. Different analysts can often have different estimates of the number of incremental jobs
created.

10 For an analysis of the 'differential treatment' of access to information requests over the period 1999–2001 by HRDC on the basis of 'political sensitivity,' see Alasdair Roberts, 'Administrative Discretion and the Access to Information Act: An "Internal Law" on Open Government,' *Canadian Public
Administration* 45, no. 2 (Summer 2002), 175–94.

11 The House of Commons Standing Committee on Human Resources Development and the Status of Persons with Disabilities, *Seeking a Balance: Final
Report on Human Resources Development Grants and Contributions* (Ottawa, June
2000).

12 Auditor General of Canada, *Report of the Auditor General of Canada: Human Resources Development Canada: Grants and Contributions* (Ottawa: The Minister of Public Works and Government Services Canada, October 2000).
13 Ibid.
14 The House of Commons Standing Committee, *Seeking a Balance.*
15 An October 1997 internal memorandum, prepared by an officer in the Office of the Ethics Counselor and released under access to information, described a process involving consultation on TJF projects with the regional minister for the province of Quebec and 'other liberal members in the field.'
16 Edwards and Langford, eds., *New Players, Partners and Process.*
17 John Langford, 'Managing Public-Private Partnerships in Canada,' in Edwards and Langford, eds., *New Players, Partners and Process*, 68–84.

Chapter 6: Looking Around

1 Christopher Pollitt and Geert Bouckaert, *Public Management Reform: A Comparative Analysis* (Oxford: Oxford University Press, 2000), 134.
2 For example, see Christopher Pollitt, *Managerialism and the Public Services* (Oxford: Basil Blackwell Ltd., 1990), and Christopher Hood, *The Art of the State: Culture, Rhetoric and Political Management* (New York: Clarenden Press, 1998).
3 For example, see Pollitt and Bouckaert, *Public Management Reform*, especially chap. 6, 'Politics and Management.'
4 Jocelyne Bourgon, *Fifth Annual Report to the Prime Minister on the Public Service of Canada* (Ottawa: Privy Council Office, 1998).
5 Christopher Hood and Michael Jackson, *Administrative Argument* (Aldershot: Dartmouth Publishing Co., 1991), 178.
6 Bourgon, *Fifth Annual Report to the Prime Minister on the Public Service of Canada.*
7 Peter Aucoin, 'The Public Service as a Learning Organization: Maintaining the Momentum in Public Service Reform' (research paper prepared for the Canadian Centre for Management Development, Ottawa, 2000).
8 This is in sharp contrast to the Neilsen Task Force on Program Review of the Mulroney government, where private sector advisors dominated public servants in the review of government programs. Poorly developed expenditure reduction proposals combined with a lack of political will resulted in none of the Task Force's recommendations being implemented.
9 G.B. Doern and R.W. Phidd, in *Canadian Public Policy: Ideas, Structure and Processes* (Toronto: Methuen, 1992), argue that there are five broad categories of

instruments of governance, including self-regulation, exhortation, expenditure, regulation (including taxation), and public ownership.

10 The most significant and visible example is the Policy Research Initiative, which has been developed to strengthen the policy capacity of the federal government by providing leadership and a government-wide focal point for policy research communities. See 'Policy Research Initiative: Preparing for Tomorrow's Issues Today.' *Canada. Policy Research Initiative* <http://www.theworld.ca>.

11 Gordon Robertson, 'The Changing Role of the Privy Council Office,' *Canadian Public Administration* 14, no. 4 (Winter 1971).

12 Henry Mintzberg, 'Developing a Model for Managing Publicly,' in Henry Mintzberg and Jacques Bourgault, *Managing Publicly* (Toronto: Institute of Public Administration of Canada, 2000), 31.

13 Sandford Borins, 'The New Public Management Is Here to Stay,' *Canadian Public Administration* (Spring 1995), 122.

14 Auditor General of Canada, *Public Service Management Reform: Progress, Setbacks and Challenges* (Ottawa: Minister of Public Works and Government Services, 2001).

15 See, for example, John Fryer, *Final Report of the Advisory Committee on Labour Management Relations in the Public Service* (Ottawa: Treasury Board Secretariat, 2001).

16 Donald J. Savoie, 'La gouvernance des sociétiés d'Etat au gouvernement fédéral: un bilan,' *Canadian Public Administration* 44, no. 2 (Summer 2001), 139–60.

17 Tip O'Neill, the Speaker in the U.S. House of Representatives for a decade, is often quoted as saying that 'all politics is local.'

18 See, for example, Philip Resnick, *The Politics of Resentment: British Columbia Regionalism and Canadian Unity* (Vancouver: University of British Columbia Press, 2000).

19 Canada, *A Framework to Improve the Social Union for Canadians. An Agreement between the Government of Canada and the Governments of the Provinces and Territories* (Ottawa, February 4, 1999).

20 Canada, Constitutional Act, 1982 [en. by the Canada Act 1982 (U.K.), c.11, s.11].

21 Jacques Bourgault, 'The Satisfaction of Ministers with the Performance of their Deputy Ministers During the Mulroney Government,' research paper no. 22, Canadian Centre for Management Development, Ottawa, 1997.

22 Jeffrey Simpson, *The Friendly Dictatorship* (Toronto: McClelland and Stewart Ltd., 2001), 121.

23 Peter Aucoin, *The New Public Management in Canada: Canada in Comparative Perspective* (Montreal: Institute for Research on Public Policy, 1995), 218.

24 Peter Aucoin, 'Administrative Reform in Public Management: Paradigms, Principles, Paradoxes and Pendulums,' *Governance* 3, no. 2 (April 1990), 115–37.

25 Paul Thomas, 'The Changing Nature of Accountability,' in B. Guy Peters and Donald J. Savoie, eds., *Taking Stock: Assessing Public Sector Reforms* (Montreal: McGill-Queen's University Press, 1998), 349–50.

26 Peter Aucoin and Ralph Heintzman, 'The Dialectics of Accountability for Performance in Public Management Reform,' *International Review of Administrative Sciences* 66, no. 1 (March 2000), 43–53.

27 This is similar to but goes beyond Behn's conceptualization of accountability for finances, for fairness, and for performance. See Robert D. Behn, *Rethinking Democratic Accountability* (Washington, DC: The Brookings Institution, 2001), 6–10.

28 Behn notes that this trade-off does not hold in all circumstances. See Behn, *Rethinking Democratic Accountability*, 11.

29 Paul Thomas, 'Ministerial Responsibility and Administrative Accountability,' in M. Charih and A. Daniels, eds., *New Public Administration in Canada* (Toronto: Institute of Public Administration of Canada, 1997), 144.

30 Auditor General of Canada and the Treasury Board Secretariat, 'Modernizing Accountability Practices in the Public Sector' (discussion paper, Ottawa, January 1998), 1.

31 Aucoin and Heintzman, 'The Dialectics of Accountability,' 49.

32 For a succinct description of agency theory and why it is more useful in the Canadian context than Niskanen's celebrated 'budget-maximizing bureaucrat,' see Aucoin, *The New Public Management*, 34–7.

33 Kenneth Kernaghan and John W. Langford, *The Responsible Public Servant* (Toronto: The Institute for Research on Public Policy and the Institute of Public Administration of Canada, 1990), 160.

34 Auditor General of Canada and the Treasury Board Secretariat, 'Modernizing Accountability Practices in the Public Sector,' 2.

35 Canada, *A Strong Foundation: Report of the Taskforce on Public Service Values and Ethics* (Ottawa: Canadian Centre for Management Development, 1996) 9.

36 See Donald N. Michael, 'Government by Learning: Boundaries, Myths and Metaphors,' *Futures* (January/February 1993), 81–9.

37 Canada, *Report of the Auditor General of Canada: Reflections on a Decade of Serving Parliament* (Ottawa, February, 2001), 24.

38 Ibid., 26.

39 The Canadian Centre for Management Development has begun to invest

heavily in work on the public service learning organization. For example, see Canada, *A Public Service Learning Organization* (Ottawa: Canadian Centre for Management Development, 2001). Also see Kenneth Kernaghan, Brian Marson, and Sandford Borins, *The New Public Organization* (Toronto: Institute of Public Administration of Canada, 2000), 207–28.

40 Aucoin, *The Public Service as a Learning Organization*, 167.

41 See, for example, the results of four 'action-research roundtables' on learning which deal with implementing the social union framework, building learning organizations, managing horizontal issues, and risk management. These are all part of Canada, *A Public Service Learning Organization.*

42 For a discussion of these learning traps and what public servants can do about them, see Canada, *The Learning Journey: A Guide to Achieving Excellence* (Ottawa: Canadian Centre for Management Development, 2001), 14.

43 Charles E. Lindblom and Edward J. Woodhouse, *The Policy-Making Process*, 3rd ed. (Englewood Cliffs, NJ: Prentice Hall, 1993).

44 Max Weber, 'Bureaucracy,' in H.H. Gerth and C. Wright Mills, eds, *From Max Weber: Essays in Sociology* (New York: Oxford University Press, 1946), 196–244.

45 Kernaghan, Marson, and Borins, *The New Public Organization*, 3.

Chapter 7: Looking Forward

1 H. George Frederickson, *The Spirit of Public Administration* (San Francisco: Jossey-Bass, 1997).

2 In particular, see Donald J. Savoie, *Governing from the Centre: The Concentration of Power in Canadian Politics* (Toronto: University of Toronto Press, 1999), and 'What Is Wrong with the New Public Management?' *Canadian Public Administration* (Spring 1995), 112–21.

3 See, for example, Sandford Borins, 'The New Public Management Is Here to Stay,' *Canadian Public Administration* (Spring 1995), 122–32.

4 There is, of course, an extensive literature addressing the politics-administration dichotomy. For a concise and useful overview see Donald J. Savoie, *Thatcher, Reagan, Mulroney: In Search of a New Bureaucracy* (Pittsburgh: University of Pittsburgh Press, 1994), 20–4.

5 For the virtues of steering, see Thomas Peters and Robert Waterman, *In Search of Excellence* (New York: Harper and Row, 1982).

6 See Neil Nevitte, *Decline of Deference: Canadian Value Change in Cross-national Perspective* (Peterborough, ON: Broadview Press, 1996), and Neil Nevitte, ed., *Value Change and Governance in Canada* (Toronto: University of Toronto Press, 2002).

7 The classic 'prisoner's dilemma,' based upon the work of Merrill Flood and

Melvin Dersher in 1950 as part of the Rand Corporation's investigations into game theory, was first explained publicly by Albert W. Tucker while addressing an audience of psychologists at Stanford University. Tucker began as follows: two burglars, Bob and Al, are captured near the scene of a burglary and are interrogated separately by the police. Each has to choose whether or not to confess and implicate the other. If neither man confesses, then both will serve one year on a charge of carrying a concealed weapon. If each confesses and implicates the other, and the other burglar does not confess, the one who has collaborated with the police will go free, while the other burglar will go to prison for twenty years on a maximum charge. What strategies are rational from each individual's perspective if that individual wants to minimize the time spent in jail? Al might reason as follows: 'Two things can happen: Bob can confess or Bob can keep quiet. Suppose Bob confesses. Then I get twenty years if I don't confess, ten years if I do, so in that case, it's better to confess. On the other hand, if Bob doesn't confess, and I don't either, I get a year; but in that case, if I confess I can go free. Either way, it's best if I confess. Therefore, I will confess.' But Bob can and will presumably reason the same way – so that they both confess and go to prison for ten years each. Yet, if they had 'cooperated' and kept quiet, they each could have gotten off with one year each.

8 The concept was first set out by Gardin Hardin in an article entitled 'The Tragedy of the Commons,' *Science* 162 (1968), 1243–8. In Hardin's own words, the tragedy develops this way:

> Picture a pasture open to all. It is to be expected that each herdsman will try to keep as many cattle as possible on the commons. Such an arrangement may work reasonably satisfactorily for centuries because tribal wars, poaching, and disease keep the numbers of both man and beast well below the carrying capacity of the land. Finally, however, comes the day of reckoning, that is, the day when the long-desired goal of social stability becomes a reality. At this point, the inherent logic of the commons remorselessly generates tragedy.
>
> As a rational being, each herdsman seeks to maximize his gain. Explicitly or implicitly, more or less consciously, he asks, 'What is the utility *to me* of adding one more animal to my herd?' This utility has one negative and one positive component.
>
> 1 The positive component is a function of the increment of one animal. Since the herdsman receives all the proceeds from the sale of the additional animal, the positive utility is nearly +1.
> 2 The negative component is a function of the additional overgrazing

created by one more animal. Since, however, the effects of overgraz-
ing are shared by all the herdsmen, the negative utility for any particular decisionmaking herdsman is only a fraction of –1.

Adding together the component partial utilities, the rational herdsman
concludes that the only sensible course for him to pursue is to add
another animal to his herd. And another ... But this is the conclusion
reached by each and every rational herdsman sharing a commons.
Therein is the tragedy. Each man is locked into a system that compels
him to increase his herd without limit – in a world that is limited. Ruin
is the destination toward which all men rush, each pursuing his own
best interest in a society that believes in the freedom of the commons.
Freedom in a commons brings ruin to all.

9 At the provincial level there has been more direct political interest, most
notably in Ontario, Alberta, and British Columbia.
10 Aaron Wildavsky, *Speaking Truth to Power: The Art and Craft of Policy Analysis*
(Toronto: Little, Brown, 1979).
11 Ibid.
12 Auditor General of Canada, *Report of the Auditor General of Canada to the House
of Commons* (Ottawa: Minister of Public Works and Government Services
Canada, October 2000), chap. 12, 'Values and Ethics in the Public Service.'
13 Ibid.
14 These issues and the following case examples have been developed by the
School of Public Administration, University of Victoria, as part of a 2001–2
project with the Pacific and Yukon Region of HRDC for regional employees.
The project is known as 'An Organization Dialogue on Values and Ethics.'
15 Auditor General of Canada, *Report of the Auditor General of Canada to the House
of Commons for the Fiscal Year Ending March 31, 1976* (Ottawa: Minister of Supply and Services, 1976), 9.
16 See Sharon Sutherland, 'Responsible Government and Ministerial Responsibility: Every Reform Has Its Own Problem,' *Canadian Journal of Political
Science* 24, no. 1 (March 1991), 111.
17 Auditor General and the Treasury Board Secretariat, 'Modernizing Accountability Practices in the Public Sector' (a joint draft discussion paper, Ottawa,
8 January 1998).
18 The staff levels in the Internal Audit Bureau of HRDC were reduced by
nearly 40 per cent, from fifty-four in 1994–95 to thirty-three in 1999–2000.
19 Michael Power, *The Audit Society: Rituals of Verification* (Oxford: Oxford University Press, 1997).
20 Ibid., 22.

21 Ibid., 30.
22 Human Resources Development Canada, Internal Audit Bureau, *Final Report: Program Integrity/Grants and Contributions*, Project no.: 429/98 (Ottawa, January 2000) 5.
23 Auditor General of Canada, *Report of the Auditor General of Canada to the House of Commons*, 9.
24 Auditor General of Canada, *Report of the Auditor General of Canada: Reflections on a Decade of Serving Parliament* (Ottawa: Public Works and Government Services Canada, February 2001), 4.
25 Peter Aucoin, *Auditing for Accountability: The Role of the Auditor General* (Ottawa: Institute on Governance Occasional Series, 1998), 5.
26 Aaron Wildavsky, 'The Self-evaluating Organization,' in *Speaking Truth to Power*, 216.
27 Auditor General of Canada, *Reflections on a Decade of Serving Parliament*, 26.
28 Ibid.
29 See 'Publications On-line.' *Treasury Board of Canada Secretariat.* <http://www.tbs-sct.gc.ca>.
30 Ian D. Clark, *Distant Reflections on Federal Public Service Reform in the 1990s.* Report prepared for the Office of the Auditor General (Ottawa, September 2000), 6.
31 Ibid. 7.
32 Canada, *Public Service 2000: The Renewal of the Public Service of Canada* (Ottawa: Minister of Supply and Services, December 1990).
33 See, for example, Paul Thomas, 'Ministerial Responsibility and Administrative Accountability,' in M. Charih and S. Daniels, eds., *New Public Administration in Canada* (Toronto: Institute of Public Administration of Canada, 1997), and Canada, *A Strong Foundation: Report of the Task Force on Public Service Values and Ethics* (Ottawa: Canadian Centre for Management Development, 1996).
34 It should be noted that in the United Kingdom, Members of Parliament have more expertise and a greater interest in matters of public administration as reflected, for example, in the regular hearings of the House of Commons Select Committee on Public Administration.
35 Peter Dobell, 'Reforming Parliamentary Practice: The Views of MPs,' *Policy Matters* 9 (December 2000), 27.
36 Peter Desbarats, *Guide to the News Media* (Toronto: Harcourt Brace, 1996), 144.
37 Nick Russell, *Morals and the Media – Ethics in Canadian Journalism* (Vancouver: University of British Columbia Press, 1994), 31.

38 Canadian Newspaper Association, *Statement of Principles*, rev. ed. (Toronto: Canadian Newspaper Association, 1995).
39 Radio-Television News Directors Association, *Code of Ethics and Professional Conduct* (Washington, DC: Radio-Television News Directors Association, 2000).

Index

Abbott, Jim 77
Ablonczy, Diane 22, 65, 74, 77
access to information: legislation 49; releases 3, 71, 73, 75, 143–4; requests 2, 3, 66, 71, 74–5, 80, 96, 110–11, 119, 121, 143
Access to Information Act 58, 76
accountability: 7, 10, 12, 14, 41, 48, 153–4, 157, 165–6, 173, 177–9, 186, 197–9; and audit 52, 168, 188–9, 201–3; and CJF and TJF 12, 76–7, 112–3, 138, 146–51, 165; for control 12, 167–9, 176; definitions of 166–7, 169–71; for learning 12, 169–71, 175–6; and partnerships 36–7; for performance 12, 171–3, 175
administrative reform. *See* public management reform
As It Happens (CBC Radio) 22
Asper family 61
assistant auditor general 22, 105, 193
ATI. *See* access to information
Atlantic Groundfish Strategy, The (TAGS) 5, 6, 50, 97–8, 210
Aucoin, Peter xvii, 15, 28, 31, 155, 165–6, 171, 175

audit: compliance 168–9; expectations gap in 191–2; financial 51–2, 193; ignoring constraints on the public service 194–8; internal vs. external 54, 192; performance 51, 193–4; rhetoric in 191–4; value for money 51–2, 191. *See also* grants and contributions
Auditor General 3, 17, 21, 27, 47, 50–1, 54–5, 78, 80, 82–9, 101, 104, 110, 125, 146, 165, 174, 182, 187, 190–9, 209; reports of Auditor General 7, 18, 23, 25, 28, 37, 50, 64–5, 86–7, 97–8, 101, 125–6, 142

balance and trade-offs in public management 9, 15–20, 25, 38, 48–9, 83–4, 86–8, 102, 122–3, 125, 134, 137, 144–5, 150–1, 153, 165, 173, 177–80, 184–5, 187, 199, 204, 208–9, 211
Behn, Robert 166
'billion dollar': 'boondoggle' 7, 60, 87–8, 130, 144, 206; 'job fund' 12, 130–31, 144, 151, 206; 'loss' 24, 59, 64, 66, 73–4, 88, 98–9, 102, 106, 108, 110, 206
Black, Conrad 60–1